Microsoft

W9-AUR-338

INSIDE
C#

Tom A

PUBLISHED BY
Microsoft Press
A Division of Microsoft Corporation
One Microsoft Way
Redmond, Washington 98052-6399

Library of Congress Cataloging-in-Publication Data
Archer, Tom.
     Inside C# / Tom Archer.
        p. cm.
     Includes index.
     ISBN 0-7356-1288-9
     1. C# (Computer program language)   I. Title.

  QA76.73.C154 A73 2001
  005.13'3--dc21

                                      2001030562

Printed and bound in the United States of America.

1 2 3 4 5 6 7 8 9   QWT   6 5 4 3 2 1

Distributed in Canada by Penguin Books Canada Limited.

A CIP catalogue record for this book is available from the British Library.

Microsoft Press books are available through booksellers and distributors worldwide. For further information about international editions, contact your local Microsoft Corporation office or contact Microsoft Press International directly at fax (425) 936-7329. Visit our Web site at mspress.microsoft.com. Send comments to *mspinput@microsoft.com*.

Acquisitions Editor: Danielle Bird
Project Editor: Devon Musgrave
Technical Editor: Brian Johnson

Body Part No. X08-04932

My father was always my harshest critic. This can be a good thing and a bad thing, depending on your view and the circumstances. However, he always wanted me to excel and do well. I remember the day I told him that I was writing a book for Microsoft Press. He was impressed and proud of me. It was definitely one of the happiest days of my life. Unfortunately, my father passed away last year and didn't get to see this book completed, but I know that he would have been happy for me.

As the first Houston Astros season without my father begins (it's just not the same), I'm dedicating this book in memory of my dad. I miss you, ol' man.

Contents at a Glance

Table of Contents

Part II   C# Class Fundamentals

4   The Type System   57

Foreword

I've spent my entire career at Microsoft working to enhance the developer experience, usually with a focus on increasing developer productivity. My work has spanned a wide variety of products and technologies, but I've never been as excited about the work we've done to enhance the developer experience as I am now. The breadth and depth of the technologies Microsoft .NET delivers is astounding. We're providing a great new language, knocking down the barriers that have traditionally divided developers into separate but unequal language worlds, and enabling Web sites to cooperate to meet users' needs. Any one of these would be interesting on its own, but the combination is truly compelling.

Let's look at the key building blocks of .NET and some related technologies:

- **C#, a new language**   C# is the first component-oriented language in the C and C++ family of languages. It's a simple, modern, object-oriented, and type-safe programming language derived from C and C++. C# combines the high productivity of Microsoft Visual Basic and the raw power of C++.

- **Common Language Runtime**   The high-performance Common Language Runtime (CLR) includes an execution engine, a garbage collector, just-in-time compilation, a security system, and a rich class framework (the .NET Framework). The CLR was designed from the ground up to support multiple languages.

- **Common Language Specification**   The Common Language Specification (CLS) describes a common level of language functionality. The relatively high minimum bar of the CLS enables the creation of a club of CLS-compliant languages. Each member of this club enjoys dual benefits: complete access to .NET Framework functionality and rich interoperability with other compliant languages. For example, a Visual Basic class can inherit from a C# class and override its virtual methods.

- **A rich set of languages that target the CLR**   Microsoft-provided languages that target the CLR include Visual Basic, Visual C++ with Managed Extensions, Visual C#, and JScript. Third parties are providing many other languages—too many to list here!

- **Web services**   Today's World Wide Web consists primarily of individual sites. While a user might visit multiple sites to accomplish a given task, such as making travel arrangements for a group of people, these

Web sites typically do not cooperate. The next generation of the Web will be based on cooperating networks of Web sites. The reason is simple: cooperating Web sites can do a better job of meeting users' needs. Microsoft's Web services technologies foster cooperation among Web sites by enabling communication via standard XML-based protocols that are both language-independent and platform-independent. Many important Web services will be based on C# and the CLR running on Windows, but the architecture is truly open.

■ **Visual Studio.NET**   Visual Studio.NET ties all of these pieces together and makes it easy to author a wide range of components, applications, and services in a variety of programming languages.

Now that I've touched on some important C#-related technologies, let's take a closer look at C# itself. Developers have a lot invested in their language of choice, and so the onus is on a new language to prove its worth through some combination of simple preservation, incremental improvement, and thoughtful innovation.

Simple Preservation

Hippocrates said, "Make a habit of two things: to help, or at least do no harm." The "do no harm" part played a prominent role in our design of C#. If a C or C++ feature addressed a problem well, we kept it without modification. Most significantly, C# borrows from C and C++ in core areas such as expressions, statements, and overall syntax. Because so much of a typical program consists of these features, C and C++ developers instantly feel comfortable with C#.

Incremental Improvement

Many incremental improvements have been made—too many to mention in this brief foreword—but it's worth calling attention to a few changes that eliminate some common and time-consuming C and C++ errors:

■ Variables must be initialized before use, so bugs resulting from uninitialized variables are eliminated.

■ Statements like *if* and *while* require Boolean values, so a developer who accidentally uses the assignment operator (=) instead of the equality operator (==) finds the mistake at compilation time.

■ Silent fall-through in *switch* statements is disallowed, so a developer who accidentally omits a *break* statement finds the mistake at compilation time.

Thoughtful Innovation

Deeper innovation is found in C#'s type system, which includes the following advances:

- The C# type system employs automatic memory management, thereby freeing developers from time-consuming and bug-prone manual memory management. Unlike most type systems, the C# type system also allows direct manipulation of pointer types and object addresses. (These manual memory management techniques are only permitted in certain security contexts.)

- The C# type system is unified—everything is an object. Through innovative use of concepts such as boxing and unboxing, C# bridges the gap between value types and reference types, allowing any piece of data to be treated as an object.

- Properties, methods, and events are fundamental. Many languages omit intrinsic support for properties and events, creating an unnecessary mismatch between the language and associated frameworks. For instance, if the framework supports properties and the language doesn't, incrementing a property is awkward (for example, *o.SetValue(o.GetValue( ) +1)*). If the language also supports properties, the operation is simple (*o.Value++*).

- C# supports attributes, which enable the definition and use of declarative information about components. The ability to define new kinds of declarative information has always been a powerful tool for language designers. Now all C# developers have this capability.

Inside C#

In *Inside C#*, Tom Archer lays a foundation by introducing .NET and the CLR, explains the fundamentals of C#, and delves into some advanced C# language concepts. His depth of experience—both as a developer and as an author of books on C++, J++, and Microsoft Windows—enables him to explain C# in ways that readers will find enjoyable and informative.

Readers, I hope you enjoy writing your first C# programs and that they are the first of many that you will write in the years ahead.

Scott Wiltamuth
C# Design Team Member
Microsoft Corporation

Introduction

Why I Wrote This Book

Having been a developer for twenty years—I feel older each time I think about that!—I had basically reached the point where programming was beginning to seem a bit stale to me. Don't get me wrong: if I were a multimillionaire and didn't need to work, I'd probably continue writing code because it's something I truly enjoy doing as much as anything. However, I was getting to the point of thinking, "Everything's been done!" Then along came Microsoft .NET and C#, and a whole new world of possibilities opened. I've spoken with several friends who have had this same "reawakening" of sorts with the introduction of .NET. We have this new, exciting technology that finally addresses issues we've been grappling with for years (for example, multilanguage development environments, the deployment and versioning problems of large, complex systems, and so on). I wrote this book because it's exciting to write code again. Because I once again get up in the morning thinking about the new and cool thing that I'll be learning today. I hope that, as you learn this language, you'll share in my enthusiasm.

Anyone authoring a book on C# at the time of this writing has had to learn the language while writing the book. If you've written an application while learning the SDK or language being used—who hasn't?—you know that this can be a difficult position. Now try to imagine writing something that tens of thousands of people are going to review after you're done! The biggest problem is that halfway through the project—once you know what you're doing—you're itching to redesign and redo the whole thing! Obviously, with deadlines, that's impractical. My point is that I believe this book is a good tool for learning C#. Because I was learning as I wrote it, there are going to be some inconsistencies and some things that I could have done much better. However, if I get a chance to do a second edition, I can promise that you and I both will benefit from my personal learning curve as I've written this text.

Finally, I'd like to say that I welcome any and all feedback regarding this book. I'm not one of these "I'm so good because I write books" people. I'm just a regular guy that was lucky enough to get the opportunity to write this book. I am always open to learning from others and, in fact, love doing so. I can be reached at *http://www.TheCodeChannel.com*.

Who Should Read This Book

This book is for the person looking to get started with C# and .NET development. As I mentioned, this is one exciting platform and is the wave of the future insofar as distributed Microsoft Windows development is concerned. This book assumes that you have a background in one of the C family of languages: C, C++, or Java. I think the only other prerequisite is the desire to learn and explore new dimensions in writing applications. Because you're holding the book in your hands, you've probably got that desire!

Organization of This Book

This book has been carefully organized into several logically sequenced sections; each section consists of a group of chapters addressing a specific category of C# or .NET development.

The book begins with Part I, "Laying the Groundwork," a section for entry-level C# programmers and for those new to the .NET environment. The chapters in this section provide an introduction to .NET and illustrate how to create and test your first C# applications.

In Part II, "C# Class Fundamentals," I present the basics of defining and working with classes in C#. The chapters in this section are geared toward giving you a solid foundation in what members are supported in C# (enums, properties, arrays, and so on) and in how to define and use them in a C# application.

Although you've been writing code for several chapters in terms of defining class members, in Part III, "Writing Code," you'll start to see different aspects of tasks such as controlling program flow, handling errors (with exceptions), and writing event handlers with delegates.

The book wraps up with Part IV, "Advanced C#." Being a typical geek, I enjoyed writing this section most. It includes chapters on multithreaded programming, reflection, working with unmanaged code (including COM interoperability), and versioning.

About the Companion CD

This book contains a companion CD. If you have the AutoRun feature in Windows enabled, you'll see a splash screen when you insert the CD into the CD-ROM drive that will provide you with setup options. To start this screen manually, run StartCD from the root directory of the CD. The StartCD program provides you with links to the eBook contained on the CD, an install program for the book's sample files, and a link to MSDN, where you can download the latest version of the Microsoft .NET Framework SDK, which you'll need to compile and run the sample programs.

The sample programs for the book are located in the Code folder. You can view the samples from the CD, or you can install them onto your hard disk by using the installer from StartCD.

> **Note** If you're unable to browse the files in the Samples folder, you might have an older CD driver that doesn't support long filenames. If this is the case, to browse the files you must install the samples files on your hard disk by running the setup program.

System Requirements

For you to get the most from this book, I highly recommend working through the sample applications as you read each chapter. To do this, you'll need to install the latest .NET Framework SDK. At the time of this writing, this includes the .NET runtime and the C# compiler. Additionally, I've intentionally avoided use of the Visual Studio.NET product so as to focus on the language and runtime environment and not place any restrictions on your particular development environment. Therefore, all the samples in this book will compile and run from the command line.

Acknowledgments

First off I'd like to acknowledge the help of my editor, Devon Musgrave. I make no pretense of being a "writer." I'm a programmer who happens to want to help others, and writing books is one way to do that. Without Devon's help in bending and shaping what I did say into what I wanted to say, this text would not be readable at all. Thanks, Devon!

I also want to thank Brian Johnson, the book's technical editor. Brian was invaluable when trying to match up the text in the book with the demo applications. He was also instrumental in helping to overcome several late changes to the compiler as we were attempting to go to press. I wrote this book on a beta release of C#. By the time the compiler is released to the general public, one or two of the demos in the book might not work. However, none of this is Brian's fault as he was extremely meticulous about testing each and every demo. Thanks, Brian!

Two others at Microsoft Press are also deserving of acknowledgements: Anne Hamilton and Danielle Bird. Both of these people were responsible for getting this project off the ground and giving me the opportunity to write this book. Their belief in me carried me through some rough times with this book, and I appreciate their support very much. Thanks!

I also want to thank the following Microsoft employees who were patient with my questions as I attempted to learn the C# language and the .NET BCL: Joe Nalewabau (who answered several early questions about C#), Brian Harry (who provided the information about deterministic finalization), and Steven Pratschner (who provided help on the global assembly cache and assembly versioning). Also, thanks much to Scott Wiltamuth for his wonderful Foreword!

Finally, I want to thank Aravind Corera, who helped out tremendously in the chapter on writing unmanaged code. It was his great work on the COM section that makes that chapter special. Great work, Aravind. I hope that we can work together again!

Part I

Laying the Groundwork

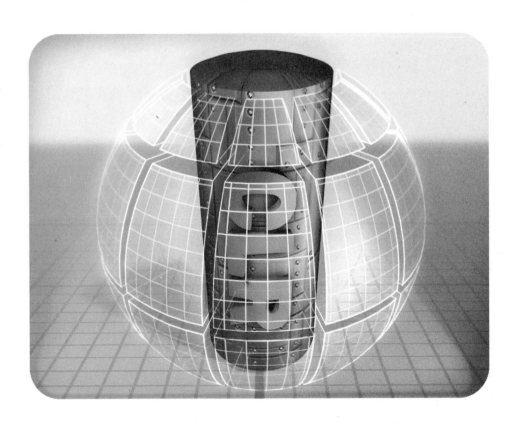

1

Fundamentals of Object-Oriented Programming

The goals of this chapter are to guide you through the terminology of object-oriented programming (OOP) and to give you an understanding of the importance of object-oriented concepts to programming. Many languages, such as C++ and Microsoft Visual Basic, are said to "support objects," but few languages actually support all the principles that constitute object-oriented programming. C# is one of these languages: it was designed from the ground up to be a truly object-oriented, component-based language. So, to get the absolute maximum out of this book, you need to have a strong grasp of the concepts presented here.

I know that conceptual chapters like this are often skipped over by readers who want to dive into the code right away, but unless you consider yourself an "object guru," I encourage you to read this chapter. For those of you only somewhat familiar with object-oriented programming, you should reap benefits from doing so. Also, keep in mind that the chapters that follow this one will refer back to the terminology and concepts discussed here.

As I've said, many languages claim to be object-oriented or object-based, but few truly are. C++ isn't, because of the undeniable, uncircumventable fact that its roots are deeply embedded in the C language. Too many OOP ideals had to be sacrificed in C++ to support legacy C code. Even the Java language, as good as it is, has some limitations as an object-oriented language. Specifically, I'm referring to the fact that in Java you have *primitive types* and *object types* that are treated and behave very differently. However, the focus of this chapter is not on comparing the faithfulness of different languages to OOP principles. Rather, this chapter will present an objective and language-agnostic tutorial on OOP principles themselves.

Before we get started, I'd like to add that object-oriented programming is much more than a marketing phrase (although it has become that for some people), a new syntax, or a new application programming interface (API). Object-oriented programming is an entire set of concepts and ideas. It's a way of thinking about the problem being addressed by a computer program and tackling the problem in a more intuitive and therefore more productive manner.

My first job involved using the Pascal language to program the box-office reporting and itinerary applications for Holiday on Ice. As I moved on to other jobs and other applications, I programmed in PL/I and RPG III (and RPG/400). After a few more years, I started programming applications in the C language. In each of these instances, I was easily able to apply knowledge I had learned from prior experience. The learning curve for each successive language was shorter regardless of the complexity of the language I was learning. This is because until I started programming in C++, all the languages I had used were procedural languages that mainly differed only in syntax.

However, if you are new to object-oriented programming, be forewarned: *prior experience with other non-object-oriented languages will not help you here!* Object-oriented programming is a different way of thinking about how to design and program solutions to problems. In fact, studies have shown that people who are new to programming learn object-oriented languages much more quickly than those of us who started out in procedural languages such as BASIC, COBOL, and C. These individuals do not have to "unlearn" any procedural habits that can hamper their understanding of OOP. They are starting with a clean slate. If you've been programming in procedural languages for many years and C# is your first object-oriented language, the best advice I can give you is to keep an open mind and implement the ideas I'm presenting here before you throw up your hands and say, "I can fake this in [insert your procedural language of choice]." Anyone who's come from a procedural background to object-oriented programming has gone through this learning curve, and it's well worth it. The benefits of programming with an object-oriented language are incalculable, both in terms of writing code more efficiently and having a system that can be easily modified and extended once written. It just might not seem that way at first. However, almost 20 years of developing software (including the past 8 with object-oriented languages) have shown me that OOP concepts, *when applied correctly,* do in fact live up to their promise. Without further ado, let's roll up our sleeves and see what all the fuss is about.

Everything Is an Object

In a true object-oriented language, all problem domain entities are expressed through the concept of *objects*. (Note that in this book I'll be using the Coad/Yourdon definition for "problem domain"—that is, that a problem domain is the problem you're attempting to solve, in terms of its specific complexities, terminology, challenges, and so on.) As you might guess, objects are the central idea behind object-oriented programming. Most of us don't walk around thinking in terms of structures, data packets, function calls, and pointers; instead, we typically think in terms of objects. Let's look at an example.

If you were writing an invoicing application and you needed to tally the detail lines of the invoice, which of the following mental approaches would be more intuitive from the client's perspective?

- **Non-object-oriented approach**   I'll have access to a data structure representing an invoice header. This invoice header structure will also include a doubly linked list of invoice detail structures, each of which contains a total line amount. Therefore, to get an invoice total, I need to declare a variable named something like *totalInvoiceAmount* and initialize it to 0, get a pointer to the invoice header structure, get the head of the linked list of detail lines, and then traverse the linked list of detail lines. As I read each detail line structure, I'll get its member variable containing the total for that line and increment my *totalInvoiceAmount* variable.

- **Object-oriented approach**   I'll have an invoice object, and I'll send a message to that object to ask it for the total amount. I don't need to think about how the information is stored internally in the object, as I had to do with the non-object-oriented data structure. I simply treat the object in a natural manner, making requests to it by sending messages. (The group of messages that an object can process are collectively called the object's *interface*. In the following paragraph, I'll explain why thinking in terms of interface rather than implementation, as I have done here, is justifiable in the object-oriented approach.)

Obviously, the object-oriented approach is more intuitive and closer to how many of us would think our way through a problem. In the second solution, the invoice object probably iterates through a *collection* of invoice detail objects, sending a message to each one requesting its line amount. However, if what you're looking for is the total, *you don't care how it's done.* You don't care because one of the main tenets of object-oriented programming is *encapsulation*—the ability of an object to hide its internal data and methods and to present an interface that makes the important parts of the object programmatically accessible. The internals of how an object carries out its job are unimportant as long as that object can carry out that job. You are simply presented with an interface to the object, and you use that interface to make the object perform a given task on your behalf. (I'll further explain the concepts of encapsulation and interfaces later in this chapter.) The point here is that programs written to simulate the real-world objects of the problem domain are much easier to design and write because they allow us to think in a more natural way.

Notice that the second approach required an object to perform work on your behalf—that is, to total the detail lines. An object doesn't contain data only, as a structure does. Objects, by definition, comprise data and the methods that work on that data. This means that when working with a problem domain we can do more than design the necessary data structures. We can also look at which methods should be associated with a given object so that the object is a fully encapsulated bit of functionality. The examples that follow here and in the coming sections help illustrate this concept.

> **Note**   The code snippets in this chapter present the concepts of object-oriented programming. Keep in mind that while I present many example code snippets in C#, the concepts themselves are generic to OOP and are not specific to any one programming language. For comparison purposes in this chapter, I'll also present examples in C, which is not object-oriented.

Let's say you're writing an application to calculate the pay of your new company's only employee, Amy. Using C, you would code something similar to the following to associate certain data with an employee:

```
struct EMPLOYEE
{
    char szFirstName[25];
    char szLastName[25];

    int iAge;

    double dPayRate;

};
```

Here's how you'd calculate Amy's pay by using the *EMPLOYEE* structure:

```c
void main()
{
    double dTotalPay;

    struct EMPLOYEE* pEmp;
    pEmp = (struct EMPLOYEE*)malloc(sizeof(struct EMPLOYEE));

    if (pEmp)
    {
        pEmp->dPayRate = 100;

        strcpy(pEmp->szFirstName, "Amy");
        strcpy(pEmp->szLastName, "Anderson");
        pEmp->iAge = 28;

        dTotalPay = pEmp->dPayRate * 40;
        printf("Total Payment for %s %s is %0.2f",
                pEmp->szFirstName, pEmp->szLastName, dTotalPay);
    }

    free(pEmp);
}
```

In this example, the code is based on data contained in a structure and some external (to that structure) code that uses that structure. So what's the problem? The main problem is one of abstraction: the user of the *EMPLOYEE* structure must know far too much about the data needed for an employee. Why? Let's say that at a later date you want to change how Amy's pay rate is calculated. For example, you might want to factor in FICA and other assorted taxes when determining a net payment. Not only would you have to change all client code that uses the *EMPLOYEE* structure, but you would also need to document—for any future programmers in your company—the fact that a change in usage had occurred.

Now let's look at a C# version of this example:

```csharp
using System;

class Employee
{
    public Employee(string firstName, string lastName,
                    int age, double payRate)
    {
        this.firstName = firstName;
        this.lastName = lastName;
        this.age = age;
        this.payRate = payRate;
    }
```

(continued)

```
        protected string firstName;
        protected string lastName;
        protected int age;
        protected double payRate;

        public double CalculatePay(int hoursWorked)
        {
            // Calculate pay here.
            return (payRate * (double)hoursWorked);
        }
    }

class EmployeeApp
{
    public static void Main()
    {
        Employee emp = new Employee ("Amy", "Anderson", 28, 100);
        Console.WriteLine("\nAmy's pay is $" + emp.CalculatePay(40));
    }
}
```

In the C# version of the EmployeeApp example, the object's user can simply call the object's *CalculatePay* method to have the object calculate its own pay. The advantage of this approach is that the user no longer needs to worry about the internals of exactly how the pay is calculated. If at some time in the future you decide to modify how the pay is calculated, that modification will have no impact on existing code. This level of abstraction is one of the basic benefits of using objects.

Now, one valid comment might be that I could have abstracted the C client's code by creating a function to access the *EMPLOYEE* structure. However, the fact that I'd have to create this function completely apart from the structure being worked on is exactly the problem. When you use an object-oriented language such as C#, an object's data and the methods that operate on that data (its interface) are always together.

Keep in mind that only an object's methods should modify an object's variables. As you can see in the previous example, each *Employee* member variable is declared with the *protected* access modifier, except for the actual *CalculatePay* method, which is defined as *public*. Access modifiers are used to specify the level of access that derived class and client code has to a given class member. In the case of the *protected* modifier, a derived class would have access to the member, but client code would not. The *public* modifier makes the member accessible to both derived classes and client code. I'll go into more detail on access modifiers in Chapter 5, "Classes," but the key thing to remember for now is that modifiers enable you to protect key class members from being used incorrectly.

Objects vs. Classes

The difference between a class and an object is a source of confusion for programmers new to the terminology of object-oriented programming. To illustrate the difference between these two terms, let's make our EmployeeApp example more realistic by assuming that we're working not with a single employee but with an entire company of employees.

Using the C language, we could define an array of employees—based on the *EMPLOYEE* structure—and start from there. Because we don't know how many employees our company might one day employ, we could create this array with a static number of elements, such as 10,000. However, given that our company currently has only Amy as its sole employee, this wouldn't exactly be the most efficient use of resources. Instead, we would normally create a linked list of *EMPLOYEE* structures and dynamically allocate memory as needed in our new payroll application.

My point is that we're doing exactly what we shouldn't be doing. We're expending mental energy thinking about the language and the machine—in terms of how much memory to allocate and when to allocate it—instead of concentrating on the problem domain. Using objects, we can focus on the business logic instead of the machinery needed to solve the problem.

There are many ways to define a class and distinguish it from an object. You can think of a class as simply a type (just like *char*, *int*, or *long*) that has methods associated with it. An object is an instance of a type or class. However, the definition I like best is that a class is a blueprint for an object. You, as the developer, create this blueprint as an engineer would create the blueprint of a house. Once the blueprint is complete, you have only one blueprint for any given type of house. However, any number of people can purchase the blueprint and have the same house built. By the same token, a class is a blueprint for a given set of functionality, and an object created based on a particular class has all the functionality of the class built right in.

Instantiation

A term unique to object-oriented programming, *instantiation* is simply the act of creating an instance of a class. That instance is an object. In the following example, all we're doing is creating a class, or specification, for an object. In other words, no memory has been allocated at this time because we have only the blueprint for an object, not an actual object itself.

```
class Employee
{
    public Employee(string firstName, string lastName,
                int age, double payRate)
```

(continued)

```
    {
        this.firstName = firstName;
        this.lastName = lastName;
        this.age = age;
        this.payRate = payRate;
    }

    protected string firstName;
    protected string lastName;
    protected int age;
    protected double payRate;

    public double CalculatePay(int hoursWorked)
    {
        // Calculate pay here.
        return (payRate * (double)hoursWorked);
    }
}
```

To instantiate this class and use it, we have to declare an instance of it in a method similar to this:

```
public static void Main()
{
    Employee emp = new Employee ("Amy", "Anderson", 28, 100);
}
```

In this example, *emp* is declared as type *Employee* and is instantiated using the *new* operator. The variable *emp* represents *an instance of the* Employee *class and is considered an* Employee *object.* After instantiation, we can communicate with this object through its public members. For example, we can call the *emp* object's *CalculatePay* method. We can't do this if we don't have an actual object. (There is one exception to this, and that's when we're dealing with static members. I'll discuss static members in both Chapter 5 and Chapter 6, "Methods.")

Have a look at the following C# code:

```
public static void Main()
{
    Employee emp = new Employee();
    Employee emp2 = new Employee();
}
```

Here we have two instances—*emp* and *emp2*—of the same *Employee* class. While programmatically each object has the same capabilities, each instance will contain its own instance data and can be treated separately. By the same token, we can create an entire array or collection of these *Employee* objects. Chapter 7, "Properties, Arrays, and Indexers," will cover arrays in detail. However, the point I want to make here is that most object-oriented languages support the ability to define an array of objects. This, in turn, gives you the ability to easily group objects and iterate through them by calling methods of the object array or by subscripting the array. Compare this to the work you'd have to do with a linked list, in which case you'd need to manually link each item in the list to the item that comes before and after it.

The Three Tenets of Object-Oriented Programming Languages

According to Bjarne Stroustrup, author of the C++ programming language, for a language to call itself object-oriented, it must support three concepts: objects, classes, and inheritance. However, object-oriented languages have come to be more commonly thought of as those languages built on the tripod of *encapsulation, inheritance,* and *polymorphism.* The reason for this shift in philosophy is that over the years we've come to realize that encapsulation and polymorphism are just as integral to building object-oriented systems as class and inheritance.

Encapsulation

As I mentioned earlier, encapsulation, sometimes called *information hiding,* is the ability to hide the internals of an object from its users and to provide an interface to only those members that you want the client to be able to directly manipulate. However, I also spoke of *abstraction* in the same context, so in this section, I'll clear up any confusion regarding these two similar concepts. Encapsulation provides the boundary between a class's external interface—that is, the public members visible to the class's users—and its internal implementation details. The advantage of encapsulation for the class developer is that he can expose the members of a class that will remain static, or unchanged, while hiding the more dynamic and volatile class internals. As you saw earlier in this chapter, encapsulation is achieved in C# by virtue of assigning an access modifier—*public, private,* or *protected*—to each class member.

Designing Abstractions

An abstraction refers to how a given problem is represented in the program space. Programming languages themselves provide abstractions. Think about it like this: When was the last time you had to worry about the CPU's registers and stack? Even if you initially learned how to program in assembler, I'll bet it's been a long time since you had to worry about such low-level, machine specific details. The reason is that most programming languages abstract you from those details such that you can focus on the problem domain.

Object-oriented languages enable you to declare classes whose names and interfaces closely mimic real-world problem domain entities such that using the objects have a more natural "feel" to them. The result of removing the elements not directly related to solving the problem at hand is that you're able to focus specifically on the problem and greater productivity. In fact, paraphrasing Bruce Eckel in *Thinking in Java* (Prentice Hall Computer Books, 2000), the ability to solve most problems will generally come down to the quality of the abstraction being used.

However, that's one level of abstraction. If you take that a step further, as a class developer you need to think in terms of how you can best design abstractions for your class's clients to allow the client to focus on the task at hand and not be mired in the details of how your class works. At this point, a good question might be, "How does a class's interface relate to abstraction?" The class's interface is the implementation of the abstraction.

I'll use a somewhat familiar analogy from programming courses to help crystallize these concepts: the internal workings of vending machines. The internals of a vending machine are actually quite involved. To fulfill its responsibilities, the machine has to accept cash and coinage, make change, and dispense the selected item. However, the vending machine has a finite set of functions it needs to express to its users. This interface is expressed through a coin slot, buttons for selecting the desired item, a lever to request change, a slot that holds the returned change, and a shoot to dispense the selected item. Each of these items represents a part of the machine's interface. Vending machines have, by and large, remained much the same since their invention. This is because despite the fact that the internals have changed as technology has evolved, the basic interface has not needed to change much. An integral part of designing a class's interface is having a deep enough understanding of the problem domain. This understanding will help you create an interface that gives the user access to the information and methods that they need yet insulates them from the internal workings of the class. You need to design an interface not only to solve today's problems but also to abstract sufficiently from the class's internals so that private class members can undergo unlimited changes without affecting existing code.

Another equally important aspect of designing a class's abstraction is keeping the client programmer in mind at all times. Imagine that you're writing a generic database engine. If you're a database guru, you might be perfectly comfortable with terms like *cursors, commitment control,* and *tuples.* However, most developers who haven't done a lot of database programming aren't going to be as knowledgeable about these terms. By using terms that are foreign to your class's clients, you have defeated the entire purpose of abstraction—to increase programmer productivity by representing the problem domain in natural terms.

Another example of when to think about the client would be when determining which class members should be publicly accessible. Once again, a little knowledge of the problem domain and your class's clients should make this obvious. In our database engine example, you'd probably not want your clients to be able to directly access members representing internal data buffers. How these data buffers are defined could easily change in the future. In addition, because these buffers are critical to the overall operation of your engine, you'd want to make sure that they are modified through your methods only. That way you can be assured that any necessary precautions are taken.

> **Note**   You might think that object-oriented systems are designed primarily to make it easier to create classes. Although this feature does provide for short-term productivity gains, long-term gains come only after realizing that OOP exists to make programming easier for the class's clients. Always consider the programmer who is going to instantiate or derive from the classes that you create when designing your classes.

Benefits of Good Abstraction

Designing the abstraction of your classes in a way most useful to the programmers using them is paramount in developing reusable software. If you can develop a stable, static interface that persists across implementation changes, less of your application will need modification over time. For example, think of our earlier payroll example code. In the case of an *Employee* object and the payroll functionality, only a few methods are going to be relevant, such as *CalculatePay*, *GetAddress*, and *GetEmployeeType*. If you know the problem domain of a payroll application, you can easily determine, to a fairly high degree, the methods that the users of this class are going to need. Having said that, if you combine intimate knowledge of the problem domain with forethought and planning in the design of this class, you can be reasonably assured that the majority of your interface for this class will remain unchanged despite future changes in the actual implementation of the class. After all, from a user's perspective, it's only an *Employee* class. From the user's vantage point, almost nothing should change from version to version.

The decoupling of user and implementation detail is what makes an entire system easier to understand and therefore easier to maintain. Contrast this with procedural languages such as C, in which each module needs to explicitly name and access the members of a given structure. In that case, each time the structure's members change, every single line of code referring to the structure must also change.

Inheritance

Inheritance relates to the programmer's ability to specify that one class has a *kind-of* relationship with another class. Through inheritance, you can create (or derive) a new class that's based on an existing class. You can then modify the class the way that you want and create new objects of the derived type. This ability is the essence of creating a class hierarchy. Outside of abstraction, inheritance is the most significant part of a system's overall design. A *derived class* is the new class being created, and the *base class* is the one from which the new class is derived. The newly derived class inherits all the members of the base class, thereby enabling you to reuse previous work.

> **Note**   In C#, the issue of which base class members are inherited is controlled by the access modifiers used to define the member. I'll get into that level of detail in Chapter 5. For the purposes of this discussion, you can assume that a derived class will inherit all its base class members.

As an example of when and how to use inheritance, let's look back at our EmployeeApp example. In that example, we would almost certainly have different types of employees, such as salaried, contractor, and hourly. While all of these *Employee* objects would have a similar interface, they would in many cases function differently internally. For instance, the *CalculatePay* method would work differently for a salaried employee than it would for a contractor. However, you want the same *CalculatePay* interface for your users regardless of employee type.

If you're new to object-oriented programming, you might be wondering, "Why do I even need objects here? Why can't I simply have an *EMPLOYEE* structure with an employee type member and then have a function similar to this?"

```
Double CalculatePay(EMPLOYEE* pEmployee, int iHoursWorked)
{
    // Validate pEmployee pointer.

    if (pEmployee->type == SALARIED)
    {
        // Do W-2 employee processing.
    }
    else if (pEmployee->type == CONTRACTOR)
    {
        // Do 1099 processing.
    }
    else if (pEmployee-> == HOURLY)
```

```
    {
        // Do hourly processing.
    }
    else
    {
        // Do corp-to-corp processing.
    }

    // Return the value from one of the
    // compound statements above.
}
```

This code has a couple of problems. First, the success of the *CalculatePay* function is tightly linked to the *EMPLOYEE* structure. As I mentioned earlier, tight coupling like this is a problem because any modification to the *EMPLOYEE* structure will break this code. As an object-oriented programmer, the last thing you want to do is burden the users of your class with needing to know the intricate details of your class's design. That would be like a vending machine manufacturer requiring you to understand the internal mechanics of the vending machine before you can purchase a soda.

Second, the code doesn't promote reuse. Once you begin to see how inheritance promotes reuse, you realize that classes and objects are good things. In this case, you would simply define all the members for the base class that would function the same regardless of employee type. Any derived class would then inherit this functionality and change anything necessary. Here's how that would look in C#:

```
class Employee
{
    public Employee(string firstName, string lastName,
                    int age, double payRate)
    {
        this.firstName = firstName;
        this.lastName = lastName;
        this.age = age;
        this.payRate = payRate;
    }

    protected string firstName;
    protected string lastName;
    protected int age;
    protected double payRate;

    public double CalculatePay(int hoursWorked)
```

(continued)

15

```
    {
        // Calculate pay here.
        return (payRate * (double)hoursWorked);
    }
}

class SalariedEmployee : Employee
{
    public string SocialSecurityNumber;

    public void CalculatePay (int hoursWorked)
    {
        // Calculate pay for a W-2 employee.
    }
}

class ContractEmployee : Employee
{
    public string FederalTaxId;

    public void CalculatePay (int hoursWorked)
    {
        // Calculate pay for a contract employee.
    }
}
```

Three features of the preceding example are worth noting:

■ The base class, *Employee*, defines a string called *EmployeeId* that is inherited by both the *SalariedEmployee* and the *ContractEmployee* classes. The two derived classes do nothing to get this member—they inherit it automatically as a by-product of being derived from the *Employee* class.

■ Both derived classes implement their own versions of *CalculatePay*. However, you'll notice that they both inherited the interface, and although they changed the internals to suit their specific needs, the user's code remains the same.

■ Both derived classes added members to the members that were inherited from the base class. The *SalariedEmployee* class defines a *SocialSecurityNumber* string, and the *ContractEmployee* class includes a definition for a *FederalTaxId* member.

You've seen in this small example that inheritance enables you to reuse code by inheriting functionality from base classes. And it goes even further, allowing you to extend the class above and beyond that point by adding your own variables and methods.

Defining Proper Inheritance

To address the all-important issue of proper inheritance, I'll use a term from Marshall Cline and Greg Lomow's *C++ FAQs* (Addison-Wesley, 1998): *substitutability*. Substitutability means that the advertised behavior of the derived class is substitutable for the base class. Think about that statement for a moment—it's the single most important rule you'll learn regarding building class hierarchies that work. (By "work," I mean stand the test of time and deliver on the OOP promises of reusable and extendable code.)

Another rule of thumb to keep in mind when creating your class hierarchies is that *a derived class should require no more and promise no less than its base class on any inherited interfaces*. Not adhering to this rule breaks existing code. A class's interface is a binding contract between itself and programmers using the class. When a programmer has a reference to a derived class, the programmer can always treat that class as though it is the base class. This is called *upcasting*. In our example, if a client has a reference to a *ContractEmployee* object, it also has an implicit reference to that object's base, an *Employee* object. Therefore, by definition, *ContractEmployee* should always be able to function as its base class. Please note that this rule applies to base class functionality only. A derived class can choose to add behavior that is more restrictive regarding its requirements and promises as little as it wants. Therefore, this rule applies only to inherited members because existing code will have a contract with only those members.

Polymorphism

The best and most concise definition I've heard for polymorphism is that it is functionality that allows old code to call new code. This is arguably the biggest benefit of object-oriented programming because it allows you to extend or enhance your system without modifying or breaking existing code.

Let's say you write a method that needs to iterate through a collection of *Employee* objects, calling each object's *CalculatePay* method. That works fine when your company has one employee type because you can then insert the exact object type into the collection. However, what happens when you start hiring other employee types? For example, if you have a class called *Employee* and it implements the functionality of a salaried employee, what do you do when you start hiring contract employees whose salaries have to be computed differently? Well, in a procedural language, you would modify the function to handle the new employee type, since old code can't possibly know how to handle new code. An object-oriented solution handles differences like this through polymorphism.

Using our example, you would define a base class called *Employee*. You then define a derived class for each employee type (as we've seen previously). Each derived employee class would then have its own implementation of the *CalculatePay* method. Here's where the magic occurs. With polymorphism, when you have an upcasted pointer to an object and you call that object's method, the language's runtime will ensure that the correct version of the method is called. Here's the code to illustrate what I'm talking about:

```
using System;

class Employee
{
    public Employee(string firstName, string lastName,
                    int age, double payRate)
    {
        this.firstName = firstName;
        this.lastName = lastName;
        this.age = age;
        this.payRate = payRate;
    }

    protected string firstName;
    protected string lastName;
    protected int age;
    protected double payRate;

    public virtual double CalculatePay(int hoursWorked)
    {
        Console.WriteLine("Employee.CalculatePay");
        return 42; // bogus value
    }
}

class SalariedEmployee : Employee
{
    public SalariedEmployee(string firstName, string lastName,
                            int age, double payRate)
    : base(firstName, lastName, age, payRate)
    {}

    public override double CalculatePay(int hoursWorked)
    {
        Console.WriteLine("SalariedEmployee.CalculatePay");
        return 42; // bogus value
    }
}
```

```
class ContractorEmployee : Employee
{
    public ContractorEmployee(string firstName, string lastName,
                              int age, double payRate)
    : base(firstName, lastName, age, payRate)
    {}

    public override double CalculatePay(int hoursWorked)
    {
        Console.WriteLine("ContractorEmployee.CalculatePay");
        return 42; // bogus value
    }
}

class HourlyEmployee : Employee
{
    public HourlyEmployee(string firstName, string lastName,
                          int age, double payRate)
    : base(firstName, lastName, age, payRate)
    {}

    public override double CalculatePay(int hoursWorked)
    {
        Console.WriteLine("HourlyEmployee.CalculatePay");
        return 42; // bogus value
    }
}

class PolyApp
{
    protected Employee[] employees;

    protected void LoadEmployees()
    {
        Console.WriteLine("Loading employees...");

        // In a real application, we'd probably get this
        // from a database.
        employees = new Employee[3];

        employees[0] = new SalariedEmployee ("Amy", "Anderson", 28, 100);
        employees[1] = new ContractorEmployee ("John", "Maffei", 35, 110);
        employees[2] = new HourlyEmployee ("Lani", "Ota", 2000, 5);

        Console.WriteLine("\n");
    }
```

(continued)

19

```
protected void CalculatePay()
{
    foreach(Employee emp in employees)
    {
        emp.CalculatePay(40);
    }
}

public static void Main()
{
    PolyApp app = new PolyApp();

    app.LoadEmployees();
    app.CalculatePay();
}
}
```

Compiling and running this application will yield the following results:

```
c:\>PolyApp

Loading employees...

SalariedEmployee.CalculatePay
ContractorEmployee.CalculatePay
HourlyEmployee.CalculatePay
```

Note that polymorphism provides at least two benefits. First, it gives you the ability to group objects that have a common base class and treat them consistently. In the example above, although technically I have three different object types—*SalariedEmployee*, *ContractorEmployee*, and *HourlyEmployee*—I can treat them all as *Employee* objects because they all derive from the *Employee* base class. This is how I can stuff them in an array that is defined as an array of *Employee* objects. Because of polymorphism, when I call one of those object's methods, the runtime will ensure that the correct derived object's method is called.

The second advantage is the one I mentioned at the beginning of this section: old code can use new code. Notice that the *PolyApp.CalculatePay* method iterates through its member array of *Employee* objects. Because this method extracts the objects as implicitly upcasted *Employee* objects and the runtime's implementation of polymorphism ensures that the correct derived class's method is called, I can add other derived employee types to the system, insert them into the *Employee* object array, and all my code continues working without me having to change any of my original code!

Summary

This chapter has taken you on a whirlwind tour through terminology and concepts that fall under the umbrella of object-oriented programming. A full discourse on the subject would require several chapters and would, therefore, take away from the focus of this book. However, a firm grasp of object-oriented fundamentals is imperative to getting the most out of the C# language.

We covered quite a few ideas in this chapter. Key to understanding object-oriented systems is knowing the difference between classes, objects, and interfaces and how these concepts relate to effective solutions. Good object-oriented solutions also depend on a sound implementation of the three tenets of object-oriented programming: encapsulation, inheritance, and polymorphism. The concepts presented in this chapter lay the groundwork for the next chapter, which introduces the Microsoft .NET Framework and the Common Language Runtime.

2

Introducing Microsoft .NET

Without a firm understanding of .NET and how the C# language plays into this Microsoft initiative, you won't fully comprehend some of the core elements of C# that are supported by the .NET runtime. The .NET overview presented in this chapter will help you understand not only the terminology used throughout this book, but also why certain features of the C# language work the way they do.

If you read any newsgroup or mailing list on the subject of .NET, you can see that some users are confused by the terminology of the technology. With the ambiguous and sometimes contradictory names being tossed about, it's been difficult just to keep track of the players. Obviously, the fact that all this is very new is part of the problem. The first thing I'd like to do is explain some terminology with regards to .NET.

The Microsoft .NET Platform

The idea behind Microsoft .NET is that .NET shifts the focus in computing from a world in which individual devices and Web sites are simply connected through the Internet to one in which devices, services, and computers work together to provide richer solutions for users. The Microsoft .NET solution comprises four core components:

- .NET Building Block Services, or programmatic access to certain services, such as file storage, calendar, and Passport.NET (an identity verification service).

- .NET device software, which will run on new Internet devices.

- The .NET user experience, which includes such features as the natural interface, information agents, and smart tags, a technology that automates hyperlinks to information related to words and phrases in user-created documents.

■   The .NET infrastructure, which comprises the .NET Framework, Microsoft Visual Studio.NET, the .NET Enterprise Servers, and Microsoft Windows.NET.

The.NET infrastructure is the part of .NET that most developers are referring to when they refer to .NET. You can assume that any time I refer to .NET (without a preceding adjective) I'm talking about the .NET infrastructure. The .NET infrastructure refers to all the technologies that make up the new environment for creating and running robust, scalable, distributed applications. The part of .NET that lets us develop these applications is the .NET Framework.

The .NET Framework consists of the Common Language Runtime (CLR) and the .NET Framework class libraries, sometimes called the Base Class Library (BCL). Think of the CLR as the virtual machine in which .NET applications function. All .NET languages have the .NET Framework class libraries at their disposal. If you're familiar with either the Microsoft Foundation Classes (MFC) or Borland's Object Windows Library (OWL), you're already familiar with class libraries. The .NET Framework class libraries include support for everything from file I/O and database I/O to XML and SOAP. In fact, the .NET Framework class libraries are so vast that it would easily take a book just to give a superficial overview of all the supported classes.

As a side note (as well as an admission of my age), when I use the term "virtual machine," I don't mean the Java Virtual Machine (JVM). I'm actually using the traditional definition of the term. Several decades ago, before Java was anything more than another word for a dark, hot beverage, IBM first coined "virtual machine." A virtual machine was a high-level operating system abstraction within which other operating systems could function in a completely encapsulated environment. When I refer to the CLR as a kind of virtual machine, I'm referring to the fact that the code that runs within the CLR runs in an encapsulated and managed environment, separate from other processes on the machine.

The .NET Framework

Let's look at what the .NET Framework is and what it delivers. The first thing I'll do is compare .NET to an earlier distributed application development environment. I'll then go through a list of the capabilities that .NET provides application developers to create powerful distributed applications more quickly.

Windows DNA and .NET

Did the phrase that I used earlier to describe .NET— "the new environment for creating and running robust, scalable, distributed applications"—sound familiar? If so, there's a reason: .NET is basically the offspring of an earlier attempt to satisfy these lofty goals. That platform was called Windows DNA. However, .NET is much more than Windows DNA was meant to be. Windows DNA was a solutions platform that focused on solving business problems through the use of Microsoft server products. The term "glue" was sometimes used with Windows DNA, as in, "DNA defines the glue used to piece together robust, scalable, distributed systems." However, aside from being a technical specification, Windows DNA didn't have any tangible pieces. This is just one of several major differences between Windows DNA and .NET. Microsoft .NET is not just a set of specifications. It also includes several tangible products, such as compilers, class libraries, and even whole end-user applications.

The Common Language Runtime

The CLR is the very core of .NET. As the name suggests, it is a run-time environment in which applications written in different languages can all play and get along nicely—otherwise known as *cross-language interoperability*. How does the CLR provide this cozy environment for cross-language interoperability? The Common Language Specification (CLS) is a set of rules that a language compiler must adhere to in order to create .NET applications that run in the CLR. Anyone, even you or me, who wants to write a .NET-compliant compiler needs simply to adhere to these rules and, *voila!*, the applications generated from our compilers will run right alongside any other .NET application and have the same interoperability.

An important concept related to the CLR is *managed code*. Managed code is just code that is running under the auspices of the CLR and is therefore being managed by the CLR. Think of it like this: In today's Microsoft Windows environments, we have disparate processes running. The only rule that applications are required to follow is that they behave well in the Windows environment. These applications are created by using one of a multitude of completely dissimilar compilers. In other words, the applications have to obey only the most general of rules to run under Windows.

The Windows environment has few global rules regarding how the applications must behave in terms of communicating with one another, allocating memory, or even enlisting the Windows operating system to do work on their behalf. However, in a managed code environment, a number of rules are in place to ensure that all applications behave in a globally uniform manner, regardless of the language they were written in. The uniform behavior of .NET applications is the essence of .NET and can't be overstated. Luckily for you and me, these global rules primarily affect the compiler writers.

The .NET Framework Class Libraries

The .NET Framework class libraries are monumentally important to providing language interoperability because they allow developers to use a single programming interface to all the functionality exposed by the CLR. If you've ever used more than one dissimilar language in development for Windows, you'll love this feature. In fact, the .NET Framework class libraries are forging a revolutionary trend in compiler development. Before .NET, most compiler writers developed a language with the ability to do most of its own work. Even a language such as C++, which was designed as a scaled-down grouping of functionality to be used in conjunction with a class library, has at least some functionality on its own. However, in the world of .NET, languages are becoming little more than syntactical interfaces to the .NET Framework class libraries.

As an example, let's first take a look at the standard "Hello, World" application in C++ and then compare it to an application that does the same thing in C#:

```
#include <iostream.h>

int main(int argc, char* argv[])
{
    cout << "Hello, World!" << endl;
    return 0;
}
```

Notice that the application first includes a header file with the declaration of the *cout* function. The application's *main* function—every C/C++ application's entry point—uses the *cout* function to write the string "Hello, World" to the standard output device. However, what's important to note here is that you can't write this application in any .NET language without the .NET Framework class libraries. That's right: .NET languages don't even have the most basic compiler features, such as the ability to output a string to the console. Now I know that technically the *cout* function is implemented in the C/C++ runtime, which is itself a library. However, basic C++ tasks such as string formatting, file I/O, and screen I/O are at least logically considered part of the base language. With C#—or any .NET language for that matter—the language itself has almost no ability to do even the most menial task without the .NET Framework class library.

Let's look at the "Hello, World" example in C# to see what I mean:

```
using System;

class Hello
{
    public static void Main()
    {
        Console.WriteLine("Hello, World");
    }
}
```

So, what does this common set of class libraries mean to you, and is it a good thing? Well, it depends on your vantage point. A common set of class libraries means that all languages, theoretically, have the same capabilities because they all have to use these class libraries to accomplish anything except declaring variables.

One gripe I've seen on discussion boards is, "Why have multiple languages if they all have the same capabilities?" For the life of me, I don't understand this complaint. As someone that has worked in many multilanguage environments, I can attest that there's a great benefit to not having to remember what language can do what with the system and how it does it. After all, our job as developers is to produce code, not to worry about whether a favorite language has this advantage or that advantage.

Another question I've seen frequently is, "If all these .NET languages can do the same thing, why do we need more than one?" The answer relates to the fact that programmers are creatures of habit. Microsoft certainly didn't want to pick one language out of the many available and force millions of programmers to toss out their years of experience in other languages. Not only might a programmer have to become familiar with a new API, he or she might have to master a completely different syntax. Instead, a developer can continue using the language that's best suited for the job. After all, the name of the game is productivity. Changing what doesn't need to be changed is not part of that equation.

> **Note**   While in theory the .NET Framework class libraries enable compilers to make all the CLR's functionality available to a language's users, this is not always the case. One point of contention at Microsoft between the .NET Framework class libraries team and the different compiler teams is that although the .NET Framework class libraries team has attempted to expose all its functionality to the different languages, there's nothing—besides meeting minimal CLS standards—that requires the different compiler teams to implement every single feature. When I asked several Microsoft developers about this discrepancy, I was told that instead of each language having access to every exposed bit of .NET Framework functionality, each compiler team has decided to implement only the features that they feel are most applicable to their users. Luckily for us, however, C# happens to be the language that seems to have provided an interface to almost all of the .NET Framework functionality.

Microsoft Intermediate Language and the JITters

To make it easy for language writers to port their languages to .NET, Microsoft developed a language akin to assembly language called Microsoft intermediate language (MSIL). To compile applications for .NET, compilers take source code as input and produce MSIL as output. MSIL itself is a complete language that you can write applications in. However, as with assembly language, you would probably never do so except in unusual circumstances. Because MSIL is its own language, each compiler team makes its own decision about how much of the MSIL it will support. However, if you're a compiler writer and you want to create a language that does interoperate with other languages, you should restrict yourself to features specified by the CLS.

When you compile a C# application or any application written in a CLS-compliant language, the application is compiled into MSIL. This MSIL is then further compiled into native CPU instructions when the application is executed for the first time by the CLR. (Actually, only the called functions are compiled the first time they are invoked.) However, since we're all geeks here and this book is called *Inside C#*, let's look at what's really happening under the hood:

1. You write source code in C#.

2. You then compile it using the C# compiler (csc.exe) into an EXE.

3. The C# compiler outputs the MSIL code and a manifest into a read-only part of the EXE that has a standard PE (Win32-portable executable) header.

   So far, so good. However, here's the important part: when the compiler creates the output, it also imports a function named _CorExeMain from the .NET runtime.

4. When the application is executed, the operating system loads the PE, as well as any dependent dynamic-link libraries (DLLs), such as the one that exports the _CorExeMain function (mscoree.dll), just as it does with any valid PE.

5. The operating system loader then jumps to the entry point inside the PE, which is put there by the C# compiler. Once again, this is exactly how any other PE is executed in Windows.

   However, since the operating system obviously can't execute the MSIL code, the entry point is just a small stub that jumps to the _CorExeMain function in mscoree.dll.

6. The _CorExeMain function starts the execution of the MSIL code that was placed in the PE.

7. Since MSIL code cannot be executed directly—because it's not in a machine-executable format—the CLR compiles the MSIL by using a just-in-time (JIT) compiler (or JITter) into native CPU instructions as it processes the MSIL. JIT compiling occurs only as methods in the program are called. The compiled executable code is cached on the machine and is recompiled only if there's some change to the source code.

Three different JITters can be used to convert the MSIL into native code, depending on the circumstances:

- **Install-time code generation**   Install-time code generation will compile an entire assembly into CPU-specific binary code, just as a C++ compiler does. An assembly is the code package that's sent to the compiler. (I'll talk about assemblies in more detail later in this chapter in "Deployment.") This compilation is done at install time, when the end user is least likely to notice that the assembly is being JIT-compiled. The advantage of install-time code generation is that it allows you to compile the entire assembly just once before you run it. Because the entire assembly is compiled, you don't have to worry about intermittent performance issues every time a method in your code is executed the first time. It's like a time-share vacation plan in which you pay for everything up front. While paying for the vacation plan is painful, the advantage is that you never have to worry about paying for accommodations again. When and if you use this utility depends on the size of your specific system and your deployment environment. Typically, if you're going to create an installation application for your system, you should go ahead and use this JITter so that the user has a fully optimized version of the system "out of the box."

- **JIT**   The default JITter is called at run time—in the manner I described in the preceding numbered list—each time a method is invoked for the first time. This is akin to a "pay-as-you-go" plan and is the default if you don't explicitly run the PreJIT compiler.

- **EconoJIT**   Another run-time JITter, the EconoJIT is specifically designed for systems that have limited resources—for example, handheld devices with small amounts of memory. The major difference between this JITter and the regular JITter is the incorporation of something called *code pitching*. Code pitching allows the EconoJIT to discard the generated, or compiled, code if the system begins to run out of memory. The benefit is that the memory is reclaimed. However, the disadvantage is that if the code being pitched is invoked again, it must be compiled again as though it had never been called.

Unified Type System

One of the key features of any development environment is its type system. After all, a development environment with a limited amount of types or a system that limits the programmer's ability to extend the system-supplied types isn't an environment with a long life expectancy. The .NET runtime does more than just give the developer a single, unified type system that is used across all CLS-compliant languages. It also lets language writers extend the type system by adding new types that look and act just like the system built-in types. This means that you, as a developer, can use *all* types in a uniform manner, regardless of whether they are .NET predefined types or user-created types. I'll discuss the details of the type system and how the C# compiler supports it in Chapter 4, "The Type System."

Metadata and Reflection

As I mentioned in the earlier section "Microsoft Intermediate Language and the JITters," the CLS-compliant compilers take your source code as input and produce MSIL code for the runtime to compile (via the JITters) and execute. In addition to mapping source code to MSIL instruction sequences, CLS-compliant compilers have another equally important task: embedding metadata into the resulting EXE.

Metadata is data that describes data. In this context, metadata is the collection of programmatic items that constitute the EXE, such as the types declared and the methods implemented. If this sounds vaguely familiar, it should. This metadata is similar to the type libraries (typelibs) generated with Component Object Model (COM) components. Not only is the metadata output from a .NET compiler substantially more expressive and complete than the COM typelibs we're accustomed to, but the metadata is also always embedded in the EXE. This way, there's no chance of losing the application's metadata or having a mismatched pair of files.

The reason for using metadata is simple. It allows the .NET runtime to know at run time what types will be allocated and what methods will be called. This enables the runtime to properly set up its environment to more efficiently run the application. The means by which this metadata is queried is called *reflection*. In fact, the .NET Framework class libraries provide an entire set of reflection methods that enable any application—not just the CLR—to query another application's metadata.

Tools such as Visual Studio.NET use these reflection methods to implement features such as IntelliSense. With IntelliSense, as you type in a method name, that method's arguments pop up in a list box on the screen. Visual Studio.NET takes that functionality even further, showing all the members of a type. I'll discuss the reflection APIs in Chapter 15, "Multithreaded Programming."

Another incredibly useful .NET tool that takes advantage of reflection is the Microsoft .NET Framework IL Disassembler (ILDASM). This powerful utility parses the target application's metadata and then displays information about the application in a treelike hierarchy. Figure 2-1 illustrates what the "Hello, World" C# application looks like in ILDASM.

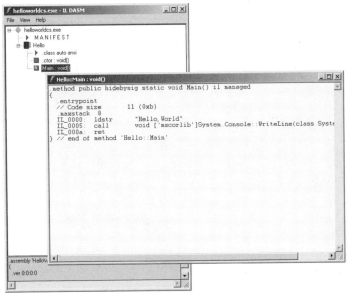

Figure 2-1 The C# "Hello, World" application displayed in ILDASM.

The window in the background of Figure 2-1 is the main IL Disassembler window. Double-clicking the *Main* method in the tree view brings up the window in the foreground that shows the *Main* method's details.

Security

The most important facet of any distributed application development environment is how it handles security. Thankfully for those of us who have long complained that Microsoft would never be taken seriously in the server-side enterprise solutions space without a completely new approach to security, .NET brings many concepts to the table. In fact, security begins as soon as a class is loaded by the CLR because the class loader is a part of the .NET security scheme. For example, when a class is loaded in the .NET runtime, security-related factors such as accessibility rules and self-consistency requirements are verified. In addition, security checks ensure that a piece of code has the proper credentials to access certain resources. Security code ensures role determination and identity information. These security checks even span process and machine boundaries to ensure that sensitive data is not compromised in distributed computing environments.

Deployment

Deployment is, by far, the most gruesome task associated with developing extremely large distributed systems. In fact, as any Windows developer can tell you, dealing with the different binary files, Registry issues, COM components, and support library installation of products such as open database connectivity (ODBC) and Data Access Objects (DAO) is enough to make you rethink your career choice. Thankfully, deployment is an area where the .NET design team obviously spent a lot of time.

The key to .NET application deployment is the concept of *assemblies*. Assemblies are simply packages of semantically related behavior that are built as either single-file or multiple-file entities. The specifics of how you deploy your application will vary based on whether you're developing a Web server application or a traditional desktop application for Windows. However, with the introduction of the assembly as a fully encapsulated set of functionality, deployment can be as simple as copying the necessary assemblies to a target location.

Many of the problems that caused so much trouble for programmers prior to the .NET Framework have now been eliminated. For example, there's no need to register components—as you do with COM components and Microsoft ActiveX controls—because with metadata and reflection, all components are self-describing. The .NET run time also keeps track of the files, and the versions of the files, associated with an application. Therefore, any application that is installed is automatically associated with the files that are part of its assembly. If a setup application attempts to overwrite a file needed by another application, the .NET runtime is smart enough to allow the setup application to install the needed file, but the CLR doesn't delete the previous version of the file because it's still required by the first application.

Interoperability with Unmanaged Code

As you might suspect, *unmanaged code* is code that isn't controlled by the .NET runtime. Let's be clear about something: this code is still run by the .NET runtime. However, unmanaged code doesn't have the advantages that managed code has, such as garbage collection, a unified type system, and metadata. You might wonder why anyone would want to run unmanaged code in the .NET environment. Well, you wouldn't do it out of choice. Rather, you would do it when faced with circumstances that offer few alternatives. Here are some situations that will make you thankful Microsoft put this feature into .NET:

- **Managed code calling unmanaged DLL functions**   Let's say your application needs to interface to a C-like DLL and the company that wrote the DLL isn't adopting .NET as quickly as your company is. In this case, you still need to call into that DLL from a .NET application. I'll cover this very example in Chapter 16, "Querying Metadata with Reflection."

- **Managed code using COM components**   For the same reason that you might need to continue supporting the ability to call a C-like DLL's functions from your .NET application, you might also need to continue supporting COM components. You do this by creating a .NET wrapper for the COM component so that the managed client thinks it's working with a .NET class. This is also covered in Chapter 16.

- **Unmanaged code using .NET services**   This is exactly the reverse problem—you want to access .NET from unmanaged code. It's solved using a reciprocal approach: a COM client is fooled into thinking it's using a COM server, which is actually a .NET service of some sort. You'll also see examples of this in Chapter 16.

Summary

Microsoft .NET represents a shift to a computing model in which devices, services, and computers work together to provide solutions for users. Central to that shift is the development of the .NET Framework and the CLR, shown in Figure 2-2 on the following page. The .NET Framework contains the class libraries shared by the languages compiled to run in the CLR. Because C# was designed for the CLR, you can't perform even the simplest tasks in C# without the CLR and .NET Framework class libraries. Understanding the features of these technologies is necessary to get the most out of C# and the remainder of this book.

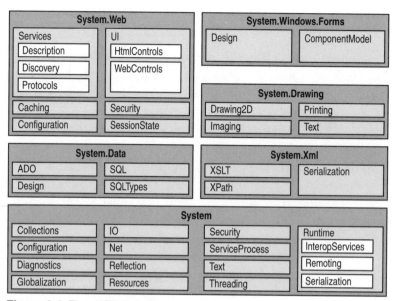

Figure 2-2 The .NET Framework contains libraries designed to facilitate interoperation between services, devices, and computers.

3

Hello, C#

Before we get to the heart of our subject—Part II, "C# Class Fundamentals," and Part III, "Writing Code"—I thought it would be a good idea to have a "getting started" chapter. In this chapter, I'll take you on a quick tour of the development process for a simple C# application. First, I'll cover the advantages and disadvantages of the different editors you can use to write in C#. Once you've selected an editor, we'll write the canonical "Hello, World" example application to get to know the basic syntax and structure of writing C# applications. You'll see that as in most languages, this syntax is formulaic and you can use this application as a template to write most basic C# applications. You'll then learn how to compile using the command-line compiler, and you'll learn how to run your new application.

Writing Your First C# Application

Let's go through the steps to get your first C# application up and running.

Choosing an Editor

Before you write a C# application, you need to choose an editor. The following sections describe the most prevalent editors and offer some pertinent facts about choosing an editor for your C# development.

Notepad

Microsoft Notepad has been the most commonly used editor during the early stages of C# for developers using the .NET Framework SDK to write C# applications. I used Notepad for this book for some other reasons I'll outline later. However, I wouldn't recommend using Notepad for the reasons described on the next page.

■ C# files should be saved with an extension of *.cs*. However, in Notepad's File Save dialog box, if you're not careful, attempting to name your file something like Test.cs will result in a file named test.cs.txt unless you remember to change the setting in the Save As Type drop-down list box to "All Files."

■ Notepad doesn't display line numbers—a major pain when the compiler reports an error on a given line.

■ Notepad inserts eight spaces for a tab, which means that writing anything beyond "Hello, World" can make applications difficult to read.

■ Notepad does not perform automatic indenting when you press the Enter key. Therefore, you have to manually tab over to the desired column to enter a line of code.

Other reasons exist, but as you can see, Notepad is *not a good choice* for developing C# applications.

Visual Studio 6

Because my background in development for Microsoft Windows is entrenched in the Microsoft Visual C++ language, Microsoft Visual Studio 6 is naturally my editor of choice. Visual Studio is a full-featured editor that includes all the features necessary to edit and save C# files.

One of the biggest advantages of using a programmer's editor is syntax highlighting. However, because Visual Studio 6 was released a couple of years before C# and was designed to develop Visual C++ applications, you'll need to do a little tweaking for Visual Studio 6 to highlight C# code correctly. The first step is to change a Visual Studio Registry key. Locate the following key in your Registry by using Regedit.exe or another Registry editor:

HKEY_CURRENT_USER\Software\Microsoft\DevStudio\6.0\ Text Editor\Tabs/Language Settings\C/C++\FileExtensions

The value will contain a string like the following:

cpp;cxx;c;h;hxx;hpp;inl;tlh;tli;rc;rc2

Add the *.cs* extension at the end of the value. (Note that an ending semicolon is optional.) The new Registry value would look like this:

cpp;cxx;c;h;hxx;hpp;inl;tlh;tli;rc;rc2;cs

Now, when you open a file in Visual Studio 6 with a .cs extension, Visual Studio will recognize it as a supported file.

Next you need to tell Visual Studio which files are keywords in C#. To do this, you create and place in the same folder as the msdev.exe file a file named usertype.dat. This is an ASCII text file that contains all the keywords that should be highlighted—place one keyword on each line. When Visual Studio starts up, it will load this file. Therefore, when you make a change to this file, you must restart Visual Studio to see your changes. I've included a copy of a usertype.dat file on this book's companion CD that lists all the keywords for the C# language. Figure 3-1 shows what your C# code will look like once you've followed these steps.

Figure 3-1 One advantage of using an editor that provides syntax highlighting like the one in Visual Studio 6 is immediate feedback as to whether a keyword is valid.

Visual Studio.NET

Obviously, if you want the maximum in productivity in the .NET environment, you should use Visual Studio.NET. Not only does it provide all the integrated tools and wizards for creating C# applications, but it also includes productivity features such as IntelliSense and Dynamic Help. With IntelliSense, as you type in a namespace or class name, members are automatically displayed so that you don't have to remember every member of every class. IntelliSense also displays all arguments and their types when you type in the name of a method and an opening parenthesis. Visual Studio 6 also provides this capability, but obviously it doesn't support the .NET types and classes. Dynamic Help is a feature new to Visual Studio. While you're typing code into the editor, a separate window displays topics related to the word the cursor is in. For example, if you type the keyword *namespace*, the window shows hyperlinks to help topics covering the usage of the *namespace* keyword.

Third-Party Editors

Let's not forget that there are also plenty of popular third-party editors out there, such as Starbase's CodeWright and Visual SlickEdit from MicroEdge. I won't go into the details of these editors, but I will make the point that you can use any third-party editor to write C# applications.

What I Used for this Book

Because I started this book while Visual Studio.NET was still in testing, I've used Visual Studio 6. I hope that using an environment that wasn't created for C# has helped me keep my promise that the book will be helpful for anyone developing C# applications, regardless of the chosen development environment. As I mentioned before, you can even write the demos in this book by using Notepad and you'll get the expected results.

"Hello, World"

Assuming you've decided on a development environment, let's look at your first C# application, the canonical "Hello, World" application. Write the following code into a file, and save it with a filename of HelloWorld.cs:

```
class HelloWorld
{
    public static void Main()
    {
        System.Console.WriteLine("Hello, World");
    }
}
```

Let's not worry yet about what each line of code does. At this point, we're just concerned with presenting the first application, getting it compiled, and executing it. Once we've done that—which will validate that you have the correct environment for creating and running C# applications—we'll look into the details of what this code does.

Using the Command-Line Compiler

If you're using an editor with a built-in feature for building C# applications, this step might be awkward. However, to stay as editor-agnostic as possible, I'm going to use the C# command-line compiler (csc.exe) throughout this book. This provides two benefits. First, it means that no matter what environment you're using, the steps for building the demos will always work. Second, learning the different compiler options will help you in the long run in situations where your editor doesn't provide you complete control over this step.

Once you've typed in the "Hello, World" code, open a command window and navigate to the folder where the HelloWorld.cs file is. Now type in the following:

```
csc helloWorld.cs
```

If everything works correctly, you should see results similar to those shown in Figure 3-2, where the compiler name and version are displayed along with any errors or warnings. As you can see, I'm using a beta version of the compiler at the time of this writing. Despite the version of the compiler you're using, you should not see any errors or warnings as a result of this simple example.

Figure 3-2 Compiling HelloWorld.cs should result in no errors or warnings.

If you receive an error along the lines of *'csc' is not recognized as an internal or external command, operable program or batch file*, it probably means that you haven't installed the .NET SDK, which includes the C# compiler.

If you invoke the C# compiler incorrectly—such as passing it an invalid file name—or you call it with the */?* argument, the compiler will list every possible switch that can be set when compiling your applications. I don't want to bog down this discussion with descriptions of all the flags that can be set for the compiler, so instead I'll focus on the switches salient to the current discussion, and you can investigate the rest at your leisure.

Running the Application

Now that you've built the "Hello, World" application, let's run it to make sure that your .NET runtime environment is set up correctly. All demos in this book will be "console applications," meaning that we're sticking to C# and not doing anything specific to Windows development. As a result, you can run these demos from the command line or from your editor if it supports running command-line applications.

If you're using the command-line option, open a command window now and type **HelloWorld** at the command prompt where you built the application. The output should be similar to this:

```
d:\>HelloWorld
Hello, World
```

If, on the other hand, you're attempting to run the application from an editor and either you do not see anything or a command prompt pops up, runs the application, and disappears quickly, alter your code as follows:

```
class HelloWorld
{
    public static void Main()
    {
        System.Console.WriteLine("Hello, World");
        String str = System.Console.ReadLine();
    }
}
```

The call to *System.Console.ReadLine* will cause the application to pause until you've pressed the Enter key, thereby giving you the opportunity to see that the application has printed what you were expecting. From here on, the demos in this book will not contain this line of code. If you're using an editor to run these demos, you'll need to remember to insert this line before the end of each application.

Code Walk-Through

Now that we've established that you can write and execute a C# application, let's walk through the code and look at the basic structure of a C# application.

One-Stop Programming

As you've seen throughout the first couple of chapters and in the "Hello, World" application, my examples have shown the methods of each class being defined within the class definition itself. This is not merely an exercise in convenience on my part, as C++ programmers might think. When programming in C++, you have two options: you can program the implementation of a class's member function directly into the class declaration—an example of *inline programming*—or you can separate the class declaration and its member function definitions into separate files. In C#, you do not have this choice.

When you define a class in C#, you must define all methods inline—header files do not exist. Why is this a good thing? It enables the writers of classes to create highly mobile code, which is one of the key concepts of the .NET environment. This way when you write a C# class, you end up with a fully encapsulated bundle of functionality that you can easily drop into any other development environment without worrying how that language processes include files or if it has a mechanism for including files within files. Using this "one-stop programming" approach, you can, for instance, take an entire class and drop it into an Active Server Pages (ASP) page and it will function just as it would if it were being compiled into a desktop Windows application!

Classes and Members

First you see in a basic C# application the name of a class or namespace. As you learned in Chapter 1, "Fundamentals of Object-Oriented Programming," you should select a class name that describes a problem domain—for example, *Invoice*, *PurchaseOrder*, or *Customer*. The beginning and ending of a class's definition is marked by the "curlies": { and }, respectively. Everything in between is considered part of that C# class. Notice above that we have a class named *HelloWorld* and everything in the application is defined within the context of that class.

All of a class's members are defined within the class's curlies. These include methods, fields, properties, indexers, attributes, and interfaces. I'll cover the specific details of how to define these different C# elements in the next several chapters.

The *Main* Method

Every C# application must have a method named *Main* defined in one of its classes. It doesn't matter which class contains the method—you can have as many classes as you want in a given application—as long as one class has a method named *Main*. In addition, this method must be defined as *public* and *static*. The *public* keyword is an access modifier that tells the C# compiler that anyone can call this method. As you saw in Chapter 1, the *static* keyword tells the compiler that the *Main* method is a global method and that the class does not need to be instantiated for the method to be called. This makes sense once you think about it because otherwise the compiler would not know how or when to instantiate your class. Because the method is static, the compiler stores the address of the method as the entry point so that the .NET runtime knows where to begin the execution of your application.

> **Note**   The demos in this chapter show the *Main* method as returning *void* and not receiving any arguments. However, you can define your *Main* method as returning a value as well as taking an array of arguments. These options, as well as how to iterate through the passed arguments to an application's *Main* method, are covered in Chapter 5, "Classes."

The *System.Console.WriteLine* Method

The *System.Console.WriteLine* method writes the provided string—followed by a line terminator—to the standard output device. In most cases, unless you do something fancy to change this or are using an editor that redirects the output to a window, this means the string will be output in a console window.

Namespaces and the *using* Directive

In Chapter 2, "Introducing Microsoft .NET," you learned that the .NET Framework class library is organized into a hierarchical lattice of namespaces. This can result in some rather lengthy names when a desired class or type is nested several layers deep. Therefore, to save on typing, C# provides the *using* directive. Let's look at an example of how this directive works. In our "Hello, World" application, we have the following line of code:

```
System.Console.WriteLine("Hello, World");
```

Typing this once isn't such a big deal, but imagine having to fully qualify every type or class in a large application. The *using* directive gives you the ability to list a kind of search path so that if the compiler can't understand something you've typed, it will search the listed namespaces for the definition. When we incorporate the *using* directive into our example, it looks like this:

```
using System;

class HelloWorld
{
    public static void Main()
    {
        Console.WriteLine("Hello, World");
    }
}
```

When the compiler parses the *Console.WriteLine* method, it will determine that the method is undefined. However, it will then search through the namespaces specified with the *using* directives and, upon finding the method in the *System* namespace, will compile the code without error.

Note that the *using* directive applies to namespaces and not classes. In the example we're using, *System* is the namespace, *Console* is the class, and *WriteLine* is a static method belonging to *Console*. Therefore, the following code would be invalid:

```
using System.Console; //ERROR Can't use a using
                      //directive with a class.

class HelloWorld
{
    public static void Main()
    {
        WriteLine("Hello, World");
    }
}
```

Although you can't specify a class in a *using* directive, the following variant of the *using* directive does enable you to create aliases for classes:

using *alias* = *class*

Using this form of the *using* directive, you can write code like the following:

```
using ouput = System.Console;

class HelloWorld
{
    public static void Main()
    {
        output.WriteLine("Hello, World");
    }
}
```

This gives you the flexibility to apply meaningful aliases to classes that are nested several layers deep in the .NET hierarchy, thus making your code a little easier to both write and maintain.

Skeleton Code

Let's quickly look at what can be viewed as skeleton code for most any C# application, code that illustrates a basic outline for a simple, no-frills C# application. You might want type this into a file and save it to use as a template in the future. Notice that the angle brackets denote where you need to supply information.

```
using <namespace>
namespace <your optional namespace>
class <your class>
{
    public static void Main()
    {
    }
}
```

Class Ambiguity

In the case of a type being defined in more than one referenced namespace, the compiler will emit an error denoting the ambiguity. Therefore, the following code will not compile because the class *C* is defined in two namespaces that are both referenced with the *using* directive:

```
using A;
using B;

namespace A
{
    class C
    {
        public static void foo()
        {
            System.Console.WriteLine("A.C.foo");
        }
    }
}

namespace B
{
    class C
    {
        public static void foo()
        {
            System.Console.WriteLine("B.C.foo");
        }
    }
}

class MultiplyDefinedClassesApp
{
    public static void Main()
    {
        C.foo();
    }
}
```

To avoid this type of error, make sure to give your classes and methods unique, descriptive names.

Something Went Wrong!

So what do we know so far? We know how to write, compile, and execute C#
applications, and we have a basic outline of a C# application to build from. And
when bad things happen to good C# applications? First, let's define a "bad thing":
anything that happens that I didn't expect to happen. With regards to programming, these come in two flavors: compile-time errors and run-time errors. Let's
look at a couple examples of each and how to rectify them.

Compile-Time Errors

When a compiler, including the C# compiler, can't interpret what you're attempting
to convey, it will print an error message and your application will fail to build.
Type the following code into a file named HelloErrors.cs, and compile it:

```
using Syste;

class HelloErrors
{
    public static void Main()
    {
        xConsole.WriteLine("Hello, World");
        Console.WriteLinex("Hello, World");
    }
}
```

Running the compiler will result in this output:

```
HelloErrors.cs(1,7): error CS0234: The type or namespace name
' Syste' does not exist in the class or namespace ''
```

Keeping in mind that there's always a default, global namespace, this means that
the compiler could not locate anything called *Syste*, for obvious reasons. However,
what I want to illustrate here is what to expect when the compiler encounters
syntax errors in your code. First you'll see the name of the current file being
compiled, followed by the line number and column position of the error. Next
you'll see the error code as defined by the compiler—in this case, *CS0234*.

Finally, after the error code, you'll see a short description of the error. Many
times, this description will give you enough to make the error clear. However,
if it doesn't, you can search for the error code in the .NET Framework SDK
Documentation, which is installed with the .NET Framework SDK, for a more
detailed description. The online help associated with the CS0234 error code is
shown in Figure 3-3.

45

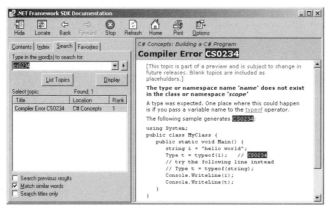

Figure 3-3 You can use the error code supplied by the C# compiler to find a description of the error in the online help documentation.

Notice that although we introduced three errors—the *System* namespace is misspelled, the *Console* class is misspelled, and the call to the *WriteLine* method is misspelled—the compiler will report only one error. This is because certain errors, once they are encountered, cause the compiler to abort the compilation process and print the errors accrued up to that point. In this example, the compiler stopped its compilation process once it could not resolve the *using* directive because that error could be the cause of many more errors. Once you've correctly spelled the *System* namespace in the *using* directive, the compiler will report the line numbers and column positions of the remaining two errors.

Spelunking with ILDASM

As you read in Chapter 2, when you create an EXE or a DLL by using a .NET compiler, the file is not your ordinary executable. Instead, it comprises a manifest, which lists the types and classes included in the file, and MSIL (Microsoft intermediate language) opcodes that are later compiled and executed by your installation application or the .NET runtime using a just-in-time compiler (JITter).

One huge advantage of this is that the generated MSIL looks like assembly language and can be used as an incredible teaching tool to illustrate what the compiler has done with our code. For this reason, many times in this book I'll "drop down" to the C# compiler's MSIL output to illustrate how something works under the covers or to explain why you should use a particular feature of the language in a specific manner. To see the MSIL output by the .NET compilers, Microsoft has included a disassembler named the Microsoft .NET Framework IL

Disassembler (ILDASM) to enable you to open a .NET executable file (EXE or DLL) and peruse its namespaces, classes, types, and code. We'll begin getting comfortable with ILDASM in the next section.

"Hello, World" in MSIL

In the Start menu's Run dialog box, type **ildasm** and click OK. You'll see a nondescript application with a few menu options. At this point, from the File menu, click Open. When the File Open dialog box appears, browse to the folder containing the HelloWorld.exe application you created earlier (on page 39) and select it. As shown in Figure 3-4, things start to look a bit more promising.

Figure 3-4 ILDASM lets you spelunk in the caverns of the manifest and the IL opcodes that make up your .NET application.

Notice the tree view that ILDASM uses to list the contents of a managed binary. Figure 3-5 shows the various icons used in the ILDASM tree view to describe the parts of a .NET application. As you can see by cross-referencing the icons shown in Figure 3-5 and the "Hello, World" program in ILDASM, HelloWorld.exe consists of a manifest, one class (*HelloWorld*), two methods (a class constructor and the static method *Main*), and a bit of class information.

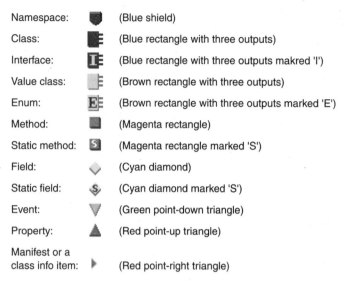

Namespace:		(Blue shield)
Class:		(Blue rectangle with three outputs)
Interface:		(Blue rectangle with three outputs makred 'I')
Value class:		(Brown rectangle with three outputs)
Enum:		(Brown rectangle with three outputs marked 'E')
Method:		(Magenta rectangle)
Static method:		(Magenta rectangle marked 'S')
Field:		(Cyan diamond)
Static field:		(Cyan diamond marked 'S')
Event:		(Green point-down triangle)
Property:		(Red point-up triangle)
Manifest or a class info item:		(Red point-right triangle)

Figure 3-5 The different icons used to denote the parts of a .NET application in ILDASM.

The most interesting part of "Hello, World" is in the *Main* method. Double-click the *Main* method in the ILDASM tree view, and ILDASM will present a window displaying the MSIL for the *Main* method, as shown in Figure 3-6.

Figure 3-6 To look at the generated MSIL for a method, open the binary in ILDASM and double-click the method.

"Hello, World," even in MSIL, isn't too exciting, but you can learn a few facts about the generated MSIL to carry over to any .NET application. Let's look at this method line by line to see what I mean.

```
.method public hidebysig static void Main() il managed
{
    .entrypoint
    // Code size    11 (0xb)
    .maxstack 8
    IL_0000:          ldstr      "Hello, World"
    IL_0005:      call void [mscorlib]System.Console::WriteLine
                          (class System.String)
} // end of method HelloWorld::Main
```

The first line defines the *Main* method by using the *.method* MSIL keyword. We can also see that the method is defined as being *public* and *static*, which are the default modifiers for the *Main* method. In addition, however, we see that this method is defined as *managed*. This is an important distinction because you can also write "unmanaged," or "unsafe," code in C#. Chapter 17, "Interoperating with Unmanaged Code," discusses unmanaged C# code.

The next line of code uses the MSIL *.entrypoint* keyword to designate this particular method as the entry point to the application. When the .NET runtime executes this application, this is where control will be passed to the program.

The next items of interest are the actual MSIL opcodes on lines IL_0000 and IL0005. The first uses the *ldstr* (Load String) opcode to load a hard-coded literal ("Hello, World") onto the stack. The next line of code calls the *System.Console.WriteLine* method. Notice that the MSIL prefixes the method name with the name of the assembly that defines the method. What's nice about this level of detail in the MSIL is that it means you can more easily write tools like dependency walkers that can look through an application to determine what files are needed for it to execute properly. Additionally, you can see the number of arguments (and their types) that are expected by the method. In this case, the *System.Console.WriteLine* method will expect a *System.String* object to be on the stack when it's called. Finally, line IL000a is a simple *ret* MSIL opcode to return from the method.

ILDASM is a powerful tool. When I refer to the C# compiler's generated MSIL, you can fire up ILDASM and follow along.

> **Note**   To tell whether an EXE or DLL is managed, attempt to open it with ILDASM. If the file is a valid managed file containing MSIL and a manifest, it will be opened. If it's not, you'll receive an error message stating that *<your file> has no valid CLR header and cannot be disassembled.*

C# Programming Guidelines

I'll close this chapter with some guidelines on writing C# applications.

When to Define Your Own Namespaces

In the "Hello, World" application, we used the *Console.WriteLine* method that's defined in the *System* namespace. In fact, all .NET types and classes are defined in namespaces. However, we didn't create a namespace for our application, so let's address that issue.

Namespaces are a great way of categorizing your types and classes so as to avoid name collisions. Microsoft places all the .NET class and type definitions in specific namespaces because it wants to make sure that its names don't conflict with the names of anyone using its compilers. However, whether you should use namespaces comes down to one question: will the types and classes you create be used in an environment not controlled by you? In other words, if your code is being used only by members of your own team, you can easily create naming rules such that name collision doesn't occur. However, if you're writing classes that will be used by third-party developers, in which case you don't have any control over naming practices, you should definitely use namespaces. In addition, since Microsoft recommends using your company name as the top-level namespace, I would recommend using namespaces anytime someone else might see your code. Call it free advertising.

Naming Guidelines

Statistically, the largest cost associated with application development has always been maintenance. Before we continue, I want to take a few minutes to talk about naming conventions because choosing a stable and easily understood naming convention will enable you to write code that's easier to read and, therefore, to maintain.

As most of us know, naming conventions are a touchy subject. The issue was easier back when Visual C++ and MFC first came out. I remember facing this question when I was a lead developer of a team at Peachtree Software that was tasked with writing the company's first accounting application in MFC. It was one of those beginning-of-the-project meetings with everyone raring to go and prepared to fight tooth-and-nail over any philosophical point, as opposed to later in the project when people just want to ship the darn product. As developers filed in, you could just sense from the gleam in their eyes and the texts under their arms that these guys were ready to do battle. In the face of what was surely going to be a bloody free-for-all, what did I do? I punted, of course! I stated that because much of MFC development was spent diving into Microsoft's code, we should use the naming conventions Microsoft used in writing MFC. After all, it would be counterproductive to have two naming systems in the source code—one for MFC and one for ours. Of course, the fact that I *like* Hungarian notation didn't exactly hurt.

However, it's a new day, and we have in C# a new language with a new set of challenges. In this environment, we don't see the Microsoft code. Even so, after many conversations with Microsoft's C# design team, I've found that a standard is evolving. It might end up slightly different than what I present here, but this will at least give you a place to start.

Naming Convention Standards

Before I explain where and how to name the different elements of your application, let's briefly look at the different standards employed today.

Hungarian Notation

Hungarian notation is the system used by most C and C++ developers (including those at Microsoft). It's a complete naming system created by Microsoft Distinguished Engineer Charles Simonyi. Back in the early 1980s, Microsoft adopted this famous—or infamous, depending on your point of view—naming system based on ideas from Simonyi's doctoral thesis, "Meta-Programming: A Software Production Method."

Hungarian notation specifies that a prefix be added to each variable to indicate its type. However, not every type was given a standard prefix. In addition, as other languages were introduced and new types created, new prefixes had to be created. This is why even if you go into a shop that employs Hungarian notation, you might see some prefixes you're not accustomed to seeing. (By the way, the term "Hungarian notation" comes from the fact that the prefixes make the variables look as if they are written in a language other than English; plus, Mr. Simonyi is from Hungary.)

Perhaps the most important publication that encouraged the use of Hungarian notation was the first book read by almost every Windows and OS/2 developer: Charles Petzold's *Programming Windows* (Microsoft Press), which used a dialect of Hungarian notation throughout its demo applications. In addition, Microsoft employed the notation in its own development. When MFC was released, a bunch of new prefixes specific to C++ development were released with its source code, thereby guaranteeing the continued use of Hungarian notation.

So why not simply continue using Hungarian notation? Because Hungarian notation is useful in situations where it's beneficial to know the type, or scope, of a variable being used. However, as you'll see in more detail in the next chapter, all types in C# are objects and based on the .NET *System.Object* class. Therefore, all variables have a basic set of functionality and behavioral characteristics. For this reason, the need for Hungarian notation is lessened in the .NET environment.

> **Note**   For the curious, or for those suffering from insomnia, the original paper that presented Hungarian notation can be found at *http://msdn.microsoft.com/library/techart/hunganotat.htm*.

Pascal Casing and Camel Casing

Although it's been impossible to pin down the C# team on a "hard" standard, it is obvious from their writings that they're following the notation set forth by fellow Microsoft employee Rob Caron, who suggests using a mixture of Pascal and camel casing when naming variables. In his paper "Coding Techniques and Programming Practices," available at MSDN (*http://msdn.microsoft.com/library/techart/cfr.htm*), he suggests using Pascal casing on method names where the first character is capitalized and camel casing on variable names. Accordingly, I've chosen to use the same naming convention in this book's demo applications. However, because C# contains more elements than just methods and variables, in the following sections I've listed the different elements and the naming conventions that I've seen Microsoft use internally and that I've chosen to use as well.

> **Note**   For more information on this topic, you can refer to the .NET Framework guidelines included in the .NET Framework SDK documentation under .NET Framework Developer Specifications\.NET Framework Design Guidelines\Naming Guidelines.

Namespaces

Use your company or product name, and employ mixed casing with an initial capital letter—for example, *Microsoft*. If you're in the business of selling component software, create a top-level namespace that is the same as your company name and then for each product, create a nested namespace with its embedded types, which will prevent name collision with other products. An example of this can be found in the .NET Framework SDK: *Microsoft.Win32*. This strategy might result in more long-winded names, but remember that the users of your code need only specify the *using* directive to save typing. If your company is called Trey Research, and you sell two products—a grid and a database—name your namespaces *TreyResearch.Grid* and *TreyResearch.Database.*

Classes

Because objects are supposed to be living, breathing entities that have abilities, name classes by using nouns that describe the class's problem domain. In cases where the class is more generic (that is, less specific to the problem domain) than that—for example, a type that represents an SQL string—use Pascal casing.

Methods

Use Pascal casing on all methods. Methods are meant to act—they carry out work. Therefore, let the names of your methods depict *what* they do. Examples of this are *PrintInvoice* and *OpenDatabase.*

In the case of methods that will be used in Boolean expressions, prefix the method with a verb that indicates what the method will do. For example, if you have a method that will return a Boolean value based on whether a workstation is locked, name the method something like *IsWorkStationLocked.* That way, if the method is used in an *if* statement, its meaning will be much clearer, as shown here:

```
if (IsWorkStationLocked) ...
```

Method Arguments

Use Pascal casing on all arguments. Give meaningful names to arguments so that when IntelliSense is used, the user can see immediately what each argument is used for.

Interfaces

Use Pascal casing on all interfaces. It's common to prefix interface names with a capital "I"—for example, *IComparable.* (This is the only Hungarian notation–like convention that I know of in C#.)

Many developers use the same rules when naming interfaces as they do when naming classes. However, there's a fundamental philosophical difference between the two. Classes represent an encapsulation of data and the functions that work on that data. Interfaces, on the other hand, represent behavior. By implementing an interface, you're saying that a class can exhibit that behavior. Therefore, a common technique is naming interfaces with adjectives. For example, an interface that declares methods for serializing data might be called *ISerializable* to easily denote the capability being taken on by the implementing class.

Class Members

This is probably the stickiest issue with regards to C# developers. Those of us coming over from C++ and MFC are accustomed to prefixing member names with *m_*. However, I would recommend using camel casing, in which the first letter is not capitalized. That way if you have a method that takes as an argument something called *Foo*, you can differentiate it from the internal representation of that variable by creating the internal member named *foo*.

It's redundant to prefix a member name with the class name. Take, for example, a class name of *Author*. Instead of creating a member named *AuthorName*, which would then be written out as *Author.AuthorName*, instead use *Name* as the member name.

Summary

Writing, compiling, and executing a program written in C# is an important first step in the exploration of the language. Although in general it doesn't matter what program you use to edit your C# source files, there are benefits to using more powerful editors and environments designed for C# development. Knowing the options and switches of the C# compiler will allow you to take control of how MSIL code is generated by the compiler. You can explore that code by using tools such as ILDASM, included with the Microsoft .NET Framework SDK.

The structure of C# programs provides for a number of features designed to make programs safer, easier to write, and less bug-prone. Included in this feature set are namespaces and the *using* directive. Finally, naming conventions, which include specific casing conventions, can make programs more readable and easier to maintain.

Part II

C# Class Fundamentals

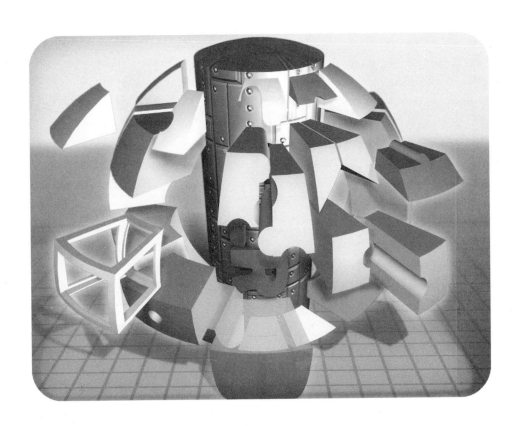

4

The Type System

At the center of the Microsoft .NET Framework is a universal type system called the .NET Common Type System (CTS). In addition to defining all types, the CTS also stipulates the rules that the Common Language Runtime (CLR) follows with regard to applications declaring and using these types. In this chapter, we'll look at this new type system so that you can learn the types available to C# developers and understand the ramifications of using the different types in C# programs. We'll begin by exploring the concept that every programming element is an object in .NET. We'll then look at how .NET divides types into the two categories—value types and reference types—and we'll discover how boxing enables a completely object-oriented type system to function efficiently. Finally, we'll cover how type casting works in C#, and we'll start looking at namespaces.

Everything Is an Object

Most object-oriented languages have two distinct types: those types that are intrinsic to the language (*primitive types*), and those types that can be created by users of the language (*classes*). As you might guess, primitive types are usually simple types such as characters, strings, and numbers, and classes tend to be more elaborate types.

Having two discrete sets of types causes a lot of problems. One problem relates to compatibility. For example, let's say you wanted to have a collection of *int*s in a traditional system with these two sets of types. You'd need to create a class specifically to hold values of type *int*. And if you wanted a class to hold a collection of *double*s, you'd have to do the same for that type. The reason for this is that these primitive types normally have nothing in common. They aren't real objects, so they don't derive from a common base class. They are more like magic types that have to be dealt with individually on their own terms. A similar problem surfaces in these traditional systems when you want to specify that a method can take an argument of *any* type supported by the language. Because these primitive types are incompatible, you can't specify an argument like this unless you write wrapper classes for each primitive type.

Thankfully, this is no longer an issue in the world of .NET and C# because everything in the CTS is an object. In fact, not only is everything an object but, even more importantly, all objects implicitly derive from a single base class defined as part of the CTS. This base class, called *System.Object*, will be covered in the section "Boxing and Unboxing."

Value Types and Reference Types

Creating a language where everything is an object is not a new concept. Other languages have tried this, the most famous being SmallTalk. The biggest disadvantage to making everything an object has always been poor performance. For example, if you attempt to add two values of type *double* in SmallTalk, an object is actually allocated on the heap. Needless to say, the allocation of an object is extremely inefficient when all you wanted to do was sum two numbers.

The designers of the CTS were faced with the task of creating a type system in which everything is an object but the type system works in an efficient manner, when applicable. Their solution was to separate the CTS types into two categories: *value types* and *reference types*. These terms, as you'll soon see, reflect how variables are allocated and how they function internally.

Value Types

When you have a variable that is a value type, you have a variable that contains actual data. Thus, the first rule of value types is that they cannot be *null*. For example, below I have allocated memory by creating a variable of the CTS type *System.Int32* in C#. In this declaration, what happens is that a 32-bit space is allocated on the stack.

```
int i = 32;
```

In addition, the act of assigning a value to *i* results in that 32-bit value being moved into this allocated space.

There are several value types defined in C#, including enumerators, structures, and primitives. Anytime you declare a variable of one of these types, you have allocated the number of bytes associated with that type on the stack and are working directly with that allocated array of bits. In addition, when you pass a variable that is a value type, you're passing that variable's value and not a reference to its underlying object.

Reference Types

Reference types are similar to references in C++ in that they are type-safe pointers. The type-safe part means that instead of merely being an address, which might or might not point to what you think it does, a reference (when not *null*) is always guaranteed to point to an object that is of the type specified and that has already been allocated on the heap. Also take note of the fact that a reference can be *null*.

In the following example, a reference type (*string*) is being allocated. However, what's happening under the covers is that the value has been allocated on the heap and a reference to that value has been returned.

```
string s = "Hello, World";
```

As with value types, there are several types defined as reference types in C#: classes, arrays, delegates, and interfaces. Any time you declare a variable of one of these types, you allocate the number of bytes associated with that type on the heap, and you are working with a reference to that object instead of directly with the bits (as with value types).

Boxing and Unboxing

So, the question becomes, "How do these different categories of types make the system more efficient?" This is done through the magic of *boxing*. At its simplest, boxing is the conversion of a value type to a reference type. The reciprocal case is when a reference type is *unboxed* back to a value type.

What makes this technique so great is that an object is only an object when it needs to be. For example, let's say you declare a value type such as *System.Int32*. Memory for this variable is allocated from the stack. You can pass this variable to any method defined as taking a *System.Object* type, and you access any of its members for which you have access. Therefore, to you it looks and feels just like an object. However, in reality, it's just four bytes on the stack.

It's only when you attempt to use that variable in a way consistent with its implied *System.Object* base class interface that the system automatically boxes the variable so that it becomes a reference type and can be used like any object. Boxing is how C# enables everything to appear to be an object, thereby avoiding the overhead required if everything actually were an object. Let's look at some examples to bring this into focus.

```
int foo = 42;        // Value type.
object bar = foo;    // foo is boxed to bar.
```

In the first line of this code, we're creating a variable (*foo*) of type *int*. As you know, the type *int* is a value type (because it's a primitive type). In the second line, the compiler sees that the variable *foo* is being copied to a reference type, which is represented by the variable *bar*. The compiler then spits out the MSIL code necessary to box this value.

Now, to convert *bar* back to a value type, you can perform an explicit cast:

```
int foo = 42;        // Value type.
object bar = foo;    // foo is boxed to bar.
int foo2 = (int)bar; // Unboxed back to int.
```

Notice that when boxing—that is, once again, when converting from a value type to a reference type—there is no explicit cast needed. However, when unboxing—converting from a reference type to a value type—the cast is needed. This is because in the case of unboxing, an object could be cast to any type. Therefore, the cast is necessary so that the compiler can verify that the cast is valid per the specified variable type. Because casting involves strict rules and because these rules are governed by the CTS, we'll take a look at this issue in more detail later in this chapter in "Casting Between Types."

The Root of All Types: *System.Object*

As I've mentioned, all types are ultimately derived from the *System.Object* type, thereby guaranteeing that every type in the system has a minimum set of abilities. Table 4-1 describes the four public methods that all types get for free.

Table 4-1 Public Methods of the *System.Object* Type

Method Name	Description
bool Equals()	This method compares two object references at run time to determine whether they are the exact same object. If the two variables refer to the same object, the return value is true. In the case of value types, which are discussed in the next section, this method returns true if the two types are identical and have the same value.
int GetHashCode()	Retrieves the hash code specified for an object. Hash functions are used when the implementor of a class wants to put an object's hash code in a hash table for performance reasons.
Type GetType()	Used with the reflection methods (discussed in Chapter 16, "Querying Metadata with Reflection") to retrieve the type information for a given object.
string ToString	By default, this method is used to retrieve the name of the object. It can be overridden by derived classes to return a more user-friendly string representation of the object.

Table 4-2 describes the protected methods of *System.Object*.

Table 4-2 Protected Methods of the *System.Object* Type

Method Name	Description
void Finalize()	This method is called by the runtime to allow for cleanup prior to garbage collection. Note that this method may or may not be called. Therefore, do not put code that must run into this method. This rule gets into something called *deterministic finalization,* which I'll cover in detail in Chapter 5, "Classes."
Object MemberwiseClone	This member represents a *shallow copy* of the object. By that I mean a copy of an object containing references to other objects that does not include copies of the objects referenced. If you need your class to support a *deep copy*, which does include copies of the referenced objects, you must implement the *ICloneable* interface and manually do the cloning, or copying, yourself.

Types and Aliases

While the CTS is responsible for defining the types that can be used across .NET languages, most languages choose to implement aliases to those types. For example, a four-byte integer value is represented by the CTS type *System.Int32*. C# then defines an alias for this called *int*. There is no advantage to using one technique over the other. Table 4-3 lists the different CTS types and their C# aliases.

Table 4-3 CTS Types and Aliases

CTS Type Name	C# Alias	Description
System.Object	*object*	Base class for all CTS types
System.String	*string*	String
System.SByte	*sbyte*	Signed 8-bit byte
System.Byte	*byte*	Unsigned 8-bit byte
System.Int16	*short*	Signed 16-bit value
System.UInt16	*ushort*	Unsigned 16-bit value
System.Int32	*int*	Signed 32-bit value
System.UInt32	*uint*	Unsigned 32-bit value

(continued)

| *System.Int64* | *long* | Signed 64-bit value |

Table 4-3 *(continued)*

CTS Type Name	C# Alias	Description
System.UInt64	*ulong*	Unsigned 64-bit value
System.Char	*char*	16-bit Unicode character
System.Single	*float*	IEEE 32-bit float
System.Double	*double*	IEEE 64-bit float
System.Boolean	*bool*	Boolean value (*true/false*)
System.Decimal	*decimal*	128-bit data type exact to 28 or 29 digits—mainly used for financial applications where a great degree of accuracy is required

Casting Between Types

At this point, let's look at one of the most important aspects of types: casting. Assuming a base class named *Employee* and a derived class named *ContractEmployee*, the following code works because there's always an implied upcast from a derived class to its base class:

```
class Employee { }

class ContractEmployee : Employee { }

class CastExample1
{
    public static void Main ()
    {
        Employee e = new ContractEmployee();
    }
}
```

However, the following is illegal, because the compiler cannot provide an implicit downcast:

```
class Employee { }

class ContractEmployee : Employee { }

class CastExample2
{
```

```
public static void Main ()
{
    ContractEmployee ce = new Employee(); // Won't compile.
}
}
```

The reason for the different behavior goes back to the Chapter 1, "Fundamentals of Object-Oriented Programming," and the concept of substitutability. Remember that the rules of substitutability state that a derived class can be used in place of its base class. Therefore, an object of type *ContractEmployee* should always be able to be used in place of or as an *Employee* object. That's why the first example compiles.

However, you cannot cast an object of type *Employee* down to an object of type *ContractEmployee* because there's no guarantee that the object supports the interface defined by the *ContractEmployee* class. Therefore, in the case of a downcast, an explicit cast is used as follows:

```
class Employee { }

class ContractEmployee : Employee { }

class CastExample3
{
    public static void Main ()
    {
        //Downcast will fail.
        ContractEmployee ce = (ContractEmployee)new Employee();
    }
}
```

But what happens if we lie and try to trick the CTS by explicitly casting a base class to a derived class as follows?

```
class Employee { }

class ContractEmployee : Employee { }

class CastExample4
{
    public static void Main ()
    {
        Employee e = new Employee();
        ContractEmployee c = (ContractEmployee)e;
    }
}
```

The program compiles, but running the program generates a run-time exception. There are two things to note here. First, the result is not a compile-time error because *e* might have really been an upcasted *ContractEmployee* object. Therefore, the true nature of the upcasted object can't be known until run time. Second, the CLR determines the object types at run time. When the CLR recognizes an invalid cast, it throws a *System.InvalidCastException*.

There is one other way of casting objects: using the *as* keyword. The advantage to using this keyword instead of a cast is that if the cast is invalid, you don't have to worry about an exception being thrown. What will happen instead is that the result will be *null*. Here's an example:

```
using System;

class Employee { }

class ContractEmployee : Employee { }

class CastExample5
{
    public static void Main ()
    {
        Employee e = new Employee();
        Console.WriteLine("e = {0}",
                    e == null ? "null" : e.ToString());

        ContractEmployee c  = e as ContractEmployee;
        Console.WriteLine("c = {0}",
                        c == null ? "null" : c.ToString());
    }
}
```

If you run this example, you'll see the following result:

```
c:>CastExample5
e = Employee
c = null
```

Note that the ability to compare an object to *null* means that you don't have to run the risk of using a null object. In fact, if the example had attempted to call a *System.Object* method on the *c* object, the CTS would have thrown a *System.NullReferenceException*.

Namespaces

Namespaces are used to define scope in C# applications. By declaring a namespace, an application developer can give a C# application a hierarchical structure based on semantically related groups of types and other (nested) namespaces. Multiple source code files can contribute to the same namespace. To that extent, if you're packaging several classes in a given namespace, you can define each of these classes in its own source code file. A programmer employing your classes can get access to all the classes within a namespace through the *using* keyword.

> **Note**   It is recommended that, where applicable, a company name be used as the name of the root namespace to help ensure uniqueness. See Chapter 3, "Hello, C#," for more on naming guidelines.

The *using* Keyword

Sometimes you'll want to use the fully qualified name for a given type in the form *namespace.type*. However, this can be rather tedious and sometimes isn't necessary. In the following example, we're using the *Console* object that exists in the *System* namespace.

```
class Using1
{
    public static void Main()
    {
        System.Console.WriteLine("test");
    }
}
```

However, what if we know that the *Console* object exists only in the *System* namespace? The *using* keyword allows us to specify a search order of namespaces so that when the compiler encounters a nonqualified type, it can look at the listed namespaces to search for the type. In the following example, the compiler locates the *Console* object in the *System* namespace without the developer having to specify it each time.

```
using System;

class Using2
{
    public static void Main()
    {
        Console.WriteLine("test");
    }
}
```

As you start building real-world applications with a few hundreds of calls to various *System* objects, you'll quickly see the advantage of not having to prepend each one of these object references with the name of the namespace.

You cannot specify a class name with the *using* keyword. Therefore, the following would be invalid:

```
using System.Console; // Invalid.

class Using3
{
    public static void Main()
    {
        WriteLine("test");
    }
}
```

What you can do, however, is use a variation of the *using* keyword to create a *using* alias:

```
using console = System.Console;

class Using4
{
    public static void Main()
    {
        console.WriteLine("test");
    }
}
```

This is especially advantageous in cases where nested namespaces combined with long class names make it tedious to write code.

CTS Benefits

One of the key features of any language or run-time environment is its support for types. A language that makes available a limited number of types or that limits the programmer's ability to extend the language's built-in types isn't a language with a long life expectancy. However, having a unified type system has many other benefits as well.

Language Interoperability

The CTS plays an integral role in allowing language interoperability because it defines the set types that a .NET compiler must support in order to interoperate with other languages. The CTS itself is defined in the Common Language Specification (CLS). The CLS defines a single set of rules for every .NET compiler, ensuring that each compiler will output code that interacts with the CLR consistently. One of the CLS requirements is that the compiler must support certain types defined in the CTS. The benefit being that because all .NET languages are using a single type system, you are assured that objects and types created in different languages can interact with one another in a seamless manner. It's this CTS/CLS combination that helps make language interoperability more than just a programmer's dream.

Singly Rooted Object Hierarchy

As I mentioned earlier, an important CTS characteristic is the singly rooted object hierarchy. In the .NET Framework, every type in the system derives from the *System.Object* base class. An important diversion from the C++ language, in which there is no implied base class for all classes, this single base class approach is endorsed by OOP theorists and is implemented in most mainstream object-oriented language. The benefits to a singly rooted hierarchy aren't immediately apparent, but over time you'll come to question how languages were designed before this type of hierarchy was adopted.

A singly rooted object hierarchy is the key to a unified type system because it guarantees that each object in the hierarchy has a common interface and therefore everything in the hierarchy will ultimately be of the same base type. One of the main drawbacks of C++ is its lack of support for such a hierarchy. Let's consider a simple example to see what I mean.

Say you've built up an object hierarchy in C++ based on a base class of your own making. We'll call this base class *CFoo*. Now say you want to integrate with another object hierarchy whose objects all derive from a base class called *CBar*. In this example, the object hierarchies have incompatible interfaces and it's going to require a lot of effort to integrate these two hierarchies. You might have to use some sort of wrapper class with aggregation or use multiple inheritance to make this work. With a singly rooted hierarchy, compatibility is not an issue because each object has the same interface (inherited from *System.Object*). As a result, you know that each and every object in your hierarchy—and, crucially, in the hierarchies of third-party .NET code—has a certain minimal set of functionality.

Type Safety

The last benefit of the CTS that I want to mention is type safety. Type safety guarantees that types are what they say they are and that only appropriate operations can be performed on a particular type. Type safety provides a number of advantages and capabilities—as described on the next page—most of which stem from the singly rooted object hierarchy.

- Every reference to an object is typed, and the object it's referencing is also typed. The CTS guarantees that a reference always points to what it implies it points to.

- Because the CTS tracks every type in the system, there's no way to trick the system into thinking that one type is actually another. This is obviously a major concern for distributed applications in which security is a priority.

- Each type is responsible for defining the accessibility of its members by specifying an access modifier. This is done on a member-by-member basis and includes allowing any access (by declaring the member *public*), limiting the visibility to inherited classes only (by declaring the member *protected*), allowing no access at all (by declaring the member *private*), and allowing access only to other types in the current compilation unit (by declaring the member *internal*). I'll discuss access modifiers in more detail in the next chapter.

Summary

The Common Type System is an important feature of the .NET Framework. The CTS defines the type system rules that applications must follow to run properly in the CLR. CTS types are divided into two categories: reference types and value types. Namespaces can be used to define scope in an application. The benefits of a common type system include language interoperability, a singly rooted object hierarchy, and type safety. Types can be converted in C# through boxing and unboxing, and compatible types can be made to share characteristics and functionality through casting.

5

Classes

Classes are at the heart of every object-oriented language. As discussed in Chapter 1, "Fundamentals of Object-Oriented Programming," a class is the encapsulation of data and the methods that work on that data. That's true in any object-oriented language. What differentiates the languages from that point on are the types of data you can store as members and the capabilities of each class type. With classes, as with a lot of the language's features, C# borrows a little from C++ and Java and adds some ingenuity to create elegant solutions to old problems.

In this chapter, I'll first describe the basics of defining classes in C#, including instance members, access modifiers, constructors, and initialization lists, and then I'll move on to defining static members and the difference between constant and read-only fields. After that, I'll cover destructors and something called deterministic finalization. Finally, the chapter will wrap up with a quick discussion of inheritance and C# classes.

Defining Classes

The syntax used for defining classes in C# is simple, especially if you usually program in C++ or Java. You place the *class* keyword in front of the name of your class and then insert the class's members between the "curlies," like so:

```
class Employee
{
    private long employeeId;
}
```

As you can see, this class is as basic as it gets. We have a class named *Employee* that contains a single member named *employeeId*. Notice the keyword *private* that precedes our member. This is called an *access modifier*. Four valid access modifiers are defined by C#, and I'll cover them in a moment.

Class Members

In Chapter 4, "The Type System," I discussed the different types defined by the Common Type System (CTS). These types are supported as members of C# classes and include the following:

- **fields**   A field is a member variable used to hold a value. In OOP parlance, fields are sometimes referred to as the object's data. You can apply several modifiers to a field, depending on how you want the field used. These modifiers include *static*, *readonly*, and *const*. We'll get to what these modifiers signify and how to use them shortly.

- **methods**   A method is the actual code that acts on the object's data (or fields). In this chapter, we'll focus on defining class data—Chapter 6, "Methods," will cover methods in a lot more detail.

- **properties**   Properties are sometimes called *smart fields* because they are actually methods that look like fields to the class's clients. This allows a greater degree of abstraction for the client in that the client doesn't have to know whether it's accessing the field directly or an accessor method is being called. Chapter 7, "Properties, Arrays, and Indexers," covers properties in detail.

- **constants**   As the name suggests, a constant is a field with a value that cannot be changed. Later in this chapter, I'll discuss constants and compare them to something called *read-only* fields.

- **indexers**   As a property is a smart field, an indexer is a smart array—that is, a member that lets an object be indexed through *get* and *set* accessor methods. An indexer enables you to easily index into an object for purposes of setting or retrieving values. Indexers and properties are both covered in Chapter 7.

- **events**   An event is something that causes some piece of code to run. Events are an integral part of Microsoft Windows programming. An event is fired, for example, when the mouse is moved or a window is clicked or resized. C# events use the standard publish/subscribe design pattern seen in Microsoft Message Queuing (MSMQ) and the COM+ asynchronous event model—which gives an application asynchronous event-handling capabilities—but in C# this design pattern is a "first-class" concept built into the language. Chapter 14, "Delegates and Event Handlers," describes how to use events.

■   **operators**   C# gives you the ability, via operator overloading, to add the standard mathematical operators to a class so that you can write more intuitive code by using those operators. Operator overloading is covered in detail in Chapter 13, "Operator Overloading and User-Defined Conversions."

Access Modifiers

Now that we've noted the different types that can be defined as members of a C# class, let's look at an important modifier used to specify how visible, or accessible, a given member is to code outside its own class. These modifiers are called *access modifiers* and are listed in Table 5-1.

Table 5-1 C# Access Modifiers

Access Modifier	Description
public	Signifies that the member is accessible from outside the class's definition and hierarchy of derived classes.
protected	The member is not visible outside the class and can be accessed by derived classes only.
private	The member cannot be accessed outside the scope of the defining class. Therefore, not even derived classes have access to these members.
internal	The member is visible only within the current compilation unit. The *internal* access modifier creates a hybrid of *public* and *protected* accessibility depending on where the code resides.

Note that unless you want a member to have the default access modifier of *private*, you must specify an access modifier for the member. This is in contrast to C++ where a member not explicitly decorated with an access modifier takes on the visibility characteristics of the previously stated access modifier. For example, in the following C++ code, the members *a*, *b*, and *c* are defined with *public* visibility, and the members *d* and *e* are defined as *protected* members:

```
class CAccessModsInCpp
{
    public:
    int a;
    int b;
    int c;
```

(continued)

```
    protected:
        int d;
        int e;
}
```

To accomplish the same goal in C#, this code would have to be changed to the following:

```
class AccessModsInCSharp
{
    public int a;
    public int a;
    public int a;
    protected int d;
    protected int d;
}
```

The following C# code results in the member *b* being declared as *private*:

```
public MoreAccessModsInCSharp
{
    public int a;
    int b;
}
```

The *Main* Method

Every C# application must have a *Main* method defined as a method in one of its classes. In addition, this method must be defined as *public* and *static*. (We'll get into what *static* means shortly.) It doesn't matter to the C# compiler which class has the *Main* method defined, nor does the class you choose affect the order of compilation. This is unlike C++ where dependencies must be monitored closely when building an application. The C# compiler is smart enough to go through your source files and locate the *Main* method on its own. However, this all-important method is the entry point to all C# applications.

Although you can place the *Main* method in any class, I would recommend creating a class specifically for the purpose of housing the *Main* method. Here's an example of doing that using our—so far—simple *Employee* class:

```
class Employee
{
    private int employeeId;
}
```

```
class AppClass
{
    static public void Main()
    {
        Employee emp = new Employee();
    }
}
```

As you can see, the example has two classes. This is a common approach to C# programming even in the simplest applications. The first class (*Employee*) is a problem domain class, and the second class (*AppClass*) contains the needed entry point (*Main*) for the application. In this case, the *Main* method instantiates the *Employee* object, and, if this were a real application, it would use the *Employee* object's members.

Command-Line Arguments

You can access the command-line arguments to an application by declaring the *Main* method as taking a string array type as its only argument. At that point, the arguments can be processed as you would any array. Although arrays won't be covered until Chapter 7, here's some generic code for iterating through the command-line arguments of an application and writing them out to the standard output device:

```
using System;
class CommandLineApp
{
    public static void Main(string[] args)
    {
        foreach (string arg in args)
        {
            Console.WriteLine("Argument: {0}", arg);
        }
    }
}
```

And here's an example of calling this application with a couple of randomly selected values:

```
e:>CommandLineApp 5 42
Argument: 5
Argument: 42
```

The command-line arguments are given to you in a string array. To process the parameters as flags or switches, you'll have to program that capability yourself.

> **Note**   Developers in Microsoft Visual C++ are already accustomed to iterating through an array that represents the command-line arguments to an application. However, unlike Visual C++, the array of command-line arguments in C# does not contain the application name as the first entry in the array.

Return Values

Most examples in this book define *Main* as follows:

```
class SomeClass
{
    ⋮
public static void Main()
{
    ⋮
}
    ⋮
}
```

However, you can also define *Main* to return a value of type *int*. Although not common in GUI applications, this can be useful when you're writing console applications that are designed to be run in batch. The *return* statement terminates execution of the method and the returned value is used as an error level to the calling application or batch file to indicate user-defined success or failure. To do this, use the following prototype:

```
public static int Main()
{
⋮
    // Return some value of type int
    // that represents success or value.
    return 0;
}
```

Multiple *Main* Methods

The designers of C# included a mechanism by which you can define more than one class with a *Main* method. Why would you want to do that? One reason is to place test code in your classes. You can then use the */main:<className>* switch with the C# compiler to specify which class's *Main* method is to be used. Here's an example in which I have two classes containing *Main* methods:

```
using System;

class Main1
{
    public static void Main()
    {
        Console.WriteLine("Main1");
    }
}

class Main2
{
    public static void Main()
    {
        Console.WriteLine("Main2");
    }
}
```

To compile this application such that the *Main1.Main* method is used as the application's entry point, you'd use this switch:

```
csc MultipleMain.cs /main:Main1
```

Changing the switch to */main:Main2* would then use the *Main2.Main* method.

Obviously, because C# is case-sensitive, you must be careful to use the correct case of the class in the switch as well. In addition, attempting to compile an application consisting of multiple classes with defined *Main* methods and not specifying the */main* switch will result in a compiler error.

Constructors

One of the biggest advantages of an OOP language such as C# is that you can define special methods that are always called whenever an instance of the class is created. These methods are called *constructors*. C# introduces a new type of constructor called a *static constructor,* which you'll see in the next section, "Static Members and Instance Members."

A key benefit of using a constructor is that it guarantees that the object will go through proper initialization before being used. When a user instantiates an object, that object's constructor is called and must return before the user can perform any other work with that object. It's this guarantee that helps ensure the integrity of the object and helps make applications written with object-oriented languages much more reliable.

But what do you name a constructor such that the compiler will know to call it when the object is instantiated? The C# designers followed the lead of

Stroustrup and dictated that constructors in C# must have the same name as the class itself. Here's a simple class with an equally simple constructor:

```
using System;

class Constructor1App
{
    Constructor1App()
    {
        Console.WriteLine("I'm the constructor.");
    }

    public static void Main()
    {
        Constructor1App app = new Constructor1App();
    }
}
```

Constructors do not return values. If you attempt to prefix the constructor with a type, the compiler will emit an error stating that you cannot define members with the same names as the enclosing type.

You should also note the way in which objects are instantiated in C#. This is done using the *new* keyword with the following syntax:

<class> <object> = new *<class>(constructor arguments)*

If you come from a C++ background, pay special attention to this. In C++, you can instantiate an object in two ways. You can declare it on the stack, like this:

```
// C++ code. This creates an instance of CMyClass on the stack.
CMyClass myClass;
```

Or you can instantiate the object on the free store (or heap) by using the C++ *new* keyword:

```
// C++ code. This creates an instance of CMyClass on the heap.
CMyClass myClass = new CMyClass();
```

Instantiating objects is different in C#, and this is a cause for confusion for new C# developers. The confusion stems from the fact that both languages share a common keyword for creating objects. Although using the *new* keyword in C++ lets you dictate where an object gets created, where an object is created in C# depends upon the type being instantiated. As we saw in Chapter 4, reference types are created on the heap and value types are created on the stack. Therefore, the *new* keyword lets you create a new instance of a class, but it doesn't determine where that object is created.

Having said that, the following code is valid C# code, but if you're a C++ developer it doesn't do what you might think:

```
MyClass myClass;
```

In C++, this would create an instance of *MyClass* on the stack. As mentioned, you can create objects in C# only by using the *new* keyword. Therefore, this line of code in C# merely declares that *myClass* is a variable of type *MyClass*, but it does not instantiate the object.

As an example of this, if you compile the following program, the C# compiler will warn you that the variable has been declared but is never used in the application:

```
using System;

class Constructor2App
{
    Constructor2App()
    {
        Console.WriteLine("I'm the constructor");
    }

    public static void Main()
    {
        Constructor2App app;
    }
}
```

Therefore, if you declare an object type, you need to instantiate it someplace in your code by using the *new* keyword:

```
Constructor2App app;
app = new Constructor2App();
```

Why would you declare an object without instantiating it? Declaring objects before using them—or "*new*-ing" them—is done in cases in which you're declaring one class inside of another class. This nesting of classes is called *containment*, or *aggregation*.

Static Members and Instance Members

As with C++, you can define a member of a class as being a *static member* or an *instance member*. By default, each member is defined as an instance member, which means that a copy of that member is made for every instance of the class. When a member is declared as a static member, there is only one copy of the member. A static member is created when the application containing the class is loaded, and it exists for the life of the application. Therefore, you can access the member even before the class has been instantiated. But why would you do this?

One example involves the *Main* method. The Common Language Runtime (CLR) needs to have a common entry point to your application. So that the CLR doesn't have to instantiate one of your objects, the rule is to define a static method called *Main* in one of your classes. You'd also want to use static members when you have a method that, from an object-oriented perspective, belongs to a class in terms of semantics but doesn't need an actual object—for example, if you want to keep track of how many instances of a given object are created during the lifetime of an application. Because static members live across object instances, the following would work:

```
using System;

class InstCount
{
    public InstCount()
    {
    instanceCount++;
    }

    static public int instanceCount = 0;
}

class AppClass
{
    public static void Main()
    {
        Console.WriteLine(InstCount.instanceCount);

        InstCount ic1 = new InstCount();
        Console.WriteLine(InstCount.instanceCount);

        InstCount ic2 = new InstCount();
        Console.WriteLine(InstCount.instanceCount);
    }
}
```

In this example, the output would be as follows:

```
0
1
2
```

A last note on static members: a static member must have a valid value. You can specify this value when you define the member, as follows:

```
static public int instanceCount1 = 10;
```

If you do not initialize the variable, the CLR will do so upon application startup by using a default value of 0. Therefore, the following two lines are equivalent:

```
static public int instanceCount2;
static public int instanceCount2 = 0;
```

Constructor Initializers

All C# object constructors—with the exception of the *System.Object* constructors—include an invocation of the base class's constructor immediately before the execution of the first line of the constructor. These constructor initializers enable you to specify which class and which constructor you want called. This takes two forms:

- An initializer of the form *base(...)* enables the current class's base class constructor—that is, the specific constructor implied by the form of the constructor called—to be called.

- An initializer taking the form *this(...)* enables the current class to call another constructor defined within itself. This is useful when you have overloaded multiple constructors and want to make sure that a default constructor is always called. Overloaded methods are covered in Chapter 6, but here's a quick and dirty definition: overloaded methods are two or more methods with the same name but different argument lists.

To see the order of events in action, note that the following code will execute the constructor for class A first and then the constructor for class B:

```
using System;

class A
{
    public A()
    {
        Console.WriteLine("A");
    }
}

class B : A
```

(continued)

```
{
    public B()
    {
        Console.WriteLine("B");
    }
}

class DefaultInitializerApp
{
    public static void Main()
    {
        B b = new B();
    }
}
```

This code is the functional equivalent to the following code in which the base class's constructor is called explicitly:

```
using System;

class A
{
    public A()
    {
        Console.WriteLine("A");
    }
}

class B : A
{
    public B() : base()
    {
        Console.WriteLine("B");
    }
}

class BaseDefaultInitializerApp
{
    public static void Main()
    {
        B b = new B();
    }
}
```

Let's look at a better example of when constructor initalizers are useful. Once again, I have two classes: *A* and *B*. This time, class *A* has two constructors, one that takes no arguments and one that takes an *int*. Class *B* has one constructor that takes an *int*. The problem arises in the construction of class *B*. If I run the following code, the class *A* constructor that takes no arguments will be called:

```
using System;

class A
{
    public A()
    {
        Console.WriteLine("A");
    }

    public A(int foo)
    {
        Console.WriteLine("A = {0}", foo);
    }
}

class B : A
{
    public B(int foo)
    {
        Console.WriteLine("B = {0}", foo);
    }
}

class DerivedInitializer1App
{
    public static void Main()
    {
        B b = new B(42);
    }
}
```

So, how do I ensure that the desired class *A* constructor will be called? By explicitly telling the compiler which constructor I want called in the initalizer list, like so:

```
using System;

class A
{
    public A()
    {
        Console.WriteLine("A");
    }
```

(continued)

```
    public A(int foo)
    {
        Console.WriteLine("A = {0}", foo);
    }
}

class B : A
{
    public B(int foo) : base(foo)
    {
        Console.WriteLine("B = {0}", foo);
    }
}

class DerivedInitializer2App
{
    public static void Main()
    {
        B b = new B(42);
    }
}
```

> **Note**   Unlike in Visual C++, you cannot use constructor initializers to access instance members, aside from constructors, of the current class.

Constants vs. Read-Only Fields

There will certainly be times when you have fields that you do not want altered during the execution of the application—for example, data files your application depends on, the value of *pi* for a math class, or any value that you use in your application that you know will never change. To address these situations, C# allows for the definition of two closely related member types: constants and read-only fields.

Constants

As you can guess from the name, *constants*—represented by the *const* keyword—are fields that remain constant for the life of the application. There are only two rules to keep in mind when defining something as a *const*. First, a constant is a member whose value is set at compile time, either by the programmer or defaulted by the compiler. Second, a constant member's value must be written as a literal.

To define a field as a constant, specify the *const* keyword before the member being defined, as follows:

```
using System;

class MagicNumbers
{
    public const double pi = 3.1415;
    public const int answerToAllLifesQuestions = 42;
}

class ConstApp
{
    public static void Main()
    {
        Console.WriteLine("pi = {0}, everything else = {1}",
            MagicNumbers.pi, MagicNumbers.answerToAllLifesQuestions);
    }
}
```

Notice one key point about this code. There's no need for the client to instantiate the *MagicNumbers* class because by default *const* members are static. To get a better picture of this, take a look at the following MSIL that was generated for these two members:

```
answerToAllLifesQuestions : public static literal int32 = int32(0x0000002A)
pi : public static literal float64 = float64(3.1415000000000002)
```

Read-Only Fields

A field defined as a *const* is useful because it clearly documents the programmer's intention that the field contain an immutable value. However, that only works if you know the value at compile time. So what does a programmer do when the need arises for a field with a value that won't be known until run time and should not be changed once it's been initialized? This issue—typically not addressed in other languages—was resolved by the designers of the C# language with what's called a *read-only field*.

When you define a field with the *readonly* keyword, you have the ability to set that field's value in one place: the constructor. After that point, the field cannot be changed by either the class itself or the class's clients. Let's say you want to keep track of the screen's resolution for a graphics application. You can't address this problem with a *const* because the application cannot determine the end user's screen resolution until run time, so you use code like that at the top of the following page.

```
using System;

class GraphicsPackage
{
    public readonly int ScreenWidth;
    public readonly int ScreenHeight;

    public GraphicsPackage()
    {
        this.ScreenWidth = 1024;
        this.ScreenHeight = 768;
    }
}

class ReadOnlyApp
{
    public static void Main()
    {
        GraphicsPackage graphics = new GraphicsPackage();
        Console.WriteLine("Width = {0}, Height = {1}",
                          graphics.ScreenWidth,
                          graphics.ScreenHeight);
    }
}
```

At first glance, this code seems to be just what you would need. However, there's one small issue: the read-only fields that we defined are instance fields, meaning that the user would have to instantiate the class to use the fields. This might not be a problem and could even be what you want in cases in which the way the class is instantiated will determine the read-only field's value. But what if you want a constant, which is static by definition, that can be initialized at run time? In that case, you would define the field with both the *static* and the *readonly* modifiers. Then you'd create a special type of constructor called a *static constructor*. Static constructors are constructors that are used to initialize static fields, read-only or otherwise. Here I've modified the previous example to make the screen resolution fields static and read-only, and I've added a static constructor. Note the addition of the *static* keyword to the constructor's definition:

```
using System;

class GraphicsPackage
{
    public static readonly int ScreenWidth;
    public static readonly int ScreenHeight;
```

```
    static GraphicsPackage()
    {
        // Code would be here to
        // calculate resolution.
        ScreenWidth = 1024;
        ScreenHeight = 768;
    }
}

class ReadOnlyApp
{
    public static void Main()
    {
        Console.WriteLine("Width = {0}, Height = {1}",
                          GraphicsPackage.ScreenWidth,
                          GraphicsPackage.ScreenHeight);
    }
}
```

Object Cleanup and Resource Management

One of the most important features of a component-based system is its ability to provide for cleanup and release of resources upon termination of components. By "cleanup and release of resources," I mean the timely release of references to other components as well as the release of scarce resources or limited resources over which there might be contention, such as database connections, file handles, and communication ports. By "termination," I mean that point at which the object is no longer in use.

In C++, cleanup is straightforward because it's done in the object's *destructor*, a function defined for every C++ object that automatically executes when the object goes out of scope. In the Microsoft .NET world, object cleanup is handled automatically by the .NET Garbage Collector (GC). This strategy is somewhat controversial because, in contrast to the predictability in C++ of when an object's termination code is executed, the .NET solution is a based on a "lazy" model. The GC uses threads running in the background that determine when an object is no longer being referenced. Other GC threads are then responsible for running that object's termination code. This is fine in most situations, but it's a less-than-optimal solution when dealing with resources that need to be released in a timely manner and in a predictable order. As you might be aware, this is not an easy problem to solve. In this section, I'll address the problems of object termination and resource management and your role in creating objects with predictable lifetimes. (Note that this section is heavily based on an excellent explanation of C# resource management made in an online public forum by Brian Harry, a member of Microsoft's .NET team. Thanks to Brian for allowing my use of his explanation.)

A Bit of History

A few years ago when the .NET project first started, a massive debate on the issue of resource management raged. Early contributors to .NET came from the COM and Microsoft Visual Basic teams, as well as many other teams across Microsoft. One of the big problems these teams faced was how to handle issues regarding reference counting, including cycles and errors resulting from misuse. One such example is the circular reference problem: one object contains a reference to another object that then contains a reference back to the first object. When and how one releases a circular reference can cause problems. Not releasing one or both references results in memory leak, which is extremely difficult to track down. And anyone who's done a lot of COM work can recount the stories of schedule time lost to chasing down bugs that resulted from reference-counting problems. Microsoft, realizing that reference-counting problems are fairly common in substantial component-based applications (such as COM applications), set out to provide a uniform solution in .NET.

The initial solution to the problem was based on automatic reference counting—so that if the programmer had forgotten reference counting it wouldn't matter—in addition to methods of detecting and handling cycles automatically. In addition, the .NET team looked at adding conservative reference collection, tracing collection, and GC algorithms that could collect a single object without doing an entire graph trace. However, for a variety of reasons—I'll cover these different approaches shortly—it was concluded that these solutions were not going to function in the typical case.

One major obstacle was that in the beginning days of .NET development, maintaining a high degree of Visual Basic compatibility was a primary goal. Therefore, the solution had to be complete and transparent with no semantic changes to the Visual Basic language itself. After much debate, the final solution was a context-based model where everything existing in a deterministic context would use reference counting on top of the GC and everything not in this context would use only the GC. This did help avoid some of the type bifurcation issues (described shortly) but did not yield a good solution for the fine-grained mixing of code between languages. So, the decision was made to make a series of changes to the Visual Basic language to "modernize" it and make it more capable. A part of that decision was the dropping of Visual Basic's lifetime compatibility requirements. This decision also generally ended investigation into deterministic lifetime issues.

Deterministic Finalization

With a bit of the history out of the way, let's define deterministic finalization. Once an object is determined to no longer be in use, its termination code executes and releases the references it holds to other objects. This termination process then naturally cascades through the graph of objects, starting from the topmost object. Ideally, this would work for both shared and single-use objects.

Note that there is no promise regarding time here. Once a GC thread discovers that a reference is no longer being used, that particular thread won't do anything else until the object termination code is executed. However, a CPU context switch can always occur during processing, meaning that an arbitrary—from the application's perspective—amount of time might pass before completion of this step. As mentioned above, many situations exist in which an application might care about the timeliness or order of execution regarding the termination code. These situations are generally tied to resources, for which there is a high degree of contention. Here are some examples of resources that an object might need to release as soon as the object is no longer in use:

- **Memory**   Freeing the memory for an object graph quickly returns the memory to the pool for use.

- **Window handles**   The footprint of the window object in the GC does not reflect the actual cost. There is some footprint inside the operating system to represent the window, and there might even be a limit, other than available memory, on the total number of window handles that can be allocated.

- **Database connections**   Concurrent database connections are frequently licensed, and therefore there might be a limited number of them available. It's important that these be returned to a pool promptly so that they can be reused.

- **Files**   Because there's a single instance of a given file and exclusive access is required for many operations, it's important that file handles be closed when not in use.

Reference-Counting Collection

Reference counting does a reasonable job of providing deterministic finalization in many cases. However, it's worth noting that in quite a few cases it doesn't, the most commonly cited example being cycles. In fact, straightforward reference counting *never collects objects that participate in cycles*. Most of us have painfully learned manual techniques to manage this, but using these techniques is an undesirable source of bugs. Also, if you start remoting objects across apartments, you can get apartment reentrancy and thus introduce a great deal of nondeterminism in your program. Some would argue that as soon as you hand a reference to an object outside the immediate control of a tightly coupled program, you have lost your deterministic finalization because you have no idea when or if that "foreign" code will release the reference. Others believe a complex system dependent on the order of termination of a complex graph of objects is an inherently brittle design likely to create a significant maintenance problem as the code evolves.

Tracing Collection

A tracing collector makes some weaker promises than reference counting does. It's a somewhat more lazy system with respect to executing termination code. Objects have *finalizers*, methods that are executed when the object is no longer reachable by the program. Tracing has the advantage that cycles are not an issue and the larger advantage that assigning a reference is a simple move operation—more on this shortly. The price that you pay is that there's no promise about termination code running "immediately" after a reference is no longer used. So, what's promised? The truth is that for well-behaved programs—an ill-behaved program is one that crashes or puts the finalizer thread in an infinite loop—the finalizers will be called for objects. The online documentation tends to be overly cautious about promises in this respect, but if an object has a *Finalize* method, the system will call it. This doesn't address the issue of deterministic finalization, but it's important to understand that resources will get collected and finalizers are an effective way to prevent resource leaks in a program.

Performance

Performance as it's related to the problem of finalization is an important issue. The .NET team believes that some kind of tracing collector must exist to handle cycles, which necessitates a big part of the cost of a tracing collector. It's also believed that code-execution performance can be substantially affected by the cost of reference counting. The good news is that in the context of all objects allocated in a running program, the number of those objects that really need deterministic finalization is small. However, it's usually difficult to isolate the performance cost to just those objects. Let's look at some pseudocode for a simple reference assignment when using a tracing collector and then at the pseudocode when using reference counting:

```
// Tracing.
a = b;
```

That's it. The compiler turns that into a single move instruction and might even optimize the whole thing away in some circumstances.

```
// Ref counting.
if (a != null)
    if (InterlockedDecrement(ref a.m_ref) == 0)
        a.FinalRelease();

if (b != null)
    InterlockedIncrement(ref b.m_ref);

a = b;
```

The bloat in this code is very high—the working set is bigger and the execution performance is obscenely higher, especially given the two interlocked instructions. You can limit code bloat by putting this stuff in a "helper" method and further increasing the length of the code path. In addition, code generation will ultimately suffer when you put in all the necessary *try* blocks because the optimizer has its hands somewhat tied in the presence of exception handling code—this is true even in unmanaged C++. It's also worth noting that every object is four bytes bigger because of the extra ref count field, again increasing memory usage and the size of the working set.

Two example applications follow that demonstrate the cost of this—they are provided courtesy of the .NET team. This particular benchmark loops, allocating objects, doing two assignments, and exiting the scope of one reference. As with any benchmark, it's open to some subjective interpretation. One might even argue that in the context of this routine, most of the reference counting can be optimized away. That's probably true; however, here it's intended to demonstrate the effect. In a real program, those kinds of optimizations are difficult, if not impossible, to perform. In fact, in C++ programmers make those optimizations manually, which leads to reference-counting bugs. Therefore, note that in a real program the ratio of assignment to allocation is much higher than here.

Here's the first example, ref_gc.cs—this version relies on the tracing GC:

```
using System;

public class Foo
```

(continued)

```
{
    private static Foo m_f;
    private int m_member;

    public static void Main(String[] args)
    {
        int ticks = Environment.TickCount;

        Foo f2 = null;

        for (int i=0; i < 10000000; ++i)
        {
            Foo f = new Foo();

            // Assign static to f2.
            f2 = m_f;

            // Assign f to the static.
            m_f = f;

            // f goes out of scope.
        }

        // Assign f2 to the static.
        m_f = f2;

        // f2 goes out of scope.

        ticks = Environment.TickCount - ticks;
        Console.WriteLine("Ticks = {0}", ticks);
    }

    public Foo()
    {
    }
}
```

And here's the second, ref_rm.cs—a ref counted version that uses interlocked operations for thread safety:

```
using System;
using System.Threading;

public class Foo
{
    private static Foo m_f;
    private int m_member;
    private int m_ref;
```

```
public static void Main(String[] args)
{
    int ticks = Environment.TickCount;

    Foo f2 = null;

    for (int i=0; i < 10000000; ++i)
    {
        Foo f = new Foo();

        // Assign static to f2.
        if (f2 != null)
        {
            if (Interlocked.Decrement(ref f2.m_ref) == 0)
                f2.Dispose();
        }
        if (m_f != null)
            Interlocked.Increment(ref m_f.m_ref);
        f2 = m_f;

        // Assign f to the static.
        if (m_f != null)
        {
            if (Interlocked.Decrement(ref m_f.m_ref) == 0)
                m_f.Dispose();
        }
        if (f != null)
            Interlocked.Increment(ref f.m_ref);
        m_f = f;

        // f goes out of scope.
        if (Interlocked.Decrement(ref f.m_ref) == 0)
            f.Dispose();
    }

    // Assign f2 to the static.
    if (m_f != null)
    {
        if (Interlocked.Decrement(ref m_f.m_ref) == 0)
            m_f.Dispose();
    }
    if (f2 != null)
        Interlocked.Increment(ref f2.m_ref);
    m_f = f2;

    // f2 goes out of scope.
    if (Interlocked.Decrement(ref f2.m_ref) == 0)
        f2.Dispose();
```

(continued)

```
        ticks = Environment.TickCount - ticks;
        Console.WriteLine("Ticks = {0}", ticks);
    }

    public Foo()
    {
        m_ref = 1;
    }

    public virtual void Dispose()
    {
    }
}
```

Note there's only one thread and therefore no bus contention, making this the "ideal" case. You could probably fine-tune this a bit but not much. It's also worth noting that Visual Basic has not historically had to worry about using interlocked operations for its reference counting (although Visual C++ has). In prior releases of Visual Basic, a component ran in a single-threaded apartment and was guaranteed that only a single thread at a time would be executing in it. One of the goals for Visual Basic.NET is multithreaded programming, and another is getting rid of the complexity of COM's multiple threading models. However, for those of you who want to see a version that doesn't use lock prefixes, another example follows, again courtesy of the .NET team: ref_rs.cs, a ref counted version that assumes it's running in a single-threaded environment. This program is not nearly as slow as the multithreaded version, but it's still quite a bit slower than the GC version.

```
using System;

public class Foo
{
    private static Foo m_f;
    private int m_member;
    private int m_ref;

    public static void Main(String[] args)
    {
        int ticks = Environment.TickCount;

        Foo f2 = null;

        for (int i=0; i < 10000000; ++i)
        {
            Foo f = new Foo();
```

```
            // Assign static to f2.
            if (f2 != null)
            {
                if (--f2.m_ref == 0)
                    f2.Dispose();
            }
            if (m_f != null)
                ++m_f.m_ref;
            f2 = m_f;

            // Assign f to the static.
            if (m_f != null)
            {
                if (--m_f.m_ref == 0)
                    m_f.Dispose();
            }
            if (f != null)
                ++f.m_ref;
            m_f = f;

            // f goes out of scope.
            if (--f.m_ref == 0)
                f.Dispose();
        }

        // Assign f2 to the static.
        if (m_f != null)
        {
            if (--m_f.m_ref == 0)
                m_f.Dispose();
        }
        if (f2 != null)
            ++f2.m_ref;
        m_f = f2;

        // f2 goes out of scope.
        if (--f2.m_ref == 0)
            f2.Dispose();

        ticks = Environment.TickCount - ticks;
        Console.WriteLine("Ticks = {0}", ticks);
    }

    public Foo()
    {
        m_ref = 1;
    }
```

(continued)

```
public virtual void Dispose()
{
}
}
```

Obviously, there are many variables here. Still, running all three of these applications results in the GC version running almost twice as fast as the single-threaded reference-counting example and four times faster than the reference-counting example with locking prefixes. My personal experience was as follows—note that these numbers represent the mean average on an IBM ThinkPad 570 running the .NET Framework SDK Beta 1 compiler:

```
GC Version (ref_gc)                     1162ms
Ref Counting (ref_rm)(multi-threaded)   4757ms
Ref Counting (ref_rs)(single-threaded)  1913ms
```

The Perfect Solution

Most would agree that the perfect solution to this problem would result in a system in which every object is cheap to allocate, use, and reclaim. In such an ideal system, every object goes away in a deterministic, orderly fashion the instant the programmer believes the object is no longer needed (regardless of whether cycles exist). Having invested countless hours into solving this problem, the .NET team believes that the only means of accomplishing this is by combining a tracing GC with reference counting. The benchmark data reflects that reference counting is too expensive to be used in a general-purpose way for all of the objects in programming environment. The code paths are longer, and the code and data working set is larger. If you then combine this already high price with the additional cost of implementing a tracing collector to reclaim cycles, you're spending an exorbitant price for memory management.

It should be noted that in the beginning days of .NET development, various techniques were researched to find a way to improve reference-counting performance. There have been reasonably high performance systems built on reference counting before. Alas, after surveying the literature, it was determined that such systems accomplished the improved performance by giving up some of their determinism.

As an aside, it might be worth noting that C++/COM programs don't suffer from this problem. Most high performance C++ programs that use COM use C++ classes internally where the programmer is required to explicitly manage the memory. C++ programmers generally use COM only to create the interfaces for their clients. This is a key characteristic that allows those programs to perform well. However, this is obviously not the goal of .NET, in which the issues of memory management are intended to be handled by the GC and not the programmer.

The (Almost) Perfect Solution

So, like most things in life, you can't have it all with regards to the resource management solution. But what if you could have deterministic finalization on just those objects that you need it on? The .NET team spent a lot of time thinking about this. Remember that this was in the context of exactly duplicating Visual Basic 6 semantics within the new system. Most of that analysis still applies, but some ideas that were discarded a long time ago now look more palatable as resource management techniques rather than transparent Visual Basic 6 lifetime semantics.

The first attempt was to simply mark a class as requiring deterministic finalization either with an attribute or by inheriting from a "special" class. This would cause the object to be reference counted. Many different designs were investigated that included both subclasses of *System.Object* and changing the root of the class hierarchy to some other class that would bind the reference-counting world to the non-reference-counting world. Unfortunately, there were a number of issues that could not be circumvented, as described in the following sections.

Composition

Any time you take an object that requires deterministic finalization and store it in an object that doesn't, you've lost the determinism (because determinism is not transitive). The problem is that this strikes at the heart of the class hierarchy. For example, what about arrays? If you want arrays of deterministic objects, arrays need to be deterministic. And what about collections and hash tables? The list goes on—before you know it, the entire class library is reference counted, thereby defeating the purpose.

Another alternative was to bifurcate (or split into two branches) the .NET Framework class library and have two versions of many types of classes—for example, deterministic arrays and nondeterministic arrays. This was seriously considered. However, the final decision was that having two copies of the entire framework would be confusing, perform horribly—two copies of every class would be loaded—and in the end wouldn't be practical.

Specific solutions to specific classes were examined, but none of these solutions came close to being a general purpose solution scalable for the entire framework. Making the fundamental problem—if a nondeterministic object contains a reference to a deterministic one, the system is not deterministic—an error was also considered, but it was concluded that this restriction would make it difficult to write real programs.

Casting

A somewhat related issue involves casting. Consider these questions: Can I cast a deterministic object to *System.Object*? If so, is it reference counted? If the answer is yes, everything is reference counted. If the answer is no, the object loses determinism. If the answer is "error," the fundamental premise that *System.Object* is the root of the object hierarchy has been violated.

Interfaces

By now, you should be seeing just how complex this issue is. If a deterministic object implements interfaces, is the reference typed as an interface reference counted? If the answer is yes, you reference count all objects that implement interfaces. (Note that *System.Int32* implements interfaces.) If the answer is no, once again the object loses determinism. If the answer is "error," deterministic objects can't implement interfaces. If the answer is "it depends on whether the interface is marked deterministic," you have another bifurcation problem. Interfaces aren't supposed to dictate object lifetime semantics. What if someone implements an API that takes an *ICollection* interface, and your object that implements it needs determinism, but the interface wasn't defined that way? You'd be out of luck. In this scenario, two interfaces would need to be defined—one deterministic and one nondeterministic—with each method being implemented twice. Believe it or not, a means of automatically generating the two versions of the methods was also considered. That line of thought bogged down in immense complexity, and the idea was dropped.

The Dispose Design Pattern

So where does that leave us? Currently, it would appear that we're left with deterministic finalization that works like this:

- The GC keeps track of which objects are being referenced.

- The GC always has a low-priority thread scanning its objects to determine when an object is no longer referenced.

- A second low-priority thread is then responsible for cleanup. This thread calls the object's *Finalize* method.

This approach does solve the circular reference problem, but it causes other problems. For example, there's no guarantee that the *Finalize* method will ever be called by the runtime! This is what is meant by *deterministic* in deterministic finalization. So the question becomes, "How can I do necessary cleanup and know that my cleanup code is called every time?"

In the case of releasing scarce resources, Microsoft proposes a solution based on the Dispose design pattern. This design pattern recommends that the object expose a public method, called something generic like *Cleanup* or *Dispose*, that the user is then instructed to call when finished using the object. It's then up to the class's designer to do any necessary cleanup in that method. In fact, you'll see that many of the classes in the .NET Framework class library implement a *Dispose* method for this purpose. As an example, the documentation for the *System.Winforms.TrayIcon* class says, "Call *Dispose* when you are finished using the *TrayIcon.*"

Inheritance

As I mentioned in Chapter 1, inheritance is used when a class is built upon another class—in terms of data or behavior—and it adheres to the rules of substitutability—namely, that the derived class can be substituted for the base class. An example of this would be if you were writing a hierarchy of database classes. Let's say you wanted to have a class for handling Microsoft SQL Server databases and Oracle databases. Since these databases differ in some respects, you'd want to have a class for each database. However, both databases do share enough functionality that you'd want to put common functionality into a base class, derive the other two classes from the base class, and override or modify the inherited base class behavior at times.

To inherit one class from another, you would use the following syntax:

class *<derivedClass>* : *<baseClass>*

Here's what this database example would look like:

```
using System;

class Database
{
    public Database()
    {
        CommonField = 42;
    }

    public int CommonField;

    public void CommonMethod()
    {
        Console.WriteLine("Database.Common Method");
    }
}

class SQLServer : Database
```

(continued)

```
{
    public void SomeMethodSpecificToSQLServer()
    {
        Console.WriteLine("SQLServer.SomeMethodSpecificToSQLServer");
    }
}

class Oracle : Database
{
    public void SomeMethodSpecificToOracle()
    {
        Console.WriteLine("Oracle.SomeMethodSpecificToOracle");
    }
}

class InheritanceApp
{
    public static void Main()
    {
        SQLServer sqlserver = new SQLServer();

        sqlserver.SomeMethodSpecificToSQLServer();
        sqlserver.CommonMethod();
        Console.WriteLine("Inherited common field = {0}",
                        sqlserver.CommonField);
    }
}
```

Compiling and executing this application results in the following output:

```
SQLServer.SomeMethodSpecificToSQLServer
Database.Common Method
Inherited common field = 42
```

Notice that the *Database.CommonMethod* and *Database.CommonField* methods are now a part of the *SQLServer* class's definition. Because the *SQLServer* and *Oracle* classes are derived from the base *Database* class, they both inherit almost all of its members that are defined as *public, protected,* or *internal.* The only exception to this is the constructor, which cannot be inherited. Each class must implement its own constructor irrespective of its base class.

Method overriding is covered in Chapter 6. However, for completeness in this section, let me mention that method overriding enables you to inherit a method from a base class and then to change that method's implementation. Abstract classes tie in heavily with method overriding—these too will be covered in Chapter 6.

Multiple Interfaces

Let me be clear on this because multiple inheritance has become a controversial subject on many newsgroups and mailing lists: C# *does not* support multiple inheritance through derivation. You can, however, aggregate the behavioral characteristics of multiple programmatic entities by implementing multiple interfaces. Interfaces and how to work with them will be covered in Chapter 9, "Interfaces." For now, think of C# interfaces as you would a COM interface.

Having said that, the following program is invalid:

```
class Foo
{
}

class Bar
{
}

class MITest : Foo, Bar
{
    public static void Main ()
    {
    }
}
```

The error that you'll get in this example has to do with how you implement interfaces. The interfaces you choose to implement are listed after the class's base class. Therefore, in this example, the C# compiler thinks that *Bar* should be an interface type. That's why the C# compiler will give you the following error message:

```
'Bar' : type in interface list is not an interface
```

The following, more realistic, example is perfectly valid because the *MyFancyGrid* class is derived from *Control* and implements the *ISerializable* and *IDataBound* interfaces:

```
class Control
{
}

interface ISerializable
{
}
```

(continued)

```
interface IDataBound
{
}

class MyFancyGrid : Control, ISerializable, IDataBound
{
}
```

The point here is that the only way you can implement something like multiple inheritance in C# is through the use of interfaces.

Sealed Classes

If you want to make sure that a class can never be used as a base class, you use the *sealed* modifier when defining the class. The only restriction is that an abstract class cannot be used as a sealed class because by their nature abstract classes are meant to be used as base classes. Another point to make is that although the purpose of a sealed class is to prevent unintended derivation, certain run-time optimizations are enabled as a result of defining a class as sealed. Specifically, because the compiler guarantees that the class can never have any derived classes, it's possible to transform virtual function member invocations on sealed class instances into nonvirtual invocations. Here's an example of sealing a class:

```
using System;

sealed class MyPoint
{
    public MyPoint(int x, int y)
    {
        this.x = x;
        this.y = y;
    }

    private int X;
    public int x
    {
        get
        {
            return this.X;
        }
        set
        {
            this.X = value;
        }
    }
}
```

```
        private int Y;
        public int y
        {
            get
            {
                return this.Y;
            }
            set
            {
                this.Y = value;
            }
        }
    }

    class SealedApp
    {
        public static void Main()
        {
            MyPoint pt = new MyPoint(6,16);
            Console.WriteLine("x = {0}, y = {1}", pt.x, pt.y);
        }
    }
```

Note that I used the *private* access modifier on the internal class members *X* and *Y*. Using the *protected* modifier would result in a warning from the compiler because of the fact that protected members are visible to derived classes and, as you now know, sealed classes don't have any derived classes.

Summary

The concept of classes and their relationship to objects is the basis for the idea of programming based on objects. The object-oriented features of C# build on a heritage handed down from C++ and are molded and enhanced by the features of the .NET Framework. In managed systems like the Common Language Runtime, resource management is a subject of great concern to developers. The CLR strives to free programmers from the drudgery of reference counting through garbage collection based on deterministic finalization. Also, inheritance in C# is handled differently than in C++. Although only single inheritance is supported, developers can still reap some of the benefits of multiple inheritance by implementing multiple interfaces.

6

Methods

As you learned in Chapter 1, "Fundamentals of Object-Oriented Programming," classes are encapsulated bundles of data and the methods that work on that data. Put another way, methods give classes their behavioral characteristics, and we name methods after the actions we want the classes to carry out on our behalf. So far, I haven't gotten into the more specific issues regarding defining and calling methods in C#. That's where this chapter comes in—you'll discover the *ref* and *out* method parameter keywords and how they enable you to define a method such that it can return more than a single value to the caller. You'll also learn how to define overloaded methods so that multiple methods with the same name can function differently depending on the types and/or number of arguments passed to them. Then you'll learn how to handle situations in which you don't know the exact number of arguments a method will have until run time. Finally, I'll wrap up the chapter with a discussion of virtual methods—which will build on the inheritance discussion in Chapter 5, "Classes"—and how to define static methods.

ref and *out* Method Parameters

When attempting to retrieve information by using a method in C#, you receive only a return value. Therefore, at first glance it would appear that you can retrieve only one value per method call. Obviously, calling one method for every piece of necessary data would be cumbersome in many situations. For example, let's say you have a *Color* class that represents a given color with three values by using the standard RGB (red-green-blue) model for describing colors. Using only return values, you'd be forced to write code similar to that at the top of the following page to retrieve all three values.

```
// Assuming color is an instance of a Color class.
int red = color.GetRed();
int green = color.GetGreen();
int blue = color.GetBlue();
```

But what we want is something similar to this:

```
int red;
int green;
int blue;
color.GetRGB(red, green, blue);
```

However, there's a problem here. When the *color.GetRGB* method is called, the values for the *red*, *green*, and *blue* arguments are copied into the method's local stack and any changes that the method makes will not be made to the caller's variables.

In C++, this problem is circumvented by having the calling method pass pointers or references to the variables so that the method works on the caller's data. The solution in C# is similar. Actually, C# offers two similar solutions. The first involves the keyword *ref*. This keyword tells the C# compiler that the arguments being passed point to the same memory as the variables in the calling code. That way, if the called method modifies these values and then returns, the calling code's variables will have been modified. The following code illustrates how to use the *ref* keyword with the *Color* class example:

```
using System;

class Color
{
    public Color()
    {
        this.red = 255;
        this.green = 0;
        this.blue = 125;
    }

    protected int red;
    protected int green;
    protected int blue;

    public void GetColors(ref int red, ref int green, ref int blue)
    {
        red = this.red;
        green = this.green;
        blue = this.blue;
    }
}
```

```
class RefTest1App
{
    public static void Main()
    {
        Color color = new Color();
        int red;
        int green;
        int blue;
        color.GetColors(ref red, ref green, ref blue);
        Console.WriteLine("red = {0}, green = {1}, blue = {2}",
red, green, blue);
    }
}
```

Using the *ref* keyword has one drawback, and, in fact, because of this limitation, the code above will not compile. When you use the *ref* keyword, you must initialize the passed arguments before calling the method. Therefore, for this code to work, it must be modified like this:

```
using System;

class Color
{
    public Color()
    {
        this.red = 255;
        this.green = 0;
        this.blue = 125;
    }

    protected int red;
    protected int green;
    protected int blue;

    public void GetColors(ref int red, ref int green, ref int blue)
    {
        red = this.red;
        green = this.green;
        blue = this.blue;
    }
}

class RefTest2App
{
    public static void Main()
```

(continued)

```
    {
        Color color = new Color();
        int red = 0;
        int green = 0;
        int blue = 0;
        color.GetColors(ref red, ref green, ref blue);
        Console.WriteLine("red = {0}, green = {1}, blue = {2}",
red, green, blue);
    }
}
```

In this example, initializing the variables that are going to be overwritten seems pointless, doesn't it? Therefore, C# provides an alternative means of passing an argument whose changed value needs to be seen by the calling code: the *out* keyword. Here's the same *Color* class example using the *out* keyword:

```
using System;

class Color
{
    public Color()
    {
        this.red = 255;
        this.green = 0;
        this.blue = 125;
    }

    protected int red;
    protected int green;
    protected int blue;

    public void GetColors(out int red, out int green, out int blue)
    {
        red = this.red;
        green = this.green;
        blue = this.blue;
    }
}

class OutTest1App
{
    public static void Main()
    {
        Color color = new Color();
        int red;
        int green;
        int blue;
```

```
        color.GetColors(out red, out green, out blue);
        Console.WriteLine("red = {0}, green = {1}, blue = {2}",
                     red, green, blue);
    }
}
```

The only difference between the *ref* keyword and the *out* keyword is that the *out* keyword doesn't require the calling code to initialize the passed arguments first. So when would the *ref* keyword be used? You should use the *ref* keyword when you need to be assured that the calling method has initialized the argument. In the examples above, *out* could be used because the method being called wasn't dependent on the value of the variable being passed. But what if a parameter value is used by the called method? Take a look at this code:

```
using System;

class Window
{
    public Window(int x, int y)
    {
        this.x = x;
        this.y = y;
    }

    protected int x;
    protected int y;

    public void Move(int x, int y)
    {
        this.x = x;
        this.y = y;
    }

    public void ChangePos(ref int x, ref int y)
    {
        this.x += x;;
        this.y += y;

        x = this.x;
        y = this.y;
    }
}

class OutTest2App
```

(continued)

```
{
    public static void Main()
    {
        Window wnd = new Window(5, 5);

        int x = 5;
        int y = 5;

        wnd.ChangePos(ref x, ref y);
        Console.WriteLine("{0}, {1}", x, y);

        x = -1;
        y = -1;
        wnd.ChangePos(ref x, ref y);
        Console.WriteLine("{0}, {1}", x, y);
    }
}
```

As you can see, the method being called—*Window.ChangePos*—bases its work on the values being passed in. In this case, the *ref* keyword forces the caller to initialize the value so that the method will function properly.

Method Overloading

Method overloading enables the C# programmer to use the same method name multiple times with only the passed arguments being different. This is extremely useful in at least two scenarios. The first involves situations in which you want to expose a single method name where the behavior of the method is slightly different depending on the value types passed. For example, let's say you have a logging class that enables your application to write diagnostic information to disk. To make the class a bit more flexible, you might have several forms of the *Write* method used to specify the information to be written. Besides accepting the string that's to be written, the method could also accept a string resource id. Without the ability to overload methods, you'd have to implement a method for both of these situations, something like *WriteString* and *WriteFromResourceId*. However, using method overloading, you could implement the following methods—both named *WriteEntry*—with each method differing only in parameter type:

```
using System;

class Log
{
    public Log(string fileName)
```

```
    {
        // Open fileName and seek to end.
    }

    public void WriteEntry(string entry)
    {
        Console.WriteLine(entry);
    }

    public void WriteEntry(int resourceId)
    {
        Console.WriteLine
        ("Retrieve string using resource id and write to log");
    }
}

class Overloading1App
{
    public static void Main()
    {
        Log log = new Log("My File");
        log.WriteEntry("Entry one");
        log.WriteEntry(42);
    }
}
```

A second scenario in which method overloading is helpful is when you use constructors, which are essentially methods called when an object is instantiated. Let's say you want to create a class that can be constructed in more than one way— for example, one that takes either a file handle (an *int*) or a file name (a *string*) to open a file. Because C# rules dictate that a class's constructor must have the same name as the class itself, you can't simply create different method names for each of the different variable types. Instead, you need to overload the constructor:

```
using System;

class File
{
}

class CommaDelimitedFile
{
    public CommaDelimitedFile(String fileName)
    {
        Console.WriteLine("Constructed with a file name");
    }
```

(continued)

```
        public CommaDelimitedFile(File file)
        {
            Console.WriteLine("Constructed with a file object");
        }
    }

class Overloading2App
{
    public static void Main()
    {
        File file = new File();
        CommaDelimitedFile file2 = new CommaDelimitedFile(file);
        CommaDelimitedFile file3 =
new CommaDelimitedFile("Some file name");
    }
}
```

One important point to remember about method overloading is that each method's argument list must be different. Therefore, the following code will not compile because the only difference between the two versions of the *Overloading3App.Foo* method is the return type:

```
using System;

class Overloading3App
{
    void Foo(double input)
    {
        Console.WriteLine("Overloading3App.Foo(double)");
    }

    // ERROR: Only differs by return value. Won't compile.
    double Foo(double input)
    {
        Console.WriteLine("Overloading3App.Foo(double)
                        (second version)");
    }

    public static void Main()
    {
        Overloading3App app = new Overloading3App();

        double i = 5;
        app.Foo(i);
    }
}
```

Variable Method Parameters

Sometimes the number of arguments that will be passed to a method won't be known until run time. For example, say you wanted a class that would plot a line on a graph according to a series of x-coordinates and y-coordinates. You could have the class expose a method that would take as its only argument a single *Point* object representing both an *x* value and a *y* value. This method would then store each *Point* object in a linked list or array member until the caller wanted to print out the entire sequence of points. However, this is a poor design decision for a couple of reasons. First, it requires the user to perform the unnecessary work of calling one method for each point of the line to be drawn—very tedious if the line will be long—and then calling another method to have the line drawn. The second drawback is that it requires the class to store these points in some fashion when the only reason the points are needed is for the use of a single method, the *DrawLine* method. Variable arguments work great to solve this sort of problem.

You can specify a variable number of method parameters by using the *params* keyword and by specifying an array in the method's argument list. Here's an example of the *Draw* class in C# allowing the user to make a single call that would take a variable number of *Point* objects and print each one:

```csharp
using System;

class Point
{
    public Point(int x, int y)
    {
        this.x = x;
        this.y = y;
    }

    public int x;
    public int y;
}

class Chart
{
    public void DrawLine(params Point[] p)
    {
        Console.WriteLine("\nThis method would print a line " +
                        "along the following points:");
        for (int i = 0; i < p.GetLength(0); i++)
```

(continued)

111

```
            {
                Console.WriteLine("{0}, {1}", p[i].x, p[i].y);
            }
        }
    }

    class VarArgsApp
    {
        public static void Main()
        {
            Point p1 = new Point(5,10);
            Point p2 = new Point(5, 15);
            Point p3 = new Point(5, 20);

            Chart chart = new Chart();
            chart.DrawLine(p1, p2, p3);
        }
    }
```

The *DrawLine* method tells the C# compiler that it can take a variable number
of *Point* objects. At run time, the method then uses a simple *for* loop to iterate
through the *Point* objects that are passed, printing each one.

Note that in a real application it would be far better to use properties to
have access to the *Point* object's *x* and *y* members, instead of making the members *public*. In addition, it would also be better to use the *foreach* statement in
the *DrawLine* method instead of a *for* loop. However, for reasons of continuity
in this book, I haven't presented these features of the language yet. I'll cover
properties in Chapter 7, "Properties, Arrays, and Indexers," and the *foreach* statement in Chapter 11, "Program Flow Control."

Virtual Methods

As we saw in Chapter 5, you can derive one class from another so that one class
can inherit and build on the capabilities of an existing class. Because I hadn't
discussed methods yet, that discussion touched on the inheritance of fields and
methods only. In other words, I didn't look at the ability to modify the base class's
behavior in the derived class. This is done by using virtual methods and is the
subject of this section.

Method Overriding

Let's first look at how to override the base class functionality of an inherited
method. We'll begin with a base class that represents an employee. To keep the
example as simple as possible, we'll give this base class a single method called

CalculatePay with the body of this method doing nothing more than letting us know the name of the method that was called. This will help us determine which methods in the inheritance tree are being called later.

```
class Employee
{
    public void CalculatePay()
    {
        Console.WriteLine("Employee.CalculatePay()");
    }
}
```

Now, let's say that you want to derive a class from *Employee* and you want to override the *CalculatePay* method to do something specific to the derived class. To do this, you need to use the *new* keyword with the derived class's method definition. Here's the code to show how easy that is:

```
using System;

class Employee
{
    public void CalculatePay()
    {
        Console.WriteLine("Employee.CalculatePay()");
    }
}

class SalariedEmployee : Employee
{
    // The new keyword enables you to override the
    // base class' implementation.
    new public void CalculatePay()
    {
        Console.WriteLine("SalariedEmployee.CalculatePay()");
    }
}

class Poly1App
{
    public static void Main()
    {
        Poly1App poly1 = new Poly1App();

        Employee baseE = new Employee();
        baseE.CalculatePay();
```

(continued)

```
        SalariedEmployee s = new SalariedEmployee();
        s.CalculatePay();
    }
}
```

Compiling and executing this application generates the following output:

```
c:\>Poly1App
Employee.CalculatePay()
Salaried.CalculatePay()
```

Polymorphism

Method overriding with the *new* keyword works fine if you have a reference to the derived object. However, what happens if you have an upcasted reference to a base class and want the compiler to call the derived class's implementation of a method? This is where polymorphism comes in. Polymorphism enables you to define a method multiple times throughout your class hierarchy in such a way that the runtime calls the appropriate version of that method depending on the exact object being used.

Let's look at our employee example to see what I mean. The Poly1App application runs correctly because we have two objects: an *Employee* object and a *SalariedEmployee* object. In a more practical application, we'd probably read all the employee records from a database and populate an array. Although some of these employees would be contractors and some would be salaried employees, we'd need to place them all in our array as the same type—the base class type, *Employee*. However, when we iterate through this array, retrieving and calling each object's *CalculatePay* method, we'd want the compiler to call the correct object's implementation of the *CalculatePay* method.

In the following example, I've added a new class, *ContractEmployee*. The main application class now contains an array of type *Employee* and two additional methods—*LoadEmployees* loads the employee objects into the array, and *DoPayroll* iterates through the array, calling each object's *CalculatePay* method.

```
using System;

class Employee
{
    public Employee(string name)
    {
        this.Name = name;
    }

    protected string Name;
```

```
    public string name
    {
        get
        {
            return this.Name;
        }
    }

    public void CalculatePay()
    {
        Console.WriteLine("Employee.CalculatePay called for {0}",
                        name);
    }
}

class ContractEmployee : Employee
{
    public ContractEmployee(string name)
    : base(name)
    {
    }

    public new void CalculatePay()
    {
        Console.WriteLine("ContractEmployee.CalculatePay called for {0}",
                        name);
    }
}

class SalariedEmployee : Employee
{
    public SalariedEmployee (string name)
    : base(name)
    {
    }

    public new void CalculatePay()
    {
        Console.WriteLine("SalariedEmployee.CalculatePay called for {0}",
                        name);
    }
}

class Poly2App
{
    protected Employee[] employees;
```

(continued)

```
    public void LoadEmployees()
    {
        // Simulating loading from a database.
        employees = new Employee[2];
        employees[0] = new ContractEmployee("Kate Dresen");
        employees[1] = new SalariedEmployee("Megan Sherman");
    }

    public void DoPayroll()
    {
        foreach(Employee emp in employees)
        {
            emp.CalculatePay();
        }
    }

    public static void Main()
    {
        Poly2App poly2 = new Poly2App();
        poly2.LoadEmployees();
        poly2.DoPayroll();
    }
}
```

However, running this application results in the following output:

```
c:\>Poly2App
Employee.CalculatePay called for Kate Dresen
Employee.CalculatePay called for Megan Sherman
```

Obviously, this is not what we wanted—the base class's implementation of *CalculatePay* is being called for each object. What happened here is an example of a phenomenon called *early binding*. When the code was compiled, the C# compiler looked at the call to *emp.CalculatePay* and determined the address in memory that it would need to when the call is made. In this case, that would be the memory location of the *Employee.CalculatePay* method.

Take a look at the following MSIL that was generated from the Poly2App application, and specifically take note of line *IL_0014* and the fact that it explicitly calls the *Employee.CalculatePay* method:

```
.method public hidebysig instance void DoPayroll() il managed
{
  // Code size       34 (0x22)
  .maxstack  2
  .locals (class Employee V_0,
           class Employee[] V_1,
           int32 V_2,
           int32 V_3)
```

```
IL_0000:    ldarg.0
IL_0001:    ldfld       class Employee[] Poly2App::employees
IL_0006:    stloc.1
IL_0007:    ldloc.1
IL_0008:    ldlen
IL_0009:    conv.i4
IL_000a:    stloc.2
IL_000b:    ldc.i4.0
IL_000c:    stloc.3
IL_000d:    br.s        IL_001d
IL_000f:    ldloc.1
IL_0010:    ldloc.3
IL_0011:    ldelem.ref
IL_0012:    stloc.0
IL_0013:    ldloc.0
IL_0014:    call        instance void Employee::CalculatePay()
IL_0019:    ldloc.3
IL_001a:    ldc.i4.1
IL_001b:    add
IL_001c:    stloc.3
IL_001d:    ldloc.3
IL_001e:    ldloc.2
IL_001f:    blt.s       IL_000f
IL_0021:    ret
} // end of method Poly2App::DoPayroll
```

That call to the *Employee.CalculatePay* method is the problem. What we want instead is for *late binding* to occur. Late binding means that the compiler does not select the method to execute until run time. To force the compiler to call the correct version of an upcasted object's method, we use two new keywords: *virtual* and *override*. The *virtual* keyword must be used on the base class's method, and the *override* keyword is used on the derived class's implementation of the method. Here's the example again—this time functioning properly!

```
using System;

class Employee
{
    public Employee(string name)
    {
        this.Name = name;
    }

    protected string Name;
    public string name
```

(continued)

```
        {
            get
            {
                return this.Name;
            }
        }

        virtual public void CalculatePay()
        {
            Console.WriteLine("Employee.CalculatePay called for {0}",
                              name);
        }
    }

    class ContractEmployee : Employee
    {
        public ContractEmployee(string name)
        : base(name)
        {
        }
        override public void CalculatePay()
        {
            Console.WriteLine("ContractEmployee.CalculatePay called for {0}",
                              name);
        }
    }

    class SalariedEmployee : Employee
    {
        public SalariedEmployee (string name)
        : base(name)
        {
        }
        override public void CalculatePay()
        {
            Console.WriteLine("SalariedEmployee.CalculatePay called for {0}",
                              name);
        }
    }

    class Poly3App
    {
        protected Employee[] employees;
        public void LoadEmployees()
        {
            // Simulating loading from a database.
            employees = new Employee[2];
```

```
        employees[0] = new ContractEmployee("Kate Dresen");
        employees[1] = new SalariedEmployee("Megan Sherman");
    }

    public void DoPayroll()
    {
        foreach(Employee emp in employees)
        {
            emp.CalculatePay();
        }
    }

    public static void Main()
    {
        Poly3App poly3 = new Poly3App();
        poly3.LoadEmployees();
        poly3.DoPayroll();
    }
}
```

Before running this application, let's take a peek at the IL code that's generated, this time noting that line *IL_0014* uses the MSIL opcode *callvirt*, which tells the compiler that the exact method to be called won't be known until run time because it's dependent on which derived object is being used:

```
.method public hidebysig instance void DoPayroll() il managed
{
  // Code size       34 (0x22)
  .maxstack  2
  .locals (class Employee V_0,
           class Employee[] V_1,
           int32 V_2,
           int32 V_3)
  IL_0000:  ldarg.0
  IL_0001:  ldfld      class Employee[] Poly3App::employees
  IL_0006:  stloc.1
  IL_0007:  ldloc.1
  IL_0008:  ldlen
  IL_0009:  conv.i4
  IL_000a:  stloc.2
  IL_000b:  ldc.i4.0
  IL_000c:  stloc.3
  IL_000d:  br.s       IL_001d
  IL_000f:  ldloc.1
  IL_0010:  ldloc.3
  IL_0011:  ldelem.ref
  IL_0012:  stloc.0
  IL_0013:  ldloc.0
```

(continued)

```
IL_0014:  callvirt    instance void Employee::CalculatePay()
IL_0019:  ldloc.3
IL_001a:  ldc.i4.1
IL_001b:  add
IL_001c:  stloc.3
IL_001d:  ldloc.3
IL_001e:  ldloc.2
IL_001f:  blt.s       IL_000f
IL_0021:  ret
} // end of method Poly3App::DoPayroll
```

Running the code at this point should yield the following results:

```
c:\>Poly3App
ContractEmployee.CalculatePay called for Kate Dresen
SalariedEmployee.CalculatePay called for Megan Sherman
```

> **Note**   Virtual methods cannot be declared as *private* because, by defi-
> nition, they would not be visible in the derived classes.

Static Methods

A static method is a method that exists in a class as a whole rather than in a specific instance of the class. As with other static members, the key benefit to static methods is that they reside apart from a particular instance of a class without polluting the application's global space and without going against the object-oriented grain by not being associated with a class. An example of this is a database API I wrote in C#. Within my class hierarchy, I had a class called *SQLServerDb*. Along with the basic NURD (new, update, read, and delete) capabilities, the class also exposed a method to repair the database. In the class's *Repair* method, I had no need to open the database itself. In fact, the ODBC function I used (*SQLConfigDataSource*) mandated that the database be closed for the operation. However, the *SQLServerDb* constructor opened a database specified in a database name passed to it. Therefore, a static method was perfect. It allowed me to place a method in the *SQLServerDb* class where it belonged and yet not go through my class's constructor. Obviously, on the client side, the benefit was that the client didn't have to instantiate the *SQLServerDb* class either. In the next example, you can see a static method (*RepairDatabase*) being called from within the *Main* method. Notice that we don't create an instance of *SQLServerDB* to do this:

```
using System;

class SQLServerDb
{
    // Bunch of other nonsalient members.
    public static void RepairDatabase()
    {
        Console.WriteLine("repairing database...");
    }
}

class StaticMethod1App
{
    public static void Main()
    {
        SQLServerDb.RepairDatabase();
    }
}
```

Defining a method as static involves using the *static* keyword. The user then employs the *Class.Method* syntax to call the method. Note that this syntax is necessary even if the user has a reference to an instance of the class. To illustrate this point, the following code would fail to compile:

```
// This code will fail to compile.
using System;

class SQLServerDb
{
    // Bunch of other nonsalient members.
    public static void RepairDatabase()
    {
        Console.WriteLine("repairing database...");
    }
}

class StaticMethod2App
{
    public static void Main()
    {
        SQLServerDb db = new SQLServerDb();
        db.RepairDatabase();
    }
}
```

Access to Class Members

The last point I'll make about static methods is the rule governing which class members can be accessed from a static method. As you might imagine, a static method can access any static member within the class, but it cannot access an instance member. This is illustrated in the following code:

```
using System;

class SQLServerDb
{
    static string progressString1 = "repairing database...";
    string progressString2 = "repairing database...";

    public static void RepairDatabase()
    {
        Console.WriteLine(progressString1); // This will work.
        Console.WriteLine(progressString2); // Fails compilation.
    }
}

class StaticMethod3App
{
    public static void Main()
    {
        SQLServerDb.RepairDatabase();
    }
}
```

Summary

Methods give classes their behavioral characteristics and carry actions out on our behalf. Methods in C# are flexible, allowing for the return of multiple values, overloading, and variable parameters. The *ref* and *out* keywords allow a method to return more than a single value to the caller. Overloading allows multiple methods with the same name to function differently, depending on the types and/ or number of arguments passed to them. Methods can take variable parameters. The *params* keyword allows you to deal with methods where the number of arguments isn't known until run time. Virtual methods allow you to control how methods are modified in inherited classes. Finally, the *static* keyword allows for methods that exist as part of a class rather than as part of an object.

7

Properties, Arrays, and Indexers

So far, I've described the basic types supported by C# and how to declare and use them in your classes and applications. This chapter will break the pattern of presenting one major feature of the language per chapter. In this chapter, you'll learn about properties, arrays, and indexers because these language features share a common bond. They enable you, the C# class developer, to extend the basic class/field/method structure of a class to expose a more intuitive and natural interface to your class's members.

Properties as Smart Fields

It's always a good goal to design classes that not only hide the implementation of the class's methods, but that also disallow any direct member access to the class's fields. By providing *accessor methods* whose job it is to retrieve and set the values of these fields, you can be assured that a field is treated correctly—that is, according to the rules of your specific problem domain—and that any additional processing that's needed is performed.

As an example, let's say that you have an address class with a ZIP code field and a city field. When the client modifies the *Address.ZipCode* field, you want to validate the ZIP code against a database and automatically set the *Address.City* field based on that ZIP code. If the client had direct access to a *public Address.ZipCode* member, you'd have no easy way of doing either of these things because changing a member variable directly doesn't require a method. Therefore, instead of granting direct access to the *Address.ZipCode* field, a better design would be to define the *Address.ZipCode* and *Address.City* fields as *protected* and provide an accessor methods for getting and setting the *Address.ZipCode* field. This way, you can attach code to the change that performs any additional work that needs to be done.

This ZIP code example would be programmed in C# as follows. Notice that the actual *ZipCode* field is defined as *protected* and, therefore, not accessible from the client and that the accessor methods, *GetZipCode* and *SetZipCode*, are defined as *public*.

```
class Address
{
    protected string ZipCode;
    protected string City;
    public string GetZipCode()
    {
        return this.ZipCode;
    }
    public void SetZipCode(string ZipCode)
    {
        // Validate ZipCode against some datastore.
        this.ZipCode = ZipCode;
        // Update this.City based on validated ZIP code.
    }
}
```

The client would then access the *Address.ZipCode* value like this:

```
Address addr = new Address();
addr.SetZipCode("55555");
string zip = addr.GetZipCode();
```

Defining and Using Properties

Using accessor methods works well and is a technique used by programmers of several object-oriented languages, including C++ and Java. However, C# provides an even richer mechanism—properties—that has the same capabilities as accessor methods and is much more elegant on the client side. Through properties, a programmer can write a client that can access a class's fields as though they are public fields without knowing whether an accessor method exists.

A C# property consists of a field declaration and accessor methods used to modify the field's value. These accessor methods are called *getter* and *setter* methods. Getter methods are used to retrieve the field's value, and setter methods are used to modify the field's value. Here's the earlier example rewritten using C# properties:

```
class Address
{
    protected string city;
    protected string zipCode;

    public string ZipCode
    {
        get
        {
            return zipCode;
        }
        set
        {
            // Validate value against some datastore.
            zipCode = value;
            // Update city based on validated zipCode.
        }
    }
}
```

Notice that I created a field called *Address.zipCode* and a property called *Address.ZipCode*. This can confuse some people at first because they think *Address.ZipCode* is the field and wonder why it needs to be defined twice. But it's not the field. It's the property, which is simply a generic means of defining accessors to a class member so that the more intuitive *object.field* syntax can be used. If in this example I were to omit the *Address.zipCode* field and change the statement in the setter from *zipCode = value* to *ZipCode = value*, I'd cause the setter method to be called infinitely. Also notice that the setter doesn't take any arguments. The value being passed is automatically placed in a variable named *value* that is accessible inside the setter method. (You'll soon see in MSIL how this bit of magic happens.)

Now that we've written the *Address.ZipCode* property, let's look at the changes needed for the client code:

```
Address addr = new Address();
addr.ZipCode = "55555";
string zip = addr.ZipCode;
```

As you can see, how a client accesses the fields is intuitive: no more guessing or looking through documentation (aka the source code) to determine whether a field is *public* and, if not, what the name of the accessor method is.

What the Compiler Is Really Doing

So, how does the compiler allow us to call a method in the standard *object.field* syntax? Also, where does that *value* variable come from? To answer these questions, we need to look at the MSIL being produced by the compiler. Let's consider the property's getter method first.

In our ongoing example, we have the following getter method defined:

```
class Address
{
    protected string city;
    protected string zipCode;
    public string ZipCode
    {
        get
        {
            return zipCode;
        }
        ⋮
    }
    ⋮
}
```

If you look at the resulting MSIL from this method, you'll see that the compiler has created an accessor method called *get_ZipCode*, as seen here:

```
.method public hidebysig specialname instance string
        get_ZipCode() cil managed
{
  // Code size       11 (0xb)
  .maxstack  1
  .locals ([0] string _Vb_t_$00000003$00000000)
  IL_0000:  ldarg.0
  IL_0001:  ldfld      string Address::zipCode
  IL_0006:  stloc.0
  IL_0007:  br.s       IL_0009
  IL_0009:  ldloc.0
  IL_000a:  ret
} // end of method Address::get_ZipCode
```

You can tell the name of the accessor method because the compiler prefixes the property name with *get_* (for a getter method) or *set_* (for a setter method). As a result, the following code resolves to a call to *get_ZipCode*:

```
String str = addr.ZipCode; // this calls Address::get_ZipCode
```

Therefore, you might be tempted to try the following explicit call to the accessor method yourself:

```
String str = addr.get_ZipCode; // **ERROR - Won't compile
```

However, in this case, the code will not compile because it's illegal to explicitly call an internal MSIL method.

The answer to our question—how can a compiler allow us to use the standard *object.field* syntax and have a method be called?—is that the compiler actually generates the appropriate getter and setter methods for us when it parses the C# property syntax. Therefore, in the case of the *Address.ZipCode* property, the compiler emits MSIL that contains the *get_ZipCode* and *set_ZipCode* methods.

Now let's look at the generated setter method. In the *Address* class you saw the following:

```
public string ZipCode
{
    ⋮
    set
    {
        // Validate value against some datastore.
        zipCode = value;
        // Update city based on validated zipCode.
    }
}
```

Notice that nothing in this code declares a variable named *value* yet we're able to use this variable to store the caller's passed value and to set the protected *zipCode* member field. When the C# compiler generates the MSIL for a setter method, it injects this variable as an argument in a method called *set_ZipCode*.

In the generated MSIL, this method takes as an argument a string variable:

```
.method public hidebysig specialname instance void
        set_ZipCode(string 'value') cil managed
{
  // Code size       8 (0x8)
  .maxstack  8
  IL_0000:  ldarg.0
  IL_0001:  ldarg.1
  IL_0002:  stfld      string Address::zipCode
  IL_0007:  ret
} // end of method Address::set_ZipCode
```

Even though you can't see this method in the C# source code, when you set the *ZipCode* property with something like *addr.ZipCode("12345")*, it resolves to an MSIL call to *Address::set_ZipCode("12345")*. As with the *get_ZipCode* method, attempting to call this method directly in C# generates an error.

Read-Only Properties

In the example we've been using, the *Address.ZipCode* property is considered read/write because both a getter and a setter method are defined. Of course, sometimes you won't want the client to be able to set the value of a given field, in which case you'll make the field read-only. You do this by omitting the setter method. To illustrate a read-only property, let's prevent the client from setting the *Address.city* field, leaving the *Address.ZipCode* property as the only code path tasked with changing this field's value:

```
class Address
{
    protected string city;
    public string City
    {
        get
        {
            return city;
        }
    }

    protected string zipCode;
    public string ZipCode
    {
        get
        {
            return zipCode;
        }
        set
        {
            // Validate value against some datastore.
            zipCode = value;
            // Update city based on validated zipCode.
        }
    }
}
```

Inheriting Properties

Like methods, a property can be decorated with the *virtual, override,* or *abstract* modifiers I covered in Chapter 6, "Methods." This enables a derived class to inherit and override properties just as it could any other member from the base class. The key issue here is that you can specify these modifiers only at the property level. In other words, in cases where you have both a getter method and a setter method, if you override one, you must override both.

Advanced Use of Properties

So far, I've talked about properties being useful for the following reasons:

- They provide a level of abstraction to clients.

- They provide a generic means of accessing class members by using the *object.field* syntax.

- They enable a class to guarantee that any additional processing can be done when a particular field is modified or accessed.

The third item points us to another helpful use for properties: the implementation of something called *lazy initialization*. This is an optimization technique whereby some of a class's members are not initialized until they are needed.

Lazy initialization is beneficial when you have a class that contains seldom-referenced members whose initialization takes up a lot of time or chews up a lot of resources. Examples of this would be situations where the data has to be read from a database or across a congested network. Because you know these members are not referenced often and their initialization is expensive, you can delay their initialization until their getter methods are called. To illustrate this, let's say you have an inventory application that sales representatives run on their laptop computers to place customer orders and that they occasionally use to check inventory levels. Using properties, you could allow the relevant class to be instantiated without the inventory records having to be read, as shown in the code below. Then, if a sales rep did want to access the inventory count for the item, the getter method would access the remote database at that time.

```
class Sku
{
    protected double onHand;

    public string OnHand
    {
        get
        {
            // Read from central db and set onHand value.
            return onHand;
        }
    }
}
```

As you've seen throughout this chapter so far, properties enable you to provide accessor methods to fields and a generic and intuitive interface for the client. Because of this, properties are sometimes referred to as *smart fields*. Now, let's take this a step further and look at how arrays are defined and used in C#. We'll also see how properties are used with arrays in the form of *indexers*.

Arrays

So far, most of the examples in this book have shown how to define variables in finite, predetermined numbers. However, in most practical applications, you don't know the exact number of objects you need until run time. For example, if you're developing an editor and you want to keep track of the controls that are added to a dialog box, the exact number of controls the editor will display can't be known until run time. You can, however, use an array to store and keep track of a dynamically allocated grouping of objects—the controls on the editor, in this case.

In C#, arrays are objects that have the *System.Array* class defined as their base class. Therefore, although the syntax of defining an array looks similar to that in C++ or Java, you're actually instantiating a .NET class, which means that every declared array has all the same members inherited from *System.Array*. In this section, I'll cover how to declare and instantiate arrays, how to work with the different array types, and how to iterate through the elements of an array. I'll also look at some of the more commonly used properties and methods of the *System.Array* class.

Declaring Arrays

Declaring an array in C# is done by placing empty square brackets between the type and the variable name, like this:

```
int[] numbers;
```

Note that this syntax differs slightly from C++, in which the brackets are specified after the variable name. Because arrays are class-based, many of the same rules that apply to declaring a class also pertain to arrays. For example, when you declare an array, you're not actually creating that array. Just as you do with a class, you must instantiate the array before it exists in terms of having its elements allocated. In the following example, I'm declaring and instantiating an array at the same time:

```
// Declares and instantiates a single-
// dimensional array of 6 integers.
int[] numbers = new int[6];
```

However, when declaring the array as a member of a class, you need to declare and instantiate the array in two distinct steps because you can't instantiate an object until run time:

```
class YourClass
{
    ⋮
    int[] numbers;
    ⋮

    void SomeInitMethod()
    {
        ⋮
        numbers = new int[6];
        ⋮
    }
}
```

Single-Dimensional Array Example

Here's a simple example of declaring a single-dimensional array as a class member, instantiating and filling the array in the constructor, and then using a *for* loop to iterate through the array, printing out each element:

```
using System;

class SingleDimArrayApp
{
    protected int[] numbers;

    SingleDimArrayApp()
    {
        numbers = new int[6];
        for (int i = 0; i < 6; i++)
        {
            numbers[i] = i * i;
        }
    }

    protected void PrintArray()
    {
        for (int i = 0; i < numbers.Length; i++)
        {
            Console.WriteLine("numbers[{0}]={1}", i, numbers[i]);
        }
    }
```

(continued)

```
public static void Main()
{
    SingleDimArrayApp app = new SingleDimArrayApp();
    app.PrintArray();
}
}
```

Running this example produces the following output:

```
numbers[0]=0
numbers[1]=1
numbers[2]=4
numbers[3]=9
numbers[4]=16
numbers[5]=25
```

In this example, the *SingleDimArray.PrintArray* method uses the *System.Array Length* property to determine the number of elements in the array. It's not obvious here, since we have only a single-dimensional array, but the *Length* property actually returns the number of *all* the elements in all the dimensions of an array. Therefore, in the case of a two dimensional array of 5 by 4, the *Length* property would return 9. In the next section, I'll look at multidimensional arrays and how to determine the upper bound of a specific array dimension.

Multidimensional Arrays

In addition to single-dimensional arrays, C# supports the declaration of multidimensional arrays where each dimension of the array is separated by a comma. Here I'm declaring a three-dimensional array of doubles:

```
double[,,] numbers;
```

To quickly determine the number of dimensions in a declared C# array, count the number of commas and add one to that total.

In the following example, I have a two-dimensional array of sales figures that represent this year's year-to-date figures and last year's totals for the same time frame. Take special note of the syntax used to instantiate the array (in the *MultiDimArrayApp* constructor).

```
using System;

class MultiDimArrayApp
{
    protected int currentMonth;
    protected double[,] sales;

    MultiDimArrayApp()
```

```
{
    currentMonth=10;

    sales = new double[2, currentMonth];
    for (int i = 0; i < sales.GetLength(0); i++)
    {
        for (int j=0; j < 10; j++)
        {
            sales[i,j] = (i * 100) + j;
        }
    }
}

protected void PrintSales()
{
    for (int i = 0; i < sales.GetLength(0); i++)
    {
        for (int j=0; j < sales.GetLength(1); j++)
        {
            Console.WriteLine("[{0}][{1}]={2}", i, j, sales[i,j]);
        }
    }
}

public static void Main()
{
    MultiDimArrayApp app = new MultiDimArrayApp();
    app.PrintSales();
}
}
```

Running the *MultiDimArrayApp* example results in this output:

```
[0][0]=0
[0][1]=1
[0][2]=2
[0][3]=3
[0][4]=4
[0][5]=5
[0][6]=6
[0][7]=7
[0][8]=8
[0][9]=9
[1][0]=100
[1][1]=101
[1][2]=102
[1][3]=103
[1][4]=104
```

(continued)

```
[1][5]=105
[1][6]=106
[1][7]=107
[1][8]=108
[1][9]=109
```

Remember that in the single-dimensional array example I said the *Length* property will return the total number of items in the array, so in this example that return value would be 20. In the *MultiDimArray.PrintSales* method I used the *Array.GetLength* method to determine the length or upper bound of each dimension of the array. I was then able to use each specific value in the *PrintSales* method.

Querying for Rank

Now that we've seen how easy it is to dynamically iterate through a single-dimensional or multidimensional array, you might be wondering how to determine the number of dimensions in an array programmatically. The number of dimensions in an array is called an array's *rank*, and rank is retrieved using the *Array.Rank* property. Here's an example of doing just that on several arrays:

```
using System;

class RankArrayApp
{
    int[] singleD;
    int[,] doubleD;
    int[,,] tripleD;

    protected RankArrayApp()
    {
        singleD = new int[6];
        doubleD = new int[6,7];
        tripleD = new int[6,7,8];
    }

    protected void PrintRanks()
    {
        Console.WriteLine("singleD Rank = {0}", singleD.Rank);
        Console.WriteLine("doubleD Rank = {0}", doubleD.Rank);
        Console.WriteLine("tripleD Rank = {0}", tripleD.Rank);
    }

    public static void Main()
    {
        RankArrayApp app = new RankArrayApp();
        app.PrintRanks();
    }
}
```

As expected, the *RankArrayApp* application outputs the following:

```
singleD Rank = 1
doubleD Rank = 2
tripleD Rank = 3
```

Jagged Arrays

The last thing we'll look at with regard to arrays is the *jagged array*. A jagged array is simply an array of arrays. Here's an example of defining an array containing integer arrays:

```
int[][] jaggedArray;
```

You might use a jagged array if you were developing an editor. In this editor, you might want to store the object representing each user-created control in an array. Let's say you had an array of buttons and combo boxes (to keep the example small and manageable). You might have three buttons and two combo boxes both stored in their respective arrays. Declaring a jagged array enables you to have a "parent" array for those arrays so that you can easily programmatically iterate through the controls when you need to, as shown here:

```
using System;

class Control
{
    virtual public void SayHi()
    {
        Console.WriteLine("base control class");
    }
}

class Button : Control
{
    override public void SayHi()
    {
        Console.WriteLine("button control");
    }
}

class Combo : Control
{
    override public void SayHi()
    {
        Console.WriteLine("combobox control");
    }
}
```

(continued)

```
class JaggedArrayApp
{
    public static void Main()
    {
    Control[][] controls;
    controls = new Control[2][];

    controls[0] = new Control[3];
    for (int i = 0; i < controls[0].Length; i++)
    {
        controls[0][i] = new Button();
    }

    controls[1] = new Control[2];
    for (int i = 0; i < controls[1].Length; i++)
    {
        controls[1][i] = new Combo();
    }

    for (int i = 0; i < controls.Length;i++)
    {
        for (int j=0;j< controls[i].Length;j++)
        {
            Control control = controls[i][j];
            control.SayHi();
        }
    }

    string str = Console.ReadLine();
    }
}
```

As you can see, I've defined a base class (*Control*) and two derived classes (*Button* and *Combo*) and I've declared the jagged array as an array of arrays that contain *Controls* objects. That way I can store the specific types in the array and, through the magic of polymorphism, know that when it's time to extract the objects from the array (through an *upcasted* object) I'll get the behavior I expect.

Treating Objects Like Arrays by Using Indexers

In the "Arrays" section, you learned how to declare and instantiate arrays, how to work with the different array types, and how to iterate through the elements of an array. You also learned how to take advantage of some of the more commonly used properties and methods of the array types underlying the *System.Array* class. Let's continue working with arrays by looking at how a C#-specific feature called indexers enables you to programmatically treat objects as though they were arrays.

And why would you want to treat an object like an array? Like most features of a programming language, the benefit of indexers comes down to making your applications more intuitive to write. In the first section of this chapter, "Properties as Smart Fields," you saw how C# properties give you the ability to reference class fields by using the standard *class.field* syntax, yet they ultimately resolve to getter and setter methods. This abstraction frees the programmer writing a client for the class from having to determine whether getter/setter methods exist for the field and from having to know the exact format of these methods. Similarly, indexers enable a class's client to index into an object as though the object itself is an array.

Consider the following example. You have a list box class that needs to expose some way in which a user of that class can insert strings. If you're familiar with the Win32 SDK, you know that to insert a string into a list box window, you send it a *LB_ADDSTRING* or *LB_INSERTSTRING* message. When this mechanism appeared in the late 1980s, we thought we really were object-oriented programmers. After all, weren't we sending messages to an object just like those fancy object-oriented analysis and design books told us to? However, as object-oriented and object-based languages such as C++ and Object Pascal began to proliferate, we learned that objects could be used to create more intuitive programming interfaces for such tasks. Using C++ and MFC (Microsoft Foundation Classes), we were given an entire lattice of classes that enabled us to treat windows (such as list boxes) as objects with these classes exposing member functions that basically provided a thin wrapper for the sending and receiving of messages to and from the underlying Microsoft Windows control. In the case of the *CListBox* class (that is, the MFC wrapper for the Windows list box control), we were given an *AddString* and an *InsertString* member function for the tasks previously accomplished by sending the *LB_ADDSTRING* and *LB_INSERTSTRING* messages.

However, to help develop the best and most intuitive language, the C# language design team looked at this and wondered, "Why not have the ability to treat an object that is at its heart an array, like an array?" When you consider a list box, isn't it just an array of strings with the additional functionality of displaying and sorting? From this idea was born the concept of indexers.

Defining Indexers

Because properties are sometimes referred to as "smart fields" and indexers are called "smart arrays," it makes sense that properties and indexers would share the same syntax. Indeed, defining indexers is much like defining properties, with two major differences: First, the indexer takes an *index* argument. Second, because the class itself is being used as an array, the *this* keyword is used as the

name of the indexer. You'll see a more complete example shortly, but take a look
at an example indexer:

```
class MyClass
{
    public object this [int idx]
    {
        get
        {
            // Return desired data.
        }
        set
        {
            // Set desired data.
        }
    }
    ...
}
```

I haven't shown you a full example to illustrate the syntax of indexers
because the actual internal implementation of how you define your data and how
you get and set that data isn't relevant to indexers. Keep in mind that regardless
of how you store your data internally (that is, as an array, a collection, and so
on), indexers are simply a means for the programmer instantiating the class to
write code such as this:

```
MyClass cls = new MyClass();
cls[0] = someObject;
Console.WriteLine("{0}", cls[0]);
```

What you do within the indexer is your own business, just as long as the class's
client gets the expected results from accessing the object as an array.

Indexer Example

Let's look at some places where indexers make the most sense. I'll start with the
list box example I've already used. As mentioned, from a conceptual standpoint,
a list box is simply a list, or an array of strings to be displayed. In the following
example, I've declared a class called *MyListBox* that contains an indexer to set
and retrieve strings through an *ArrayList* object. (The *ArrayList* class is a .NET
Framework class used to store a collection of objects.)

```
using System;
using System.Collections;

class MyListBox
```

```
{
    protected ArrayList data = new ArrayList();

    public object this[int idx]
    {
        get
        {
            if (idx > -1 && idx < data.Count)
            {
                return (data[idx]);
            }
            else
            {
                // Possibly throw an exception here.
                return null;
            }
        }
        set
        {
            if (idx > -1 && idx < data.Count)
            {
                data[idx] = value;
            }
            else if (idx == data.Count)
            {
                data.Add(value);
            }
            else
            {
                // Possibly throw an exception here.
            }
        }
    }
}

class Indexers1App
{
    public static void Main()
    {
        MyListBox lbx = new MyListBox();
        lbx[0] = "foo";
        lbx[1] = "bar";
        lbx[2] = "baz";
        Console.WriteLine("{0} {1} {2}",
                          lbx[0], lbx[1], lbx[2]);
    }
}
```

Notice in this example that I check for out-of-bounds errors in the indexing of the data. This is not technically tied to indexers because, as I mentioned, indexers pertain only to how the class's client can use the object as an array and have nothing to do with the internal representation of the data. However, when learning a new language feature, it helps to see practical usage of a feature rather than only its syntax. So, in both the indexer's getter and setter methods, I validate the index value being passed with the data being stored in the class's *ArrayList* member. I personally would probably choose to throw exceptions in the cases where the index value being passed can't be resolved. However, that's a personal choice—your error handling might differ. The point is that you need to indicate failure to the client in cases where an invalid index has been passed.

Design Guidelines

Indexers are yet another example of the C# design team adding a subtle yet powerful feature to the language to help us become more productive in our development endeavors. However, like any feature of any language, indexers have their place. They should be used only where it would be intuitive to treat an object like an array. Let's take as an example the case of invoicing. It's reasonable that an invoicing application has an *Invoice* class that defines a member array of *InvoiceDetail* objects. In such a case, it would be perfectly intuitive for the user to access these detail lines with the following syntax:

```
InvoiceDetail detail = invoice[2]; // Retrieves the 3rd detail line.
```

However, it wouldn't be intuitive to take that a step further and try to turn all of the *InvoiceDetail* members into an array that would be accessed via an indexer. As you can see here, the first line is much more readily understood than the second:

```
TermCode terms = invoice.Terms; // Property accessor to Terms member.
TermCode terms = invoice[3];    // A solution in search of a problem.
```

In this case, the maxim holds true that just because you can do something doesn't mean you should necessarily do it. Or, in more concrete terms, think of how implementing any new feature is going to affect your class's clients, and let that thinking guide you when you're deciding whether implementing the feature will make the use of your class easier.

Summary

C# properties consist of field declaration and accessor methods. Properties enable smart access to class fields so that a programmer writing a client for the class doesn't have to try to determine whether (and how) an accessor method for the field was created. Arrays in C# are declared by placing an empty square bracket *between* the type and the variable name, a syntax slightly different than the one used in C++. C# arrays can be single-dimensional, multidimensional, or jagged. Objects in C# can be treated like arrays through the use of indexers. Indexers allow programmers to easily work with and track many objects of the same type.

8

Attributes

Most programming languages are designed with a given set of abilities in mind. For example, when you set out to design a compiler, you think about how an application written in the new language will be structured, how code will call other code, how functionality will be packaged, and many other issues that will make the language a productive medium for developing software. Most of what a compiler designer comes up with is static. For example, in C#, you define a class by placing the keyword *class* before the class name. You then signify derivation by inserting a colon after the class name followed by the name of the base class. This is an example of a decision that, once made by the language designer, can't be changed.

Now, the people who write compilers are darn good at what they do. However, even they can't anticipate all the future developments in our industry and how those developments will alter how programmers want to express their types in a given language. For example, how do you create the relationship between a class in C++ and a documentation URL for that class? Or how do you associate the specific members of a C++ class with the XML fields for your company's new business-to-business solution? Because C++ was designed many years before the advent of the Internet and protocols such as XML, it's not easy to perform either of these tasks.

Until now, the solutions to problems like these involved storing extra information in a separate file (DEF, IDL, and so on) that was then loosely associated with the type or member in question. Because the compiler has no knowledge of the separate file or the code-generated relationship between your class and the file, this approach is usually called a "disconnected solution." The main problem is that the class is no longer "self-describing"—that is, a user can no longer look at the class definition by itself and know everything about that class. One advantage of a self-describing component is that the compiler and run time can ensure that the rules associated with the component are adhered to. Additionally, a self-describing component is easier to maintain because the developer can see all the information related to the component in one place.

This has been the way of the world for many decades of compiler evolution. The language designers try to determine what you'll need the language to do, they design the compiler with those capabilities, and, for better or worse, those are the capabilities you have until another compiler comes along. That is, until now. C# offers a different paradigm, which stems from the introduction of a feature called *attributes*.

Introducing Attributes

What attributes allow you to do is nothing short of groundbreaking. They provide you a generic means of associating information (as annotations) with your defined C# types. You can use attributes to define design-time information (such as documentation information), run-time information (such as the name of a database column for a field), or even run-time behavioral characteristics (such as whether a given member is "transactionable"—that is, capable of participating in a transaction). The possibilities are endless, which is rather the point. Because you can create an attribute based on any information you like, a standard mechanism exists for defining the attributes themselves and for querying the member or type at run time as to its attached attributes.

An example will better illustrate how to use this powerful feature. Let's say you have an application that stores some of its information in the Windows Registry. One design issue would be deciding where to store the Registry key information. In most development environments, this information is typically stored in a resource file or in constants or it's even hard-coded in the calls to the Registry APIs. However, once again, what we have is a situation in which an integral part of a class is being stored apart from the rest of the class's definition. Using attributes, we could "attach" this information to the class members such that we have a completely self-describing component. Here's an example of how that would look, assuming that we had already defined the *RegistryKey* attribute elsewhere:

```
class MyClass
{
    [RegistryKey(HKEY_CURRENT_USER, "foo")]
    public int Foo;
}
```

To attach a defined attribute to a C# type or member, you simply specify the attribute data in brackets before the target type or member. Here we attached an attribute named *RegistryKey* to the *MyClass.Foo* field. At run time—which you'll see shortly—all we'll have to do is query the field as to its Registry key and then use that value to save the date into the Registry.

Defining Attributes

In the previous example, note that the syntax used to attach an attribute to a type or member looks a bit like the instantiation of a class. This is because an attribute is actually a class derived from the *System.Attribute* base class.

Now let's flesh out the *RegistryKey* attribute a little bit:

```
public enum RegistryHives
{
    HKEY_CLASSES_ROOT,
    HKEY_CURRENT_USER,
    HKEY_LOCAL_MACHINE,
    HKEY_USERS,
    HKEY_CURRENT_CONFIG
}

public class RegistryKeyAttribute : Attribute
{
    public RegistryKeyAttribute(RegistryHives Hive, String ValueName)
    {
        this.Hive = Hive;
        this.ValueName = ValueName;
    }

    protected RegistryHives hive;
    public RegistryHives Hive
    {
        get { return hive; }
        set { hive = value; }
    }

    protected String valueName;
    public String ValueName
    {
        get { return valueName; }
        set { valueName = value; }
    }
}
```

What I've done here is add an *enum* for the different Registry types, a constructor for the attribute class (which takes a Registry type and a value name), and two properties for the Registry hive and value name. There's much more you can do when defining attributes, but at this point, because we know how to define and attach attributes, let's go ahead and learn how to query for attributes at run time. That way, we'll have a fully working example to play with. Once we've done that, we'll move on to some of the more advanced issues with defining and attaching attributes.

> **Note** Note that in the examples the attribute class names are appended with the word *Attribute*. However, when I then attach the attribute to a type or member, I don't include the *Attribute* suffix. This is a shortcut thrown in for free by the C# language designers. When the compiler sees that an attribute is being attached to a type or member, it will search for a *System.Attribute* derived class with the name of the attribute specified. If a class can't be located, the compiler will append *Attribute* to the specified attribute name and search for that. Therefore, it's common practice to define attribute class names as ending in *Attribute* and then to omit that part of the name.

Querying About Attributes

We know how to define an attribute by deriving it from *System.Attribute* and how to attach it to a type or member. Now what? How can we use attributes in code? In other words, how can we query a type or member as to the attributes (and its parameters) that have been attached?

To query a type or member about its attached attributes, we must use *reflection*. Reflection is an advanced topic that's covered in Chapter 16, "Querying Metadata with Reflection," so I'll discuss only enough about it here to illustrate what's needed to retrieve attribute information at run time. If you want to learn more about reflection, refer to Chapter 16.

Reflection is a feature that allows you to dynamically determine at run time the type characteristics for an application. For example, you can use the .NET Framework *Reflection* APIs to iterate through the metadata for an entire assembly and produce a list of all classes, types, and methods that have been defined for that assembly. Let's look at some examples of attributes and how they would be queried using reflection.

Class Attributes

How you retrieve an attribute depends on the member type being queried. Let's say you want to define an attribute that will define the remote server on which an object is to be created. Without attributes, you'd save this information in a constant or in the application's resource file. Using attributes, you can simply annotate the class with its remote server like this:

```
using System;

public enum RemoteServers
{
    JEANVALJEAN,
    JAVERT,
    COSETTE
}

public class RemoteObjectAttribute : Attribute
{
    public RemoteObjectAttribute(RemoteServers Server)
    {
        this.server = Server;
    }

    protected RemoteServers server;
    public string Server
    {
        get
        {
            return RemoteServers.GetName(typeof(RemoteServers),
                                        this.server);
        }
    }
}


[RemoteObject(RemoteServers.COSETTE)]
class MyRemotableClass
{
}
```

To determine the server on which to create the object, use code like the following:

```
class ClassAttrApp
{
    public static void Main()
    {
        Type type = typeof(MyRemotableClass);
        foreach (Attribute attr in type.GetCustomAttributes())
        {
            RemoteObjectAttribute remoteAttr =
                attr as RemoteObjectAttribute;
```

(continued)

```
            if (null != remoteAttr)
            {
                Console.WriteLine("Create this object on {0}.",
                                    remoteAttr.Server);
            }
        }
    }
}
```

As you might expect, the output from this application is the following:

```
Create this object on COSETTE.
```

Because all variations of this example will use some common code, let's examine what's going on here regarding reflection and how it returns the attribute's value at run time.

The first line you'll notice in the *Main* method is the use of the *typeof* operator:

```
Type type = typeof(MyRemotableClass);
```

This operator returns the *System.Type* object associated with the type that is passed as its only argument. Once you have that object, you can start to query it.

There are two parts to explain about the next line of code:

```
foreach (Attribute attr in type.GetCustomAttributes(true))
```

The first is the call to the *Type.GetCustomAttributes* method. This method returns an array of type *Attribute* that in this case will contain all the attributes attached to the class named *MyRemotableClass*. The second is the *foreach* statement, which iterates the return array, stuffing each successive value into a variable (*attr*) of type *Attribute*.

The next statement uses the *as* operator to attempt to convert the *attr* variable to a type of *RemoteObjectAttribte*:

```
RemoteObjectAttribute remoteAttr =
        attr as RemoteObjectAttribute;
```

We then test for a null value, the result of a failed case via the *as* operator. If the value is not null—meaning that the *remoteAttr* variable holds a valid attribute attached to the *MyRemotableClass* type—we call one of the *RemoteObjectAttribute* properties to print the remote server name:

```
if (null != remoteAttr)
{
    Console.WriteLine("Create this object on {0}",
                    remoteAttr.Server);
}
```

Method Attributes

Now that we've seen how to work with class attributes, let's look at using method attributes. This discussion is a separate section because the reflection code needed to query a method attribute is different from that needed to query a class attribute. In this example, we'll use an attribute that would be used to define a method as being transactionable:

```
using System;
using System.Reflection;

public class TransactionableAttribute : Attribute
{
    public TransactionableAttribute()
    {
    }
}

class TestClass
{
    [Transactionable]
    public void Foo()
    {}

    public void Bar()
    {}

    [Transactionable]
    public void Baz()
    {}
}

class MethodAttrApp
{
    public static void Main()
    {
        Type type = Type.GetType("TestClass");
        foreach(MethodInfo method in type.GetMethods())
        {
            foreach (Attribute attr in
                    method.GetCustomAttributes())
            {
                if (attr is TransactionableAttribute)
                {
                    Console.WriteLine("{0} is transactionable.",
                                    method.Name);
                }
```

(continued)

149

```
                }
             }
         }
     }
```

The code outputs the following:

```
Foo is transactionable.
Baz is transactionable.
```

In this particular example, the mere presence of the *TransactionableAttribute* will be enough to tell the code that the method decorated with this attribute can belong in a transaction. That's why it's defined with only a bare-bones, parameterless constructor and no other members.

TestClass is then defined with three methods (*Foo*, *Bar*, and *Baz*) where two of them (*Foo* and *Baz*) are defined as transactionable. Notice that when attaching an attribute with a constructor that takes no parameters, you do not need to include the open and closed parentheses.

Now for the fun stuff. Let's look more closely at how we can query a class's methods as to the methods' attributes. We start off by using the static *Type* method *GetType* to obtain a *System.Type* object for the *TestClass* class:

```
Type type = Type.GetType("TestClass");
```

Then we use the *Type.GetMethods* method to retrieve an array of *MethodInfo* objects. Each of these objects contains the information about a method in the *TestClass* class. Using a *foreach* statement, we iterate through every method:

```
foreach(MethodInfo method in type.GetMethods())
```

Now that we have a *MethodInfo* object, we can use the *MethodInfo.-GetCustomAttributes* method to retrieve all the user-created attributes for the method. Once again, we use a *foreach* statement to iterate through the returned array of objects:

```
foreach (Attribute attr in method.GetCustomAttributes(true))
```

At this point in the code, we have an attribute for a method. Now, using the *is* operator, we query it as to whether it's a *TransactionableAttribute* attribute. If it is, we print the name of the method:

```
if (attr is TransactionableAttribute)
{
Console.WriteLine("{0} is transactionable.",
                  method.Name);
}
```

Field Attributes

In the last example of querying members as to their attached attributes, we'll look at how to query a class's fields. Let's say you have a class that contains some fields the values of which you want to save in the Registry. To do that, you could define an attribute with a constructor that takes as its parameters an *enum* representing the correct Registry hive and a string representing the Registry value name. You could then query the field at run time as to its Registry key:

```
using System;
using System.Reflection;

public enum RegistryHives
{
    HKEY_CLASSES_ROOT,
    HKEY_CURRENT_USER,
    HKEY_LOCAL_MACHINE,
    HKEY_USERS,
    HKEY_CURRENT_CONFIG
}

public class RegistryKeyAttribute : Attribute
{
    public RegistryKeyAttribute(RegistryHives Hive, String ValueName)
    {
        this.Hive = Hive;
        this.ValueName = ValueName;
    }

    protected RegistryHives hive;
    public RegistryHives Hive
    {
        get { return hive; }
        set { hive = value; }
    }

    protected String valueName;
    public String ValueName
    {
        get { return valueName; }
        set { valueName = value; }
    }
}

class TestClass
```

(continued)

```
    {
        [RegistryKey(RegistryHives.HKEY_CURRENT_USER, "Foo")]
        public int Foo;

        public int Bar;
    }

    class FieldAttrApp
    {
        public static void Main()
        {
            Type type = Type.GetType("TestClass");
            foreach(FieldInfo field in type.GetFields())
            {
                foreach (Attribute attr in field.GetCustomAttributes())
                {
                    RegistryKeyAttribute registryKeyAttr =
attr as RegistryKeyAttribute;
                    if (null != registryKeyAttr)
                    {
                        Console.WriteLine
                            ("{0} will be saved in {1}\\\\\{2}",
                            field.Name,
                            registryKeyAttr.Hive,
                            registryKeyAttr.ValueName);
                    }
                }
            }
        }
    }
}
```

I won't walk through all of this code because some of it is duplicated from the previous example. However, a couple of details are important. First notice that just as a *MethodInfo* object is defined for retrieving method information from a type object, a *FieldInfo* object provides the same functionality for obtaining field information from a type object. As in the previous example, we start by obtaining the type object associated with our test class. We then iterate through the *FieldInfo* array, and for each *FieldInfo* object, we iterate through its attributes until we find the one we're looking for: *RegistryKeyAttribute*. If and when we locate that, we print the name of the field and retrieve from the attribute its *Hive* and *ValueName* fields.

Attribute Parameters

In the examples above, I covered the use of attaching attributes by way of their constructors. Now I'll look at some issues regarding attribute constructors that I didn't cover earlier.

Positional Parameters and Named Parameters

In the *FieldAttrApp* example in the previous section, you saw an attribute named *RegistryKeyAttribute*. Its constructor looked like the following:

public RegistryKeyAttribute(RegistryHives *Hive*, String *ValueName*)

Based on that constructor signature, the attribute was then attached to a field like so:

```
[RegistryKey(RegistryHives.HKEY_CURRENT_USER, "Foo")]
public int Foo;
```

So far, this is straightforward. The constructor has two parameters, and two parameters were used in the attaching of that attribute to a field. However, we can make this easier to program. If the parameter is going to remain the same the majority of the time, why make the class's user type it in each time? We can set default values by using positional parameters and named parameters.

Positional parameters are parameters to the attribute's constructor. They are mandatory and must be specified every time the attribute is used. In the *RegistryKeyAttribute* example above, *Hive* and *ValueName* are both positional parameters. Named parameters are actually not defined in the attribute's constructor—rather, they are nonstatic fields and properties. Therefore, named parameters give the client the ability to set an attribute's fields and properties when the attribute is instantiated without you having to create a constructor for every possible combination of fields and properties that the client might want to set.

Each public constructor can define a sequence of positional parameters. This is the same as any type of class. However, in the case of attributes, once the positional parameters have been stated, the user can then reference certain fields or properties with the syntax *FieldOrPropertyName=Value*. Let's modify the attribute *RegistryKeyAttribute* to illustrate this. In this example, we'll make *RegistryKeyAttribute.ValueName* the only positional parameter, and *RegistryKeyAttribute.Hive* will become an optional named parameter. So, the question is, "How do you define something as a named parameter?" Because only positional—and, therefore, mandatory—parameters are included in the constructor's definition, simply remove the parameter from the constructor's definition. The user can then reference as a named parameter any field that is not *readonly, static,* or *const* or any property that includes a set accessor method, or setter, that is not static. Therefore, to make the *RegistryKeyAttribute.Hive* a named parameter, we would remove it from the constructor's definition because it already exists as a public read/write property:

```
public RegistryKeyAttribute(String ValueName)
```

The user can now attach the attribute in either of the following ways:

```
[RegistryKey("Foo")]
[RegistryKey("Foo", Hive = RegistryHives.HKEY_LOCAL_MACHINE)]
```

This gives you the flexibility of having a default value for a field while at the same time giving the user the ability to override that value if needed. But hold on! If the user *doesn't* set the value of the *RegistryKeyAttribute.Hive* field, how do we default it? You might be thinking, "Well, we check to see whether it has been set in the constructor." However, the problem is that the *RegistryKeyAttribute.Hive* is an *enum* with an underlying type of *int*—it is a value type. This means that by definition the compiler has initialized it to 0! If we examine the *RegistryKeyAttribute.Hive* value in the constructor and find it to be equal to 0, we don't know if that value was placed there by the caller through a named parameter or if the compiler initialized it because it's a value type. Unfortunately, at this time, the only way I know to get around this problem is to change the code such that the value 0 isn't valid. This can be done by changing the *RegistryHives enum* as follows:

```
public enum RegistryHives
{
    HKEY_CLASSES_ROOT = 1,
    HKEY_CURRENT_USER,
    HKEY_LOCAL_MACHINE,
    HKEY_USERS,
    HKEY_CURRENT_CONFIG
}
```

Now we know that the only way *RegistryKeyAttribute.Hive* can be 0 is if the compiler has initialized it to 0 and the user did not override that value via a named parameter. We can now write code similar to the following to initialize it:

```
public RegistryKeyAttribute(String ValueName)
{
    if (this.Hive == 0)
        this.Hive = RegistryHives.HKEY_CURRENT_USER;

    this.ValueName = ValueName;
}
```

Common Mistakes with Named Parameters

When using named parameters, you must specify the positional parameters first. After that, the named parameters can exist in any order because they're preceded by the name of the field or property. The following, for example, will result in a compiler error:

```
// This is an error because positional parameters can't follow
// named parameters.
[RegistryKey(Hive=RegistryHives.HKEY_LOCAL_MACHINE, "Foo")]
```

Additionally, you can't name positional parameters. When the compiler is compiling an attribute's usage, it will attempt to resolve the named parameters first. Then it will attempt to resolve what's left over—the positional parameters—with the method signature. The following will not compile because the compiler can resolve each named parameter but, when finished with the named parameters, it can't find any positional parameters and states that *"No overload for method 'RegistryKeyAttribute' takes '0'' arguments"*:

```
[RegistryKey(ValueName="Foo", Hive=RegistryHives.HKEY_LOCAL_MACHINE)]
```

Lastly, named parameters can be any publicly accessible field or property—including a setter method—that is not *static* or *const*.

Valid Attribute Parameter Types

The types of positional parameters and named parameters for an attribute class are limited to the attribute parameter types, which are listed here:

- *bool, byte, char, double, float, int, long, short, string*

- *System.Type*

- *object*

- An *enum* type, provided that it and any types in which it is nested are publicly accessible—as in the example used with the *RegistryHives* enumeration

- A one-dimensional array involving any of the types listed above

Because the parameter types are limited to the types in this list, you can't pass data structures like classes to the attribute constructor. This restriction makes sense because attributes are attached at design time and you wouldn't have the instantiated instance of the class (an object) at that point. With the valid types listed above, you can hard-code their values at design time, which is why they can be used.

The *AttributeUsage* Attribute

In addition to custom attributes that you use to annotate regular C# types, you can use the *AttributeUsage* attribute to define how you want these attributes to be used. The *AttributeUsage* attribute has the following documented calling conventions:

```
[AttributeUsage(
validon,
AllowMultiple = allowmultiple,
Inherited = inherited
)]
```

As you can see, it's easy to discern which are positional parameters and which are named parameters. I would strongly recommend that you document your attributes in this fashion so that the user of your attribute doesn't need to look through your attribute class's source code to find the public read/write fields and properties that can be used as named attributes.

Defining an Attribute Target

Now, looking again at the *AttributeUsage* attribute in the previous section, notice that the *validon* parameter is a positional—and, again, therefore mandatory—parameter. This parameter enables you to specify the types on which your attribute can be attached. Actually, the *validon* parameter in the *AttributeUsage* attribute is of the type *AttributeTargets*, which is an enumeration defined as follows:

```
public enum AttributeTargets
{
    Assembly    = 0x0001,
    Module      = 0x0002,
    Class       = 0x0004,
    Struct      = 0x0008,
    Enum        = 0x0010,
    Constructor = 0x0020,
    Method      = 0x0040,
    Property    = 0x0080,
    Field       = 0x0100,
    Event       = 0x0200,
    Interface   = 0x0400,
    Parameter   = 0x0800,
    Delegate    = 0x1000,
    All = Assembly | Module | Class | Struct | Enum | Constructor |
          Method | Property | Field | Event | Interface | Parameter |
          Delegate,
```

```
ClassMembers = Class | Struct | Enum | Constructor | Method |
               Property | Field | Event | Delegate | Interface,
}
```

Notice when using the *AttributeUsage* attribute that you can specify *AttributeTargets.All* such that the attribute can be attached to any of the types listed in the *AttributeTargets* enumeration. This is the default if you don't specify the *AttributeUsage* attribute at all. Given that *AttributeTargets.All* is the default, you might be wondering why you would ever use the *validon* value. Well, named parameters can be used on this attribute, and you might want to change one of those. Remember that if you use a named parameter, you must precede it with all the positional parameters. This gives you an easy way to specify that you want the default attribute usage of *AttriubuteTargets.All* and still lets you set the named parameters.

So, when would you specify the *validon (AttributeTargets)* parameter and why? You use it when you want to control exactly how an attribute is being used. In the examples above, we created a *RemoteObjectAttribute* attribute that would be applicable for classes only, a *TransactionableAttribute* attribute that would apply only to methods, and a *RegistryKeyAttribute* attribute that would make sense with fields only. If we wanted to make sure that these attributes were used to annotate only the types for which they were designed, we could define them as follows (with attribute bodies left out for brevity):

```
[AttributeUsage(AttributeTargets.Class)]
public class RemoteObjectAttribute : Attribute]
{
    ...
}

[AttributeUsage(AttributeTargets.Method)]
public class TransactionableAttribute : Attribute
{
    ...
}

[AttributeUsage(AttributeTargets.Field)]
public class RegistryKeyAttribute : Attribute
{
    ...
}
```

One last point regarding the *AttributeTargets* enumeration: you can combine members by using the | operator. If you have an attribute that would apply to both fields and properties, you would attach the *AttributeUsage* attribute to it as follows:

```
[AttributeUsage(AttributeTargets.Field | AttributeTargets.Property)]
```

Single-Use and Multiuse Attributes

You can use *AttributeUsage* to define attributes as either single-use or multiuse. This decision pertains to how many times a single attribute can be used on a single field. By default, all attributes are single-use, meaning that compiling the following results in a compiler error:

```
using System;
using System.Reflection;

public class SingleUseAttribute : Attribute
{
    public SingleUseAttribute(String str)
    {
    }
}

// ERROR: This results in a "duplicate attribute" compiler error.
[SingleUse("abc")]
[SingleUse("def")]
class MyClass
{
}

class SingleUseApp
{
    public static void Main()
    {
    }
}
```

To fix this problem, specify on the *AttributeUsage* line that you want to allow the attribute to be attached multiple times to a given type. This would work:

```
using System;
using System.Reflection;

[AttributeUsage(AttributeTargets.All, AllowMultiple=true)]
public class SingleUseAttribute : Attribute
{
    public SingleUseAttribute(String str)
    {
    }
}

[SingleUse("abc")]
[SingleUse("def")]
class MyClass
{
```

```
}

class MultiUseApp
{
    public static void Main()
    {
    }
}
```

A practical example of where you might want to use this approach is with the *RegistryKeyAttribute* attribute discussed in "Defining Attributes." Because it's conceivable that a field might be saved in multiple places in the Registry, you would attach the *AttributeUsage* attribute with the *AllowMultiple* named parameter as in the code here.

Specifying Inheritance Attribute Rules

The last parameter for the *AttributeUsageAttribute* attribute is the *inherited* flag, which dictates whether the attribute can be inherited. The default for this value is *false*. However, if the *inherited* flag is set to *true*, its meaning is dependent on the value of the *AllowMultiple* flag. If the *inherited* flag is set to *true* and the *AllowMultiple* flag is *false*, the attribute will override the inherited attribute. However, if the *inherited* flag is set to *true* and the *AllowMultiple* flag is also set to *true*, the attribute accumulates on the member.

Attribute Identifiers

Look at the following line of code, and try to figure out whether the attribute annotates the return value or the method:

```
class MyClass
{
    [HRESULT]
    public long Foo();
}
```

If you have some COM experience, you know that an *HRESULT* is the standard return type for all methods not named *AddRef* or *Release*. However, it's easy to see that if the attribute name could apply to both the return value and the method name, it would be impossible for the compiler to know what your intention is. Here are some other scenarios where the compiler would not know your intention by context:

■ method vs. return type

■ event vs. field vs. property

- delegate vs. return type

- property vs. accessor vs. return value of getter method vs. value parameter of setter method

In each of these cases, the compiler makes a determination based on what's considered "most common." To override this determination, you use an attribute identifier, all of which are listed here:

- assembly

- module

- type

- method

- property

- event

- field

- param

- return

To use an attribute identifier, preface the attribute name with the identifier and a colon. In the *MyClass* example, if you wanted to make sure the compiler could determine that the *HRESULT* attribute is meant to annotate the return value and not the method, you would specify it as follows:

```
class MyClass
{
    [return:HRESULT]
    public long Foo();
}
```

Summary

C# attributes provide a mechanism for annotating types and members at design time with information that can later be retrieved at run time through *reflection*. This gives you the ability to create truly self-contained, self-describing components without having to resort to stuffing necessary bits into resource files and constants. The advantage is a more mobile component that is both easier to write and easier to maintain.

9

Interfaces

The key to understanding interfaces might be to compare them with classes. Classes are objects that have properties and methods that act on those properties. While classes do exhibit some behavioral characteristics (methods), classes are *things* as opposed to *behaviors,* and that's how interfaces come in. Interfaces enable you to define behavioral characteristics, or abilities, and apply those behaviors to classes irrespective of the class hierarchy. For example, say that you have a distribution application in which some of the entities can be serialized. These might include the *Customer, Supplier* and *Invoice* classes. Some other classes, such as *MaintenanceView* and *Document*, might not be defined as serializable. How would you make only the classes you choose serializable? One obvious way would be to create a base class called something like *Serializable.* However, that approach has a major drawback. A single inheritance path won't work because we don't want all the behaviors of the class to be shared. C# doesn't support multiple inheritance, so there's no way to have a given class selectively derive from multiple classes. The answer is interfaces. Interfaces give you the ability to define a set of semantically related methods and properties that selected classes can implement regardless of the class hierarchy.

From a conceptual standpoint, interfaces are contracts between two disparate pieces of code. That is, once an interface is defined and a class is defined as implementing that interface, clients of the class are guaranteed that the class has implemented all methods defined in the interface. You'll see this soon in some examples.

In this chapter, we'll look at why interfaces are such an important part of C# and component-based programming in general. Then we'll take a look at how to declare and implement interfaces in a C# application. Finally, we'll delve into more of the specifics regarding using interfaces and overcoming the inherent problems with multiple inheritance and name collision.

> **Note**   When you define an interface and specify that a class is going to make use of that interface in its definition, the class is said to be *implementing the interface* or *inheriting from the interface*. You can use both phrases, and you'll see them used interchangeably in other texts. Personally, I believe that *implement* is the more semantically correct term—interfaces are defined behaviors and a class is defined as implementing that behavior, as opposed to inheriting from another class—but both terms are correct.

Interface Use

To understand where interfaces are useful, let's first look at a traditional programming problem in Microsoft Windows development that doesn't use an interface but in which two pieces of disparate code need to communicate in a generic fashion. Imagine that you work for Microsoft and you are the lead programmer for the Control Panel team. You need to provide a generic means for any client applet to bolt into Control Panel so that its icon appears in Control Panel and the end user can execute the program. Keeping in mind that this functionality was designed before COM was introduced, how would you provide a means for any future application to be integrated into Control Panel? The solution that was conceived has been a standard part of Windows development for years.

You, as lead programmer for the Control Panel team, design and document the function (or functions) that you need the client application to implement, along with a few rules. In the case of Control Panel applets, Microsoft determined that to write a Control Panel applet you need to create a dynamic-link library (DLL) that implements and exports a function named *CPlApplet*. You also need to append this DLL's name with an extension of .cpl and place the DLL in the Windows System32 folder. (On Windows ME or Windows 98, this will be Windows\System32, and on Windows 2000, this will be WINNT\System32.) Once Control Panel loads, it loads all DLLs in the System32 folder with the .cpl extension (by using the *LoadLibrary* function) and then uses the *GetProcAddress* function to load the *CPlApplet* function, thereby verifying that you've followed the rules and can properly communicate with Control Panel.

As I mentioned, this is a standard programming model in Windows for handling situations in which you have a piece of code that you want future unknown code to communicate with in a generic manner. However, this isn't the most elegant solution in the world, and it definitely has its problems. The biggest disadvantage to this technique is that it forces the client—the Control Panel code, in this case—to include a lot of validation code. For example, Control Panel couldn't just assume that any .cpl file in the folder is a Windows DLL. Also, Control Panel needs to verify that the correction functions are in that DLL and that those functions do what the documentation specifies. This is where interfaces come in. Interfaces let you create the same contractual arrangement between disparate pieces of code but in a more object-oriented and flexible manner. In addition, because interfaces are a part of the C# language, the compiler ensures that when a class is defined as implementing a given interface, the class does what it says it does.

In C#, an interface is a first-class concept that declares a reference type that includes method declarations only. But what do I mean when I say "first-class concept"? The term means that the feature in question is a built-in, integral part of the language. In other words, it's not something that was bolted on after the language was designed. Now let's delve deeper into the details of what interfaces are and how to declare them.

> **Note**   To the C++ developers in attendance, an interface is basically an abstract class with only pure virtual methods declared in addition to other C# class member types, such as properties, events, and indexers.

Declaring Interfaces

Interfaces can contain methods, properties, indexers, and events—none of which are implemented in the interface itself. Let's look at an example to see how to use this feature. Suppose you're designing an editor for your company that hosts different Windows controls. You're writing the editor and the routines that validate the controls users place on the editor's form. The rest of the team is writing the controls that the forms will host. You almost certainly need to provide some sort of form-level validation. At appropriate times—such as when the user explicitly tells the form to validate all controls or during form processing—the form could then iterate through all its attached controls and validate each control, or more appropriately, tell the control to validate itself.

How would you provide this control validation capability? This is where interfaces excel. Here's a simple interface example containing a single method named *Validate*:

```
interface IValidate
{
    bool Validate();
}
```

Now you can document the fact that if the control implements the *IValidate* interface, the control can be validated.

Let's examine a couple of aspects of the preceding code snippet. First, you don't need to specify an access modifier such as *public* on an interface method. In fact, prepending the method declaration with an access modifier results in a compile-time error. This is because all interface methods are public by definition. (C++ developers might also notice that because interfaces, by definition, are abstract classes, you do not need to explicitly declare the method as being *pure virtual* by appending *=0* to the method declaration.)

In addition to methods, interfaces can define properties, indexers, and events, as shown here:

```
interface IExampleInterface
{
    // Example property declaration.
    int testProperty { get; }

    // Example event declaration.
    event testEvent Changed;

    // Example indexer declaration.
    string this[int index] { get; set; }
}
```

Implementing Interfaces

Because an interface defines a contract, any class that implements an interface *must define each and every item in that interface* or the code won't compile. Using the *IValidate* example from the previous section, a client class would need to implement only the interface's methods. In the following example, I have a base class called *FancyControl* and an interface called *IValidate*. I then have a class, *MyControl*, that derives from *FancyControl* and implements *IValidate*. Note the syntax and how the *MyControl* object can be cast to the *IValidate* interface to reference its members.

```
using System;

public class FancyControl
{
    protected string Data;
        public string data
        {
            get
```

```
            {
                return this.Data;
            }
            set
            {
                this.Data = value;
            }
        }
    }

    interface IValidate
    {
        bool Validate();
    }

    class MyControl : FancyControl, IValidate
    {
        public MyControl()
        {
            data = "my grid data";
        }

        public bool Validate()
        {
            Console.WriteLine("Validating...{0}", data);
                    return true;
        }
    }

    class InterfaceApp
    {
        public static void Main()
        {
            MyControl myControl = new MyControl();

            // Call a function to place the control on
            // the form. Now, when the editor needs to
            // validate the control, it can do
            // the following:

            IValidate val = (IValidate)myControl;
            bool success = val.Validate();
        Console.WriteLine("The validation of '{0}' was {1}successful",
                        myControl.data,
                        (true == success ? "" : "not "));
        }
    }
```

Using the preceding class and interface definition, the editor can query the control as to whether the control implements the *IValidate* interface. (You'll see how to accomplish this step in the next section.) If it does, the editor can validate and then call the implemented interface methods. You might be prompted to ask, "Why don't I just define a base class to use with this editor that has a pure virtual function called *Validate*? The editor would then accept only controls that are derived from this base class, right?"

That would be a workable solution, but it would be severely limiting. Let's say you create your own controls and they all derive from this hypothetical base class. Consequently, they all implement this *Validate* virtual method. This works until the day you find a really cool control that you want to use with the editor. Let's say you find a grid that was written by someone else. As such, it won't be derived from the editor's mandatory control base class. In C++, the answer is to use multiple inheritance and derive your grid from both the third-party grid and the editor's base class. However, C# does not support multiple inheritance.

Using interfaces, you can implement multiple behavioral characteristics in a single class. In C# you can derive from a single class and, in addition to that inherited functionality, implement as many interfaces as the class needs. For example, if you wanted the editor application to validate the control's contents, bind the control to a database, and serialize the contents of the control to disk, you would declare your class as follows:

```
public class MyGrid : ThirdPartyGrid, IValidate,
                     ISerializable, IDataBound
{
  :
}
```

As promised, the next section answers the question, "How can one piece of code know when a class implements a given interface?"

Querying for Implementation by Using *is*

In the *InterfaceApp* example, you saw the following code, which was used to cast an object (*MyControl*) to one of its implemented interfaces (*IValidate*) and then call one of those interface members (*Validate*):

```
MyControl myControl = new MyControl();
  :
IValidate val = (IValidate)myControl;
bool success = val.Validate();
```

What would happen if a client attempted to use a class as if the class had implemented a method that it hadn't? The following example will compile because *ISerializable* is a valid interface. Nonetheless, at run time a *System.InvalidCastException* will be thrown because *MyGrid* doesn't implement the *ISerializable* interface. The application would then abort unless this exception was being explicitly caught.

```csharp
using System;

public class FancyControl
{
    protected string Data;
    public string data
    {
        get
        {
            return this.Data;
        }
        set
        {
            this.Data = value;
        }
    }
}

interface ISerializable
{
    bool Save();
}

interface IValidate
{
    bool Validate();
}

class MyControl : FancyControl, IValidate
{
    public MyControl()
    {
        data = "my grid data";
    }

    public bool Validate()
    {
        Console.WriteLine("Validating...{0}", data);
        return true;
    }
}
```

(continued)

```
class IsOperator1App
{
    public static void Main()
    {
        MyControl myControl = new MyControl();

        ISerializable ser = (ISerializable)myControl;

        // NOTE: This will throw a System.InvalidateCastException
        // because the class does not implement the ISerializable
        // interface.
        bool success = ser.Save();

        Console.WriteLine("The saving of '{0}' was {1}successful",
myControl.data,
(true == success ? "" : "not "));
    }
}
```

Of course, catching the exception doesn't change the fact that the code you want to execute will not execute in this case. What you need is a way to query the object *before* attempting to cast it. One way of doing this is by using the *is* operator. The *is* operator enables you to check at run time whether one type is compatible with another type. It takes the following form, where *expression* is a reference type:

expression is *type*

The *is* operator results in a Boolean value and can, therefore, be used in conditional statements. In the following example, I've modified the code to test for compatibility between the *MyControl* class and the *ISerializable* interface before attempting to use an *ISerializable* method:

```
using System;

public class FancyControl
{
    protected string Data;
    public string data
    {
        get
        {
            return this.Data;
        }
        set
        {
            this.Data = value;
        }
    }
```

```
        }
    }

interface ISerializable
{
    bool Save();
}

interface IValidate
{
    bool Validate();
}

class MyControl : FancyControl, IValidate
{
    public MyControl()
    {
        data = "my grid data";
    }

    public bool Validate()
    {
        Console.WriteLine("Validating...{0}", data);
        return true;
    }
}

class IsOperator2App
{
    public static void Main()
    {
        MyControl myControl = new MyControl();

        if (myControl is ISerializable)
        {
            ISerializable ser = (ISerializable)myControl;
            bool success = ser.Save();

            Console.WriteLine("The saving of '{0}' was {1}successful",
myControl.data,
(true == success ? "" : "not "));
        }
        else
        {
         Console.WriteLine("The ISerializable interface is not implemented.");
        }
    }
}
```

Now that you've seen how the *is* operator enables you to verify the compatibility of two types to ensure proper usage, let's look at one of its close relatives—the *as* operator—and compare the two.

Querying for Implementation by Using *as*

If you look closely at the MSIL code generated from the preceding *IsOperator2App* example—that MSIL code follows this paragraph—you'll notice one problem with the *is* operator. You can see that *isinst* is called right after the object is allocated and the stack is set up. The *isinst* opcode is generated by the compiler for the C# *is* operator. This opcode tests to see if the object is an instance of a class or interface. Notice that just a few lines later—assuming the conditional test passes— the compiler has generated the *castclass* IL opcode. The *castclass* opcode does its own verification and, while this opcode works slightly differently than *isinst*, the result is that the generated IL is doing inefficient work by checking the validity of this cast twice.

```
.method public hidebysig static void Main() il managed
{
  .entrypoint
  // Code size       72 (0x48)
  .maxstack  4
  .locals (class MyControl V_0,
           class ISerializable V_1,
           bool V_2)
  IL_0000:  newobj      instance void MyControl::.ctor()
  IL_0005:  stloc.0
  IL_0006:  ldloc.0
  IL_0007:  isinst      ISerializable
  IL_000c:  brfalse.s   IL_003d
  IL_000e:  ldloc.0
  IL_000f:  castclass   ISerializable
  IL_0014:  stloc.1
  IL_0015:  ldloc.1
  IL_0016:  callvirt    instance bool ISerializable::Save()
  IL_001b:  stloc.2
  IL_001c:  ldstr       "The saving of '{0}' was {1}successful"
  IL_0021:  ldloc.0
  IL_0022:  call        instance class System.String FancyControl::get_data()
  IL_0027:  ldloc.2
  IL_0028:  brtrue.s    IL_0031
  IL_002a:  ldstr       "not "
  IL_002f:  br.s        IL_0036
  IL_0031:  ldstr       ""
  IL_0036:  call    void [mscorlib]System.Console::WriteLine(class System.String,
                                            class System.Object,
                                            class System.Object)
```

```
    IL_003b:  br.s    IL_0047
    IL_003d:  ldstr   "The ISerializable interface is not implemented."
    IL_0042:  call    void [mscorlib]System.Console::WriteLine(class System.String)
    IL_0047:  ret
} // end of method IsOperator2App::Main
```

We can make this verification process more efficient using the *as* operator. The *as* operator converts between compatible types and takes the following form, where *expression* is any reference type:

object = *expression* as *type*

You can think of the *as* operator as a combination of the *is* operator and, if the two types in question are compatible, a cast. An important difference between the *as* operator and the *is* operator is that the *as* operator sets the object equal to *null* instead of returning a Boolean value if *expression* and *type* are incompatible. Our example can now be rewritten in the following more efficient manner:

```
using System;

public class FancyControl
{
    protected string Data;
    public string data
    {
        get
        {
            return this.Data;
        }
        set
        {
            this.Data = value;
        }
    }
}

interface ISerializable
{
    bool Save();
}

interface IValidate
{
    bool Validate();
}
```

(continued)

```
class MyControl : FancyControl, IValidate
{
    public MyControl()
    {
        data = "my grid data";
    }

    public bool Validate()
    {
        Console.WriteLine("Validating...{0}", data);
        return true;
    }
}

class AsOperatorApp
{
    public static void Main()
    {
        MyControl myControl = new MyControl();

        ISerializable ser = myControl as ISerializable;
        if (null != ser)
        {
            bool success = ser.Save();

            Console.WriteLine("The saving of '{0}' was {1}successful",
myControl.data,
(true == success ? "" : "not "));
        }
        else
        {
            Console.WriteLine("The ISerializable interface is not implemented.");
        }
    }
}
```

Now the verification to ensure a valid cast is done only once, which is obviously much more efficient. At this point, let's revisit the MSIL code to see the impact that using the *as* operator has had:

```
.method public hidebysig static void Main() il managed
{
  .entrypoint
  // Code size       67 (0x43)
  .maxstack  4
```

```
        .locals (class MyControl V_0,
                 class ISerializable V_1,
                 bool V_2)
    IL_0000:  newobj     instance void MyControl::.ctor()
    IL_0005:  stloc.0
    IL_0006:  ldloc.0
    IL_0007:  isinst     ISerializable
    IL_000c:  stloc.1
    IL_000d:  ldloc.1
    IL_000e:  brfalse.s  IL_0038
    IL_0010:  ldloc.1
    IL_0011:  callvirt   instance bool ISerializable::Save()
    IL_0016:  stloc.2
    IL_0017:  ldstr      "The saving of '{0}' was {1}successful"
    IL_001c:  ldloc.0
    IL_001d:  call       instance class System.String FancyControl::get_data()
    IL_0022:  ldloc.2
    IL_0023:  brtrue.s   IL_002c
    IL_0025:  ldstr      "not "
    IL_002a:  br.s       IL_0031
    IL_002c:  ldstr      ""
    IL_0031:  call   void [mscorlib]System.Console::WriteLine(class System.String,
                                                    class System.Object,
                                                    class System.Object)
    IL_0036:  br.s       IL_0042
    IL_0038:  ldstr      "The ISerializable interface is not implemented."
    IL_003d:  call   void [mscorlib]System.Console::WriteLine(class System.String)
    IL_0042:  ret
} // end of method AsOperatorApp::Main
```

Explicit Interface Member Name Qualification

So far, you've seen classes implement interfaces by specifying the access modifier *public* followed by the interface method's signature. However, sometimes you'll want (or even need) to explicitly qualify the member name with the name of the interface. In this section, we'll examine two common reasons for doing this.

Name Hiding with Interfaces

The most common way to call a method implemented from an interface is to cast an instance of that class to the interface type and then call the desired method. While this is valid and many people (including myself) use this technique, technically you don't have to cast the object to its implemented interface to call that interface's methods. This is because when a class implements an interface's methods, those methods are also public methods of the class. Take a look at this C# code and especially the *Main* method to see what I mean:

```
using System;

public interface IDataBound
{
    void Bind();
}

public class EditBox : IDataBound
{
    // IDataBound implementation.
    public void Bind()
    {
        Console.WriteLine("Binding to data store...");
    }
}

class NameHiding1App
{
    // Main entry point.
    public static void Main()
    {
        Console.WriteLine();

        EditBox edit = new EditBox();
        Console.WriteLine("Calling EditBox.Bind()...");
        edit.Bind();

        Console.WriteLine();

        IDataBound bound = (IDataBound)edit;
        Console.WriteLine("Calling (IDataBound)EditBox.Bind()...");
        bound.Bind();
    }
}
```

This example will now output the following:

```
Calling EditBox.Bind()...
Binding to data store...

Calling (IDataBound))EditBox.Bind()...
Binding to data store...
```

Notice that although this application calls the implemented *Bind* method in two different ways—one with a cast and one without—both calls function correctly in that the *Bind* method is processed. Although at first blush the ability to directly call the implemented method without casting the object to an interface might seem like a good thing, at times this is less than desirable. The most obvious reason is that the implementation of several interfaces—each of which might contain numerous members—could quickly pollute your class's public namespace with members that have no meaning outside the scope of the implementing class. You can prevent the implemented members of interfaces from becoming public members of the class by using a technique called *name hiding*.

Name hiding at its simplest is the ability to hide an inherited member name from any code outside the derived or implementing class (commonly referred to as the *outside world*). Let's say that we have the same example as we used earlier where an *EditBox* class needs to implement the *IDataBound* interface—however, this time the *EditBox* class doesn't want to expose the *IDataBound* methods to the outside world. Rather, it needs this interface for its own purposes, or perhaps the programmer simply doesn't want to clutter the class's namespace with a large number of methods that a typical client won't use. To hide an implemented interface member, you need only remove the member's *public* access modifier and qualify the member name with the interface name, as shown here:

```
using System;

public interface IDataBound
{
    void Bind();
}

public class EditBox : IDataBound
{
    // IDataBound implementation.
    void IDataBound.Bind()
    {
        Console.WriteLine("Binding to data store...");
    }
}

class NameHiding2App
{
    public static void Main()
    {
        Console.WriteLine();
```

(continued)

```
EditBox edit = new EditBox();
Console.WriteLine("Calling EditBox.Bind()...");

// ERROR: This line won't compile because
// the Bind method no longer exists in the
// EditBox class's namespace.
edit.Bind();

Console.WriteLine();

IDataBound bound = (IDataBound)edit;
Console.WriteLine("Calling (IDataBound)EditBox.Bind()...");

// This is OK because the object was cast to
// IDataBound first.
bound.Bind();
}
}
```

The preceding code will not compile because the member name *Bind* is no longer a part of the *EditBox* class. Therefore, this technique enables you to remove the member from the class's namespace while still allowing explicit access by using a cast operation.

One point I want to reiterate is that when you are hiding a member, you cannot use an access modifier. You'll receive a compile-time error if you try to use an access modifier on an implemented interface member. You might find this odd, but consider that the entire reason for hiding something is to prevent it from being visible outside the current class. Since access modifiers exist only to define the level of visibility outside the base class, you can see that they don't make sense when you use name hiding.

Avoiding Name Ambiguity

One of the main reasons that C# does not support multiple inheritance is the problem of name collision, which results from name ambiguity. Although C# does not support multiple inheritance at the object level (derivation from a class), it does support inheritance from one class and the additional implementation of multiple interfaces. However, with this power comes a price: name collision.

In the following example, we have two interfaces, *ISerializable* and *IDataStore*, which support the reading and storing of data in two different formats—one as an object to disk in binary form and the other to a database. The problem is that they both contain methods named *SaveData*:

```
using System;

interface ISerializable
{
    void SaveData();
}

interface IDataStore
{
    void SaveData();
}

class Test : ISerializable, IDataStore
{
    public void SaveData()
    {
        Console.WriteLine("Test.SaveData called");
    }
}

class NameCollisions1App
{
    public static void Main()
    {
        Test test = new Test();

        Console.WriteLine("Calling Test.SaveData()");
        test.SaveData();
    }
}
```

At the time of this writing, this code does compile. However, I'm told that in a future build of the C# compiler, the code will result in a compile-time error because of the ambiguity of the implemented *SaveData* method. Regardless of whether this code compiles, you'd have a problem at run time because the resulting behavior of calling the *SaveData* method would not be clear to the programmer attempting to use the class. Would you get the *SaveData* that serializes the object to disk, or would you get the *SaveData* that saves to a database?

In addition, take a look at the following code:

```
using System;

interface ISerializable
{
    void SaveData();
}
```

(continued)

```
interface IDataStore
{
    void SaveData();
}

class Test : ISerializable, IDataStore
{
    public void SaveData()
    {
        Console.WriteLine("Test.SaveData called");
    }
}

class NameCollisions2App
{
    public static void Main()
    {
        Test test = new Test();

        if (test is ISerializable)
        {
            Console.WriteLine("ISerializable is implemented");
        }

        if (test is IDataStore)
        {
            Console.WriteLine("IDataStore is implemented");
        }
    }
}
```

Here, the *is* operator succeeds for both interfaces, which indicates that both interfaces are implemented although we know that not to be the case! Even the compiler gives the following warnings upon compilation of this example:

```
NameCollisions2.cs(27,7): warning CS0183: The given expression is
always of the provided ('ISerializable') type
NameCollisions2.cs(32,7): warning CS0183: The given expression is
always of the provided ('IDataStore') type
```

The problem is that the class has implemented either a serialized version or a database version of the *Bind* method (not both). However, if the client checks for the implementation of one of the interfaces—both will succeed—and happens to try to use the one that wasn't truly implemented, unexpected results will occur.

You can turn to explicit member name qualification to get around this problem: remove the access modifier, and prepend the member name—*SaveData*, in this case—with the interface name:

```
using System;

interface ISerializable
{
    void SaveData();
}

interface IDataStore
{
    void SaveData();
}

class Test : ISerializable, IDataStore
{
    void ISerializable.SaveData()
    {
        Console.WriteLine("Test.ISerializable.SaveData called");
    }
    void IDataStore.SaveData()
    {
        Console.WriteLine("Test.IDataStore.SaveData called");
    }
}

class NameCollisions3App
{
    public static void Main()
    {
        Test test = new Test();

        if (test is ISerializable)
        {
            Console.WriteLine("ISerializable is implemented");
            ((ISerializable)test).SaveData();
        }

        Console.WriteLine();

        if (test is IDataStore)
        {
            Console.WriteLine("IDataStore is implemented");
            ((IDataStore)test).SaveData();
        }
    }
}
```

Now there's no ambiguity as to which method will be called. Both methods are implemented with their fully qualified names, and the resulting output from this application is what you'd expect:

```
ISerializable is implemented
Test.ISerializable.SaveData called

IDataStore is implemented
Test.IDataStore.SaveData called
```

Interfaces and Inheritance

Two common problems are associated with interfaces and inheritance. The first problem, illustrated here with a code example, deals with the issue of deriving from a base class that contains a method name identical to the name of an interface method that the class needs to implement.

```
using System;

public class Control
{
    public void Serialize()
    {
        Console.WriteLine("Control.Serialize called");
    }
}

public interface IDataBound
{
    void Serialize();
}

public class EditBox : Control, IDataBound
{
}

class InterfaceInh1App
{
    public static void Main()
    {
        EditBox edit = new EditBox();
        edit.Serialize();
    }
}
```

As you know, to implement an interface, you must provide a definition for every member in that interface's declaration. However, in the preceding example we don't do that, and the code still compiles! The reason it compiles is that the C# compiler looks for an implemented *Serialize* method in the *EditBox* class and finds one. However, the compiler is incorrect in determining that this is the implemented method. The *Serialize* method found by the compiler is the *Serialize* method inherited from the *Control* class and not an actual implementation of the *IDataBound.Serialize* method. Therefore, although the code compiles, it will not function as expected, as we'll see next.

Now let's make things a little more interesting. Notice that the following code first checks—via the *as* operator—that the interface is implemented and then attempts to call an implemented *Serialize* method. The code compiles and works. However, as we know, the *EditBox* class doesn't really implement a *Serialize* method as a result of the *IDataBound* inheritance. The *EditBox* already had a *Serialize* method (inherited) from the *Control* class. This means that in all likelihood the client is not going to get the expected results.

```
using System;

public class Control
{
    public void Serialize()
    {
        Console.WriteLine("Control.Serialize called");
    }
}

public interface IDataBound
{
    void Serialize();
}

public class EditBox : Control, IDataBound
{
}

class InterfaceInh2App
{
    public static void Main()
    {
        EditBox edit = new EditBox();

        IDataBound bound = edit as IDataBound;
        if (bound != null)
        {
            Console.WriteLine("IDataBound is supported...");
            bound.Serialize();
        }
```

(continued)

```
        else
        {
            Console.WriteLine("IDataBound is NOT supported...");
        }
    }
}
```

Another potential problem to watch for occurs when a derived class has a method with the same name as the base class implementation of an interface method. Let's look at that in code as well:

```
using System;

interface ITest
{
    void Foo();
}

// Base implements ITest.
class Base : ITest
{
    public void Foo()
    {
        Console.WriteLine("Base.Foo (ITest implementation)");
    }
}

class MyDerived : Base
{
    public new void Foo()
    {
        Console.WriteLine("MyDerived.Foo");
    }
}

public class InterfaceInh3App
{
    public static void Main()
    {
        MyDerived myDerived = new MyDerived();
        myDerived.Foo();

        ITest test = (ITest)myDerived;
        test.Foo();
    }
}
```

This code results in the following screen output:

```
MyDerived.Foo
Base.Foo (ITest implementation)
```

In this situation, the *Base* class implements the *ITest* interface and its *Foo* method. However, the *MyDerived* class derives from *Base* with a new class and implements a new *Foo* method for that class. Which *Foo* gets called? It depends on what reference you have. If you have a reference to the *MyDerived* object, its *Foo* method will be called. This is because even though the *myDerived* object has an inherited implementation of *ITest.Foo*, the run time will execute the *MyDerived.Foo* because the *new* keyword specifies an override of the inherited method.

However, when you explicitly cast the *myDerived* object to the *ITest* interface, the compiler resolves to the interface implementation. The *MyDerived* class has a method of the same name, but that's not what the compiler is looking for. When you cast an object to an interface, the compiler traverses the inheritance tree until a class is found that contains the interface in its base list. This is why the last two lines of code in the *Main* method result in the *ITest* implemented *Foo* being called.

Hopefully, some of these potential pitfalls involving name collisions and interface inheritance have supported my strong recommendation: always cast the object to the interface whose member you're attempting to use.

Combining Interfaces

Another powerful feature of C# is the ability to combine two or more interfaces together such that a class need only implement the combined result. For example, let's say you want to create a new *TreeView* class that implements both the *IDragDrop* and *ISortable* interfaces. Since it's reasonable to assume that other controls, such as a *ListView* and *ListBox,* would also want to combine these features, you might want to combine the *IDragDrop* and *ISortable* interfaces into a single interface:

```
using System;

public class Control
{
}

public interface IDragDrop
{
    void Drag();
    void Drop();
}
```

(continued)

```csharp
public interface ISerializable
{
    void Serialize();
}

public interface ICombo : IDragDrop, ISerializable
{
    // This interface doesn't add anything new in
    // terms of behavior as its only purpose is
    // to combine the IDragDrop and ISerializable
    // interfaces into one interface.
}

public class MyTreeView : Control, ICombo
{
    public void Drag()
    {
        Console.WriteLine("MyTreeView.Drag called");
    }

    public void Drop()
    {
        Console.WriteLine("MyTreeView.Drop called");
    }

    public void Serialize()
    {
        Console.WriteLine("MyTreeView.Serialize called");
    }
}

class CombiningApp
{
    public static void Main()
    {
        MyTreeView tree = new MyTreeView();
        tree.Drag();
        tree.Drop();
        tree.Serialize();
    }
}
```

With the ability to combine interfaces, you can not only simplify the ability to aggregate semantically related interfaces into a single interface, but also add additional methods to the new "composite" interface, if needed.

Summary

Interfaces in C# allow the development of classes that can share features but that are not part of the same class hierarchy. Interfaces play a special role in C# development because C# doesn't support multiple inheritance. To share semantically related methods and properties, classes can implement multiple interfaces. Also, the *is* and *as* operators can be used to determine whether a particular interface is implemented by an object, which can help prevent errors associated with using interface members. Finally, explicit member naming and name hiding can be used to control interface implementation and to help prevent errors.

Part III

Writing Code

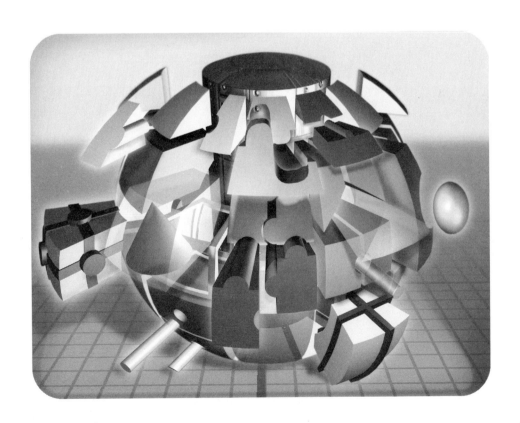

10

Expressions and Operators

In this chapter, we'll take a look at the most basic part of any programming language: its ability to express assignments and comparisons through the use of operators. We'll look at what operators are and how operator precedence is determined in C#, and then we'll delve into specific categories of expressions for doing such things as performing math, assigning values, and making comparisons between operands.

Operators Defined

An operator is a symbol that indicates an operation to be performed on one or more arguments. This operation produces a result. The syntax used with operators is a bit different than that used with method calls, but the C# format of an expression using operators should be second nature to you. Like operators in most other programming languages, C# operator semantics follow the basic rules and notations we learned as children in mathematics classes. The most basic C# operators include multiplication (*), division (/), addition and unary plus (+), subtraction and unary minus (−), modulus (%) and assignment (=).

Operators are specifically designed to produce a new value from the values that are being operated on. The values being operated on are called *operands*. The result of an operation must be stored somewhere in memory. In some cases the value produced by an operation is stored in the variable containing one of the original operands. The C# compiler generates an error message if you use an operator and no new value can be determined or stored. In the following example, the code results in nothing being changed. The compiler generates an error message because writing an arithmetic expression that doesn't result in a change to at least one value is generally a mistake on the part of the developer.

```
class NoResultApp
{
    public static void Main()
    {
        int i;
        int j;

        i + j; // Error because call is not assigned to a variable.
    }
}
```

Most operators work only with numeric data types such as *Byte*, *Short*, *Long*, *Integer*, *Single*, *Double*, and *Decimal*. Some exceptions are the comparison operators (==" and "!=) and the assignment operator (=), which can also work on objects. In addition, C# defines the + and += operators for the *String* class and even allows for the use of increment operators (++) and (−−) on unique language constructs such as delegates. I'll get into that last example in Chapter 14, "Delegates and Event Handlers."

Operator Precedence

When a single expression or statement contains multiple operators, the compiler must determine the order in which these different operators will be evaluated. The rules that govern how the complier makes this determination are called *operator precedence*. Understanding operator precedence can mean the difference between writing your expressions with confidence and staring at a single line of code as you wonder why the result isn't what you think it should be.

Take a look at the following expression: *42 + 6 * 10*. If you add 42 and 6 and then multiply the sum by 10, the product is 480. If you multiply 6 and 10 and then add that product to 42, the result is 102. When code is compiled, a special part of the compiler called the *lexical analyzer* is responsible for determining how this code should be read. It's the lexical analyzer that determines the relative precedence of operators when more than one kind of operator is present in an expression. It does this by specifying a value (or precedence) for each supported operator. The higher precedence operators are resolved first. In our example, the * operator has a higher precedence than the + operator because * *takes*—more on this term in a moment—its operands before + does. The reason for this comes from the basic rules of arithmetic: multiplication and division *always* have higher precedence than addition and subtraction. So, back to the example: 6 is said to be *taken* by the * in both *42 + 6 * 10* and *42 * 6 + 10* such that these expressions are the equivalent of *42 + (6 * 10)* and *(42 * 6) + 10*.

How C# Determines Precedence

Let's look specifically at how C# assigns precedence to operators. Table 10-1 illustrates C# operator precedence from highest precedence to lowest precedence. After this section, I'll go into more detail on the different categories of operators that are supported in C#.

Table 10-1 C# Operator Precedence

Category of Operator	Operators
Primary	(x), x.y, f(x), a[x], x++, x--, new, typeof, sizeof, checked, unchecked
Unary	+, −, !, ~, ++x, −−x, (T)x
Multiplicative	*, /, %
Additive	+, −
Shift	<<, >>
Relational	<, >, <=, >=, is
Equality	==
Logical AND	&
Logical XOR	∧
Logical OR	|
Conditional AND	&&
Conditional OR	||
Conditional	?:
Assignment	=, *=, /=, %=, +=, −=, <<=, >>=, &=, ∧=, |=

Left and Right Associativity

Associativity determines which side of an expression should be evaluated first. As an example, the following expression could result in a sum of either 21 or 33 depending on the left or right associativity of the − operator:

```
42-15-6
```

The − operator is defined as left-associative, meaning that 42−15 is evaluated and then 6 is subtracted from the result. If the − operator were defined as right-associative, the expression to the right of the operator would be evaluated first: 15−6 would be evaluated and then subtracted from 42.

All binary operators—that is, operators that take two operands—except the assignment operators, are said to be *left-associative,* meaning that the expression is evaluated from left to right. Therefore, $a + b + c$ is the same as $(a + b) + c$ where

$a + b$ is evaluated first and c is added to the resulting sum. Assignment operators and the conditional operator are said to be *right-associative*—the expression is evaluated from right to left. In other words, $a = b = c$ is equivalent to $a = (b = c)$. This trips up some people who want to place multiple assignment operations on the same line, so let's look at some code:

```
using System;

class RightAssocApp
{
    public static void Main()
    {
        int a = 1;
        int b = 2;
        int c = 3;

        Console.WriteLine("a={0} b={1} c={2}", a, b, c);
        a = b = c;
        Console.WriteLine("After 'a=b=c': a={0} b={1} c={2}", a, b, c);
    }
}
```

The results of running this example are the following:

```
a=1 b=2 c=3
After 'a=b=c': a=3 b=3 c=3
```

Seeing an expression evaluated from the right might be confusing at first, but think of it like this: If the assignment operator were left-associative, the compiler would first evaluate $a = b$, which would give a value of 2 to a, and then it would evaluate $b = c$, which would give a value of 3 to b. The end result would be *a=2 b=3 c=3*. Needless to say, that wouldn't be the expected result for $a = b = c$, and this is why the assignment and conditional operator are both right-associative.

Practical Usage

Nothing is more insidious than tracking down a bug for a long period of time only to find that the bug resulted from a developer not knowing the rules of precedence or associativity. I've seen several posts on mailing lists in which intelligent people have suggested a programming convention whereby spaces are used to indicate which operators they *think* will have precedence, a kind of self-documenting mechanism. So, for example, because we know that the multiplication operator has precedence over the addition operator, we could write code similar to the following where white space indicates the order of *intended* precedence:

```
a = b*c + d;
```

This approach is severely flawed—the compiler doesn't parse code properly without specific syntax. The compiler parses expressions based on the rules determined by the people that developed the compiler. To that end, a symbol exists that allows you to set precedence and associativity: the parenthesis. For example, you could rewrite the expression $a = b * c + d$ as either $a = (b * c) + d$ or $a = b * (c + d)$, and the compiler will evaluate what's in the parentheses first. If two or more pairs of parentheses exist, the compiler evaluates the value in each pair and then the entire statement by using the precedence and associativity rules I've described.

My firm opinion is that you should always use parentheses when using multiple operators in a single expression. I'd recommend this even if you know the order of precedence because the folks who maintain your code might not be as well informed.

C# Operators

It's helpful to think of operators according to their precedence. In this section, I'll describe the most commonly used operators in the order presented earlier in Table 10-1.

Primary Expression Operators

The first category of operators that we'll look are the primary expression operators. Because most of these operators are fairly basic, I'll just list them and give a short blurb about their function. I'll then explain the other less obvious operators a bit more thoroughly.

- **(x)** This form of the parenthesis operator is used to control precedence, either in mathematical operations or in method calls.

- **x.y** The "dot" operator is used to specify a member of a class or structure where x represents the containing entity and y represents the member.

- **f(x)** This form of the parenthesis operator is used to list the arguments to a method.

- **a[x]** Square brackets are used to index into an array. They are also used in conjunction with indexers where objects can be treated as arrays. For more information on indexers, refer to Chapter 7, "Properties, Arrays, and Indexers."

- ■   **x++**   Because there's a lot to talk about here, the increment operator is covered later in this chapter in "Increment Operators and Decrement Operators."

- ■   **x––**   The decrement operator is also covered later in this chapter.

- ■   **new**   The new operator is used to instantiate objects from class definitions.

typeof

Reflection is the ability to retrieve type information at run time. This information includes type names, class names, and structure members. Integral to this ability in the .NET Framework is a class called *System.Type*. This class is the root of all reflection operators, and it can be obtained by using the *typeof* operator. We won't be getting into reflection in great detail here—that's a task reserved for Chapter 16, "Querying Metadata with Reflection"—but here's a simple example to illustrate how easy it is to use the *typeof* operator to retrieve almost any information you want about a type or object at run time:

```
using System;
using System.Reflection;

public class Apple
{
    public int nSeeds;
    public void Ripen()
    {
    }
}

public class TypeOfApp
{
    public static void Main()
    {
        Type t = typeof(Apple);
        string className = t.ToString();

        Console.WriteLine("\nInformation about the class {0}",
            className);

        Console.WriteLine("\n{0} methods", className);
        Console.WriteLine("----------------------------");
        MethodInfo[] methods = t.GetMethods();
        foreach (MethodInfo method in methods)
        {
            Console.WriteLine(method.ToString());
        }
```

```
        Console.WriteLine("\nAll {0} members", className);
        Console.WriteLine("---------------------------");
        MemberInfo[] allMembers = t.GetMembers();
        foreach (MemberInfo member in allMembers)
        {
            Console.WriteLine(member.ToString());
        }
    }
}
```

The program contains a class called *Apple* that has only two members: a field named *nSeeds* and a method named *Ripen*. The first thing I do is to use the *typeof* operator and the class name to yield a *System.Type* object, which I then store in a variable named *t*. From that point on, I can use the *System.Type* methods to obtain all the *Apple* class methods and members. These tasks are performed using the *GetMethods* and *GetMembers* methods, respectively. The results of these method calls are printed to standard output, as shown here:

```
Information about the class Apple

Apple methods
----------------------------
Int32 GetHashCode()
Boolean Equals(System.Object)
System.String ToString()
Void Ripen()
System.Type GetType()

All Apple members
----------------------------
Int32 nSeeds
Int32 GetHashCode()
Boolean Equals(System.Object)
System.String ToString()
Void Ripen()
System.Type GetType()
Void .ctor()
```

Before we move on, there are two more points I'd like to make. First, notice that the class's inherited members are also listed in the output. Because I did not explicitly derive the class from another class, we know that all the members not defined in the *Apple* class are inherited from the implicit base class, *System.Object*. Second, note that you can also use the *GetType* method to retrieve the *System.Type* object. This is a method inherited from *System.Object* that enables you to work with objects, as opposed to classes. The two code snippets at the top of the next page could be used interchangeably to retrieve a *System.Type* object.

```
// Retrieve the System.Type object from the class definition.
Type t1 = typeof(Apple);


// Retrieve the System.Type object from the object.
Apple apple = new Apple();
Type t2 = apple.GetType();
```

sizeof

The *sizeof* operator is used to obtain the size, in bytes, of a given type. You should keep in mind two extremely important factors when using this operator. First, you can use the *sizeof* operator with value types only. Therefore, although this operator can be used on class members, it cannot be used on the class type itself. Second, this operator can be used only in a method or code block marked as *unsafe*. We'll get into unsafe code in Chapter 17, "Interoperating with Unmanaged Code." Here's an example of using the *sizeof* operator from a class method marked as *unsafe*:

```
using System;

class BasicTypes
{
    // NOTE: You must declare that code that uses the sizeof
    // operator as unsafe.
    static unsafe public void ShowSizes()
    {
        Console.WriteLine("\nBasic type sizes");
        Console.WriteLine("sizeof short = {0}", sizeof(short));
        Console.WriteLine("sizeof int = {0}", sizeof(int));
        Console.WriteLine("sizeof long = {0}", sizeof(long));
        Console.WriteLine("sizeof bool = {0}", sizeof(bool));
    }
}

class Unsafe1App
{
    unsafe public static void Main()
    {
        BasicTypes.ShowSizes();
    }
}
```

The results of running this application are the following:

```
Basic type sizes
sizeof short = 2
sizeof int = 4
```

```
sizeof long = 8
sizeof bool = 1
```

Aside from simple built-in types, the *sizeof* operator can also be used to determine the sizes of other user-created value types such as structs. However, the results of the *sizeof* operator can sometimes be less than obvious, such as in the following example:

```
// Using the sizeof operator.
using System;

struct StructWithNoMembers
{
}

struct StructWithMembers
{
    short s;
    int i;
    long l;
    bool b;
}

struct CompositeStruct
{
    StructWithNoMembers a;
    StructWithMembers b;

    StructWithNoMembers c;
}

class UnSafe2App
{
   unsafe public static void Main()
   {
   Console.WriteLine("\nsizeof StructWithNoMembers structure = {0}",
                 sizeof(StructWithNoMembers));
   Console.WriteLine("\nsizeof StructWithMembers structure = {0}",
                 sizeof(StructWithMembers));
   Console.WriteLine("\nsizeof CompositeStruct structure = {0}",
                 sizeof(CompositeStruct));
   }
}
```

While you might expect this application to print a value of *0* for the structure with no members (*StructWithNoMembers*), the value *15* for the structure with four of the basic members (*StructWithMembers*), and the value *15* for the structure that aggregates the two (*CompositeStruct*), the actual result follows.

```
sizeof StructWithNoMembers structure = 1

sizeof StructWithMembers structure = 16

sizeof CompositeStruct structure = 24
```

The reason for this is padding and structure alignment, which relates to how the compiler lays out a *struct* in the output file's image. For example, if a *struct* were three bytes long and the byte alignment were set at four bytes, the compiler would automatically pad it with an extra byte and the *sizeof* operator would report that the *struct* is four bytes in length. Therefore, you must take this into consideration when determining the size of a structure in C#.

checked and *unchecked*

These two operators control overflow checking for mathematical operations. Because these operators deal specifically with error handling, they are covered in Chapter 12, "Error Handling with Exceptions."

Mathematical Operators

The C# language supports the basic mathematical operators that almost all programming languages support: multiplication (*), division (/), addition (+), subtraction (−), and modulus (%). The first four operators are obvious in their meaning; the modulus operator produces the remainder from integer division. The following code illustrates these mathematical operators in use:

```
using System;

class MathOpsApp
{
    public static void Main()
    {
        // The System.Random class is part of the .NET
        // Framework class library. Its default constructor
        // seeds the Next method using the current date/time.
        Random rand = new Random();
        int a, b, c;

        a = rand.Next() % 100; // Limit max to 99.
        b = rand.Next() % 100; // Limit max to 99.

        Console.WriteLine("a={0} b={1}", a, b);

        c = a * b;
        Console.WriteLine("a * b = {0}", c);
```

```
// Note the following code uses integers. Therefore,
// if a is less than  b, the result will always
// be 0. To get a more accurate result, you would
// need to use variables of type double or float.
c = a / b;
Console.WriteLine("a / b = {0}", c);

c = a + b;
Console.WriteLine("a + b = {0}", c);

c = a - b;
Console.WriteLine("a - b = {0}", c);

c = a % b;
Console.WriteLine("a % b = {0}", c);
    }
}
```

Unary Operators

There are two unary operators, plus and minus. The unary minus operator indicates to the compiler that the operand is to be made negative. Therefore, the following would result in *a* being equal to *−42*:

```
using System;

using System;

class Unary1App
{
    public static void Main()
    {
        int a = 0;

        a = -42;
        Console.WriteLine("{0}", a);
    }
}
```

However, ambiguity creeps in when you do something like this:

```
using System;

class Unary2App
{
    public static void Main()
    {
```

(continued)

```
        int a;
        int b = 2;
        int c = 42;

        a = b * -c;
        Console.WriteLine("{0}", a);
    }
}
```

The *a = b * -c* can be bit confusing. Once again, the use of parentheses helps to make this line of code much clearer:

```
// With parentheses, it's obvious that you're multiplying
// b by the negative of c.
a = b * (-c);
```

If the unary minus returns the negative value of an operand, you'd think that the unary plus would return the positive value of an operand. However, the unary plus does nothing but return the operand in its original form, thereby having no effect on the operand. For example, the following code will result in the output of *–84*:

```
using System;

class Unary3App
{
    public static void Main()
    {
        int a;
        int b = 2;
        int c = -42;

        a = b * (+c);
        Console.WriteLine("{0}", a);
    }
}
```

To retrieve the positive form of an operand, use the *Math.Abs* function. The following will produce a result of *84*:

```
using System;

class Unary4App
{
    public static void Main()
    {
        int a;
        int b = 2;
        int c = -42;
```

```
        a = b * Math.Abs(c);
        Console.WriteLine("{0}", a);
    }
}
```

One last unary operator that I'll mention briefly is the (T)x operator. This is a form of the parenthesis operator that enables a cast of one type to another type. Because this operator can be overloaded by virtue of creating a user-defined conversion, it's covered in Chapter 13, "Operator Overloading and User-Defined Conversions."

Compound Assignment Operators

A *compound assignment operator* is a combination of a binary operator and the assignment (=) operator. Its syntax is

    x *op*= y

where *op* represents the operator. Note that instead of the *rvalue* being replaced by the *lvalue*, the compound operator has the effect of writing

    x = x *op* y

using the *lvalue* as the base for the result of the operation.

Note that I use the words "has the effect." The compiler doesn't literally translate something like $x += 5$ into $x = x + 5$. It just works that way logically. In fact, there's a major caveat to using an operation when the *lvalue* is a method. Let's examine that now:

```
using System;

class CompoundAssignment1App
{
    protected int[] elements;
    public int[] GetArrayElement()
    {
        return elements;
    }

    CompoundAssignment1App()
    {
        elements = new int[1];
        elements[0] = 42;
    }

    public static void Main()
```

(continued)

```
        {
            CompoundAssignment1App app = new CompoundAssignment1App();

            Console.WriteLine("{0}", app.GetArrayElement()[0]);
            app.GetArrayElement()[0] = app.GetArrayElement()[0] + 5;
            Console.WriteLine("{0}", app.GetArrayElement()[0]);
        }
}
```

Notice in the line in boldface—the call to the *CompoundAssignment1App.-GetArrayElements* method and subsequent modification of its first element—that I use the assignment syntax of

x = x *op* y

Here's the generated MSIL code:

```
// Inefficient technique of x = x op y.

.method public hidebysig static void Main() il managed
{
  .entrypoint
  // Code size        79 (0x4f)
  .maxstack  4
  .locals (class CompoundAssignment1App V_0)
  IL_0000:  newobj       instance void CompoundAssignment1App::.ctor()
  IL_0005:  stloc.0
  IL_0006:  ldstr        "{0}"
  IL_000b:  ldloc.0
  IL_000c:  call         instance int32[] CompoundAssignment1App::GetArrayElement()
  IL_0011:  ldc.i4.0
  IL_0012:  ldelema      ['mscorlib']System.Int32
  IL_0017:  box          ['mscorlib']System.Int32
  IL_001c:  call         void ['mscorlib']System.Console::WriteLine
(class System.String,
 class System.Object)
  IL_0021:  ldloc.0
  IL_0022:  call
instance int32[] CompoundAssignment1App::GetArrayElement()
  IL_0027:  ldc.i4.0
  IL_0028:  ldloc.0
  IL_0029:  call
instance int32[] CompoundAssignment1App::GetArrayElement()
  IL_002e:  ldc.i4.0
  IL_002f:  ldelem.i4
  IL_0030:  ldc.i4.5
  IL_0031:  add
```

```
  IL_0032:  stelem.i4
  IL_0033:  ldstr      "{0}"
  IL_0038:  ldloc.0
  IL_0039:  call
instance int32[] CompoundAssignment1App::GetArrayElement()
  IL_003e:  ldc.i4.0
  IL_003f:  ldelema     ['mscorlib']System.Int32
  IL_0044:  box         ['mscorlib']System.Int32
  IL_0049:  call  void ['mscorlib']System.Console::WriteLine
                            (class System.String, class System.Object)
  IL_004e:  ret
} // end of method. 'CompoundAssignment1App::Main'
```

Looking at the boldface lines in this MSIL, you can see that the *Compound-Assignment1App.GetArrayElements* method is actually being called twice! In a best-case scenario, this is inefficient. In the worst case, it could be disastrous, depending on what else the method does.

Now take a look at the following code, and note the change of the assignment to the compound assignment operator syntax:

```
using System;

class CompoundAssignment2App
{
    protected int[] elements;
    public int[] GetArrayElement()
    {
        return elements;
    }

    CompoundAssignment2App()
    {
        elements = new int[1];
        elements[0] = 42;
    }

    public static void Main()
    {
        CompoundAssignment2App app = new CompoundAssignment2App();

        Console.WriteLine("{0}", app.GetArrayElement()[0]);
        app.GetArrayElement()[0] += 5;
        Console.WriteLine("{0}", app.GetArrayElement()[0]);
    }
}
```

The use of the compound assignment operator results in the following much more efficient MSIL code:

```
// More efficient technique of x op= y.

.method public hidebysig static void Main() il managed
{
  .entrypoint
  // Code size       76 (0x4c)
  .maxstack  4
  .locals (class CompoundAssignment1App V_0, int32[] V_1)
  IL_0000:  newobj      instance void CompoundAssignment1App::.ctor()
  IL_0005:  stloc.0
  IL_0006:  ldstr       "{0}"
  IL_000b:  ldloc.0
  IL_000c:  call instance int32[] CompoundAssignment1App::GetArrayElement()
  IL_0011:  ldc.i4.0
  IL_0012:  ldelema     ['mscorlib']System.Int32
  IL_0017:  box         ['mscorlib']System.Int32
  IL_001c:  call    void ['mscorlib']System.Console::WriteLine
                          (class System.String, class System.Object)
    IL_0021:  ldloc.0
    IL_0022:  call  instance int32[] CompoundAssignment1App::GetArrayElement()

    IL_0027:  dup
    IL_0028:  stloc.1
    IL_0029:  ldc.i4.0
    IL_002a:  ldloc.1

  IL_002b:  ldc.i4.0
  IL_002c:  ldelem.i4
  IL_002d:  ldc.i4.5
  IL_002e:  add
  IL_002f:  stelem.i4
  IL_0030:  ldstr       "{0}"
  IL_0035:  ldloc.0
  IL_0036:  call      instance int32[] CompoundAssignment1App::GetArrayElement()
  IL_003b:  ldc.i4.0
  IL_003c:  ldelema     ['mscorlib']System.Int32
  IL_0041:  box         ['mscorlib']System.Int32
  IL_0046:  call    void ['mscorlib']System.Console::WriteLine
                          (class System.String, class System.Object)
  IL_004b:  ret
} // end of method 'CompoundAssignment1App::Main'
```

We can see that the MSIL *dup* opcode is being used. The *dup* opcode duplicates the top element on the stack, thereby making a copy of the value retrieved from the call to the *CompoundAssignment1App.GetArrayElements* method.

The point of this exercise has been to illustrate that although conceptually $x += y$ is equivalent to $x = x + y$, subtle differences can be found in the generated MSIL. These differences mean you need to think carefully about which syntax to use in each circumstance. A basic rule of thumb, and my recommendation, is to use compound assignment operators whenever and wherever possible.

Increment Operators and Decrement Operators

As holdovers from the same shortcuts first introduced in the C language and carried forward in both C++ and Java, increment operators and decrement operators allow you to more concisely state that you want to increment or decrement a variable representing a numeric value by 1. Therefore, $i++$ is the equivalent of adding 1 to the current value of i.

Two versions of both the increment and decrement operators exist and often are a source of confusion. Typically referred to as *prefix* and *postfix*, the type of operator indicates when the side effect modifies the variable. With the prefix versions of the increment operator and decrement operator—that is, $++a$ and $--a$, respectively—the operation is performed and then the value is produced. With the postfix versions of the increment operator and decrement operator—$a++$ and $a--$, respectively—the value is produced and then the operation is performed. Take a look at the following example:

```
using System;

class IncDecApp
{
    public static void Foo(int j)
    {
        Console.WriteLine("IncDecApp.Foo j = {0}", j);
    }

    public static void Main()
    {
        int i = 1;

        Console.WriteLine("Before call to Foo(i++) = {0}", i);
        Foo(i++);
        Console.WriteLine("After call to Foo(i++) = {0}", i);

        Console.WriteLine("\n");

        Console.WriteLine("Before call to Foo(++i) = {0}", i);
        Foo(++i);
        Console.WriteLine("After call to Foo(++i) = {0}", i);
    }
}
```

This application produces this result:

```
Before call to Foo(i++) = 1
IncDecApp.Foo j = 1
After call to Foo(i++) = 2


Before call to Foo(++i) = 2
IncDecApp.Foo j = 3
After call to Foo(++i) = 3
```

The difference here is *when* the value is produced and the operand is modified. In the call to *Foo(++i)*, the value *i* is passed (unchanged) to *Foo* and *after* the *Foo* method returns, *i* is incremented. You can see this in the following MSIL excerpt. Notice that the MSIL *add* opcode is not called until after the value has been placed on the stack.

```
IL_0013:   ldloc.0
IL_0014:   dup
IL_0015:   ldc.i4.1
IL_0016:   add
IL_0017:   stloc.0
IL_0018:   call        void IncDecApp::Foo(int32)
```

Now let's look at the preincrement operator used in the call to *Foo(++a)*. In this case, the MSIL generated looks like the code shown here. Notice that the MSIL *add* opcode is called *before* the value is placed on the stack for the subsequent call to the *Foo* method.

```
IL_0049:   ldloc.0
IL_004a:   ldc.i4.1
IL_004b:   add
IL_004c:   dup
IL_004d:   stloc.0
IL_004e:   call        void IncDecApp::Foo(int32)
```

Relational Operators

Most operators return a numeric result. Relational operators, however, are a bit different in that they generate a Boolean result. Instead of performing some mathematical operation on a set of operands, a relational operator compares the relationship between the operands and returns a value of *true* if the relationship is true and *false* if the relationship is untrue.

Comparison Operators

The set of relational operators referred to as comparison operators are less than
(<), less than or equal to (<=), greater than (>), greater than or equal to (>=),
equal to (==), and not equal to (!=). The meaning of each of these operators is
obvious when working with numbers, but how each operator works on objects
isn't so obvious. Here's an example:

```
using System;

class NumericTest
{
    public NumericTest(int i)
    {
        this.i = i;
    }

    protected int i;
}

class RelationalOps1App
{
    public static void Main()
    {
        NumericTest test1 = new NumericTest(42);
        NumericTest test2 = new NumericTest(42);

        Console.WriteLine("{0}", test1 == test2);
    }
}
```

If you're a Java programmer, you know what's going to happen here.
However, most C++ developers will probably be surprised to see that this example
prints a statement of *false*. Remember that when you instantiate an object, you
get a reference to a heap-allocated object. Therefore, when you use a relational
operator to compare two objects, the C# compiler doesn't compare the contents
of the objects. Instead, it compares the addresses of these two objects. Once again,
to fully understand what's going on here, we'll look at the MSIL for this code:

```
.method public hidebysig static void Main() il managed
{
  .entrypoint
  // Code size       39 (0x27)
  .maxstack  3
  .locals (class NumericTest V_0,
           class NumericTest V_1,
           bool V_2)
```

(continued)

```
IL_0000:  ldc.i4.s    42
IL_0002:  newobj      instance void NumericTest::.ctor(int32)
IL_0007:  stloc.0
IL_0008:  ldc.i4.s    42
IL_000a:  newobj      instance void NumericTest::.ctor(int32)
IL_000f:  stloc.1
IL_0010:  ldstr       "{0}"
IL_0015:  ldloc.0
IL_0016:  ldloc.1
IL_0017:  ceq
IL_0019:  stloc.2
IL_001a:  ldloca.s    V_2
IL_001c:  box         ['mscorlib']System.Boolean
IL_0021:  call    void ['mscorlib']System.Console::WriteLine
                            (class System.String,class System.Object)
IL_0026:  ret
} // end of method 'RelationalOps1App::Main'
```

Take a look at the *.locals* line. The compiler is declaring that this *Main* method will have three local variables. The first two are *NumericTest* objects, and the third is a Boolean type. Now skip down to lines *IL_0002* and *IL_0007*. It's here that the MSIL instantiates the *test1* object and, with the *stloc* opcode, stores the returned reference to the first local variable. However, the key point here is that the MSIL is storing the address of the newly created object. Then, in lines *IL_000a* and *IL_000f*, you can see the MSIL opcodes to create the *test2* object and store the returned reference in the second local variable. Finally, lines *IL_0015* and *IL_0016* simply load the local variables on the stack via a call to *ldloc*, and then line *IL_0017* calls the *ceq* opcode, which compares the top two values on the stack (that is, the references to the *test1* and *test2* objects). The returned value is then stored in the third local variable and later printed via the call to *System.Console.WriteLine*.

How can one produce a member-by-member comparison of two objects? The answer is in the implicit base class of all .NET Framework objects. The *System.Object* class has a method called *Equals* designed for just this purpose. For example, the following code performs a comparison of the object contents as you would expect and returns a value of *true*:

```
using System;

class RelationalOps2App
{
    public static void Main()
    {
        Decimal test1 = new Decimal(42);
        Decimal test2 = new Decimal(42);
```

```
        Console.WriteLine("{0}", test1.Equals(test2));
    }
}
```

Note that the RelationalOps1App example used a self-made class (*NumericTest*), and the second example used a .NET class (*Decimal*). The reason for this is that the *System.Object.Equals* method must be overridden to do the actual member-by-member comparison. Therefore, using the *Equals* method on the *NumericTest* class wouldn't work because we haven't overridden the method. However, because the *Decimal* class does override the inherited *Equals* method, it does work like you'd expect.

Another way to handle an object comparison is through *operator overloading*. Overloading an operator defines the operations that take place between objects of a specific type. For example, with *string* objects, the + operator concatenates the strings rather than performing an add operation. We'll be getting into operator overloading in Chapter 13.

Simple Assignment Operators

The value on the left side of an assignment operator is called the *lvalue*; the value on the right side is called the *rvalue*. The *rvalue* can be any constant, variable, number, or expression that can be resolved to a value compatible with the *lvalue*. However, the *lvalue* must be a variable of a defined type. The reason for this is that a value is being copied from the right to the left. Therefore, there must be physical space allocated in memory, which is the ultimate destination of the new value. As an example, you can state $i = 4$ because i represents a physical location in memory, either on the stack or on the heap, depending on the actual type of the i variable. However, you can't execute the statement $4 = i$ because 4 is a value, not a variable in memory the contents of which can be changed. As an aside, technically the rule in C# is that the *lvalue* can be a variable, property, or indexer. For more on properties and indexers, refer back to Chapter 7. To keep things simple, I'll stick to examples using variables found in this chapter.

Although numeric assignment is fairly straightforward, assignment operations involving objects is a much trickier proposition. Remember that when you're dealing with objects, you're not dealing with simple stack allocated elements that are easily copied and moved around. When manipulating objects, you really have only a reference to a heap-allocated entity. Therefore, when you attempt to assign an object (or any reference type) to a variable, you're not copying data as you are with value types. You're simply copying a reference from one place to another.

Let's say you have two objects: *test1* and *test2*. If you state *test1 = test2*, *test1* is not a copy of *test2*. It is the same thing! The *test1* object points to the same memory as *test2*. Therefore, any changes on the *test1* object are also changes on the *test2* object. Here's a program that illustrates this:

```
using System;

class Foo
{
    public int i;
}

class RefTest1App
{
    public static void Main()
    {
        Foo test1 = new Foo();
        test1.i = 1;

        Foo test2 = new Foo();
        test2.i = 2;

        Console.WriteLine("BEFORE OBJECT ASSIGNMENT");
        Console.WriteLine("test1.i={0}", test1.i);
        Console.WriteLine("test2.i={0}", test2.i);
        Console.WriteLine("\n");

        test1 = test2;

        Console.WriteLine("AFTER OBJECT ASSIGNMENT");
        Console.WriteLine("test1.i={0}", test1.i);
        Console.WriteLine("test2.i={0}", test2.i);
        Console.WriteLine("\n");

        test1.i = 42;

        Console.WriteLine("AFTER CHANGE TO ONLY TEST1 MEMBER");
        Console.WriteLine("test1.i={0}", test1.i);
        Console.WriteLine("test2.i={0}", test2.i);
        Console.WriteLine("\n");
    }
}
```

Run this code, and you'll see the following output:

```
BEFORE OBJECT ASSIGNMENT
test1.i=1
test2.i=2
```

```
AFTER OBJECT ASSIGNMENT
test1.i=2
test2.i=2

AFTER CHANGE TO ONLY TEST1 MEMBER
test1.i=42
test2.i=42
```

Let's walk through this example to see what happened each step of the way. *Foo* is a simple class that defines a single member named *i*. Two instances of this class—*test1* and *test2*—are created in the *Main* method and, in each case, the new object's *i* member is set (to a value of *1* and *2*, respectively). At this point, we print the values, and they look like you'd expect with *test1.i* being *1* and *test2.i* having a value of *2*. Here's where the fun begins. The next line assigns the *test2* object to *test1*. The Java programmers in attendance know what's coming next. However, most C++ developers would expect that the *test1* object's *i* member is now equal to the *test2* object's members (assuming that because the application compiled there must be some kind of implicit member-wise copy operator being performed). In fact, that's the appearance given by printing the value of both object members. However, the new relationship between these objects now goes much deeper than that. The code assigns 42 to *test1.i* and once again prints the values of both object's *i* members. What?! Changing the *test1* object changed the *test2* object as well! This is because the object formerly known as *test1* is no more. With the assignment of *test1* to *test2*, the *test1* object is basically lost because it is no longer referenced in the application and is eventually collected by the garbage collector (GC). The *test1* and *test2* objects now point to the same memory on the heap. Therefore, a change made to either variable will be seen by the user of the other variable.

Notice in the last two lines of the output that even though the code sets the *test1.i* value only, the *test2.i* value also has been affected. Once again, this is because both variables now point to the same place in memory, the behavior you'd expect if you're a Java programmer. However, it's in stark contrast to what a C++ developer would expect because in C++ the act of copying objects means just that—each variable has its own unique copy of the members such that modification of one object has no impact on the other. Because this is key to understanding how to work with objects in C#, let's take a quick detour and see what happens in the event that you pass an object to a method:

```
using System;

class Foo
```

(continued)

```
{
    public int i;
}

class RefTest2App
{
    public void ChangeValue(Foo f)
    {
        f.i = 42;
    }

    public static void Main()
    {
        RefTest2App app = new RefTest2App();

        Foo test = new Foo();
        test.i = 6;

        Console.WriteLine("BEFORE METHOD CALL");
        Console.WriteLine("test.i={0}", test.i);
        Console.WriteLine("\n");

        app.ChangeValue(test);

        Console.WriteLine("AFTER METHOD CALL");
        Console.WriteLine("test.i={0}", test.i);
        Console.WriteLine("\n");
    }
}
```

In most languages—Java excluded—this code would result in a copy of the *test* object being created on the local stack of the *RefTest2App.ChangeValue* method. If that were the case, the *test* object created in the *Main* method would never see any changes made to the *f* object within the *ChangeValue* method. However, once again, what's happening here is that the *Main* method has passed a reference to the heap-allocated *test* object. When the *ChangeValue* method manipulates its local *f.i* variable, it's also directly manipulating the *Main* method's *test* object.

Summary

A key part of any programming language is the way that it handles assignment, mathematical, relational, and logical operations to perform the basic work required by any real-world application. These operations are controlled in code through operators. Factors that determine the effects that operators have in code include precedence, and left and right associativity. In addition to providing a powerful set of predefined operators, C# extends these operators through user-defined implementations, which I'll discuss in Chapter 13.

11

Program Flow Control

The statements that enable you to control program flow in a C# application fall into three main categories: selection statements, iteration statements, and jump statements. In each of these cases, a test resulting in a Boolean value is performed and the Boolean result is used to control the application's flow of execution. In this chapter, you'll learn how to use each of these statement types to control structure flow.

Selection Statements

You use selection statements to determine what code should be executed and when it should be executed. C# features two selection statements: the *switch* statement, used to run code based on a value, and the *if* statement which runs code based on a Boolean condition. The most commonly used of these selection statements is the *if* statement.

The *if* Statement

The *if* statement executes one or more statements if the expression being evaluated is *true*. The *if* statement's syntax follows—the square brackets denote the optional use of the *else* statement (which we'll cover shortly):

```
if (expression)
    statement1
[else
    statement2]
```

Here, *expression* is any test that produces a Boolean result. If *expression* results in *true*, control is passed to *statement1*. If the result is *false* and an *else* clause exists, control is passed to *statement2*. Also note that *statement1* and *statement2* can consist of a single statement terminated by a semicolon (known as a simple statement) or of multiple statements enclosed in braces (a compound statement). The following illustrates a compound statement being used if *expression1* resolves to *true*:

```
if (expression1)
{
    statement1
    statement2
}
```

In the following example, the application requests that the user type in a number between 1 and 10. A random number is then generated, and the user is told whether the number they picked matches the random number. This simple example illustrates how to use the *if* statement in C#.

```
using System;

class IfTest1App
{
    const int MAX = 10;

    public static void Main()
    {
        Console.Write("Guess a number between 1 and {0}...", MAX);
        string inputString = Console.ReadLine();

        int userGuess = inputString.ToInt32();

        Random rnd = new Random();
        double correctNumber = rnd.NextDouble() * MAX;
        correctNumber = Math.Round(correctNumber);

        Console.Write("The correct number was {0} and you guessed {1}...",
                      correctNumber, userGuess);
        if (userGuess == correctNumber) // They got it right!
        {
            Console.WriteLine("Congratulations!");
        }
        else // Wrong answer!
        {
            Console.WriteLine("Maybe next time!");
        }
    }
}
```

Multiple *else* Clauses

The *if* statement's *else* clause enables you to specify an alternative course of action should the *if* statement resolve to *false*. In the number-guessing example, the application performed a simple compare between the number the user guessed and the randomly generated number. In that case, only two possibilities existed: the user was either correct or incorrect. You can also combine *if* and *else* to handle situations in which you want to test more than two conditions. In the example below, I ask the user which language he or she is currently using (excluding C#). I've included the ability to select from three languages, so the *if* statement must be able to deal with four possible answers: the three languages and the case in which the user selects an unknown language. Here's one way of programming this with an *if/else* statement:

```
using System;

class IfTest2App
{
    const string CPlusPlus = "C++";
    const string VisualBasic = "Visual Basic";
    const string Java = "Java";

    public static void Main()
    {
        Console.Write("What is your current language of choice " +
                    "(excluding C#)?");
        string inputString = Console.ReadLine();

        if (0 == String.Compare(inputString, CPlusPlus, true))
        {
            Console.WriteLine("\nYou'll have no problem picking " +
                        "up C# !");
        }
        else if (0 == String.Compare(inputString, VisualBasic, true))
        {
            Console.WriteLine("\nYou'll find lots of cool VB features " +
                        "in C# !");
        }
        else if (0 == String.Compare(inputString, Java, true))
        {
            Console.WriteLine("\nYou'll have an easier time " +
                        "picking up C# <G> !!");
        }
        else
        {
            Console.WriteLine("\nSorry - doesn't compute.");
        }
    }
}
```

Notice the use of the `==` operator to compare 0 to the returned value of *String.Compare*. This is because *String.Compare* will return −1 if the first string is less than the second string, 1 if the first string is greater than the second, and 0 if the two are identical. However, this illustrates some interesting details, described in the following section, about how C# enforces use of the *if* statement.

How C# Enforces *if* Rules

One aspect of the *if* statement that catches new C# programmers off guard is the fact that the expression evaluated must result in a Boolean value. This is in contrast to languages such as C++ where you're allowed to use the *if* statement to test for any variable having a value other than 0. The following example illustrates several common errors that C++ developers make when attempting to use the *if* statement in C# for the first time:

```
using System;

interface ITest
{
}

class TestClass : ITest
{
}

class InvalidIfApp
{
    protected static TestClass GetTestClass()
    {
        return new TestClass();
    }

    public static void Main()
    {
        int foo = 1;
        if (foo) // ERROR: attempting to convert int to bool.
        {
        }

        TestClass t = GetTestClass();
        if (t) // ERROR: attempting to convert TestClass to bool.
        {
            Console.WriteLine("{0}", t);

            ITest i = t as ITest;
            if (i) // ERROR: attempting to convert ITest to bool.
```

```
        {
            // ITest methods
        }
    }
}
}
```

If you attempt to compile this code, you'll receive the following errors from the C# compiler:

```
invalidIf.cs(22,7): error CS0029: Cannot implicitly convert type 'int' to 'bool'
invalidIf.cs(27,7): error CS0029: Cannot implicitly convert type 'TestClass' to 'bool'
invalidIf.cs(31,14): warning CS0183:
The given expression is always of the provided ('ITest') type
invalidIf.cs(32,8): error CS0029: Cannot implicitly convert type 'ITest' to 'bool'
```

As you can see, the compiler barks three times in response to three attempts to use the *if* statement with an operation that doesn't yield a Boolean value. The reason for this is that the C# designers want to help you avoid ambiguous code and believe that the compiler should enforce the original purpose of the *if* statement—that is, to control the flow of execution based on the result of a Boolean test. The example above is rewritten below to compile without error. Each line that caused the compiler error in the previous program has been modified to contain an expression that returns a Boolean result, thereby appeasing the compiler.

```
using System;

interface ITest
{
}

class TestClass : ITest
{
}

class ValidIfApp
{
    protected static TestClass GetTestClass()
    {
        return new TestClass();
    }

    public static void Main()
    {
        int foo = 1;
        if (foo > 0)
```

(continued)

219

```
        {
        }

        TestClass t = GetTestClass();
        if (t != null)
        {
            Console.WriteLine("{0}", t);

            ITest i = t as ITest;
            if (i != null)
            {
                // ITest methods.
            }
        }
    }
}
```

The *switch* Statement

Using the *switch* statement, you can specify an expression that returns an integral value and one or more pieces of code that will be run depending on the result of the expression. It's similar to using multiple *if/else* statements, but although you can specify multiple (possibly unrelated) conditional statements with multiple *if/else* statements, a *switch* statement consists of only one conditional statement followed by all the results that your code is prepared to handle. Here's the syntax:

```
switch (switch_expression)
{
    case constant-expression:
        statement
        jump-statement
    ⋮
    case constant-expressionN:
        statementN
    [default]
}
```

There are two main rules to keep in mind here. First, the *switch_expression* must be of the type (or implicitly convertible to) *sbyte, byte, short, ushort, int, uint, long, ulong, char,* or *string* (or an *enum* based on one of these types). Second, you must provide a *jump-statement* for each *case* statement unless that *case* statement is the last one in the switch, including the *break* statement. Because this works differently than in several other languages, I'll explain it more thoroughly later in this chapter in "No Fall-Through in *switch* Statements."

Conceptually, the *switch* statement works just as the *if* statement does. First, the *switch_expression* is evaluated, and then the result is compared to each of the *constant-expressions* or *case labels*, defined in the different *case* statements. Once a match is made, control is passed to the first line of code in that *case* statement.

In addition to letting you specify different *case* statements, the *switch* statement also allows for the definition of a *default* statement. This is like the *else clause* of an *if* statement. Note that there can be only one default label for each *switch* statement and that if no appropriate case label is found for the *switch_expression*, control is passed to the first line of code after the *switch* statement's ending brace. Here's an example—a *Payment* class is using the *switch* statement to determine which tender has been selected:

```
using System;

enum Tenders : int
{
    Cash = 1,
    Visa,
    MasterCard,
    AmericanExpress
};

class Payment
{
    public Payment(Tenders tender)
    {
        this.Tender = tender;
    }

    protected Tenders tender;
    public Tenders Tender
    {
        get
        {
            return this.tender;
        }
        set
        {
            this.tender = value;
        }
    }

    public void ProcessPayment()
```

(continued)

```
        {
            switch ((int)(this.tender))
            {
                case (int)Tenders.Cash:
                    Console.WriteLine("\nCash - Accepted");
                    break;

                case (int)Tenders.Visa:
                    Console.WriteLine("\nVisa - Accepted");
                    break;

                case (int)Tenders.MasterCard:
                    Console.WriteLine("\nMastercard - Accepted");
                    break;

                case (int)Tenders.AmericanExpress:
                    Console.WriteLine("\nAmerican Express - Accepted");
                    break;

                default:
                    Console.WriteLine("\nSorry - Invalid tender");
                    break;
            }
        }
    }

class SwitchApp
{
    public static void Main()
    {
        Payment payment = new Payment(Tenders.Visa);
        payment.ProcessPayment();
    }
}
```

Running this application results in the following output because we instantiated the *Payment* class by passing it a value of *Tenders.Visa*:

```
Visa - Accepted.
```

Combining Case Labels

In the *Payment* example, we used a different case label for each possible evaluation of the *Payment.tender* field. However, what if you want to combine case labels? For example, you might want to display a credit card authorization dialog box for any of the three credit card types deemed valid in the *Tenders enum*. In that case, you could place the case labels one right after the other, like so:

```csharp
using System;

enum Tenders : int
{
    Cash = 1,
    Visa,
    MasterCard,
    AmericanExpress
};

class Payment
{
    public Payment(Tenders tender)
    {
        this.Tender = tender;
    }

    protected Tenders tender;
    public Tenders Tender
    {
        get
        {
            return this.tender;
        }
        set
        {
            this.tender = value;
        }
    }

    public void ProcessPayment()
    {
        switch ((int)(this.tender))
        {
            case (int)Tenders.Cash:
                Console.WriteLine
                        ("\nCash - Everyone's favorite tender.");
                break;

            case (int)Tenders.Visa:
            case (int)Tenders.MasterCard:
            case (int)Tenders.AmericanExpress:
                Console.WriteLine
("\nDisplay Credit Card Authorization Dialog.");
                break;
```

(continued)

```
        default:
            Console.WriteLine("\nSorry - Invalid tender.");
            break;
        }
    }
}

class CombiningCaseLabelsApp
{

    public static void Main()
    {
        Payment payment = new Payment(Tenders.MasterCard);
        payment.ProcessPayment();
    }
}
```

If you instantiate the *Payment* class with *Tenders.Visa*, *Tenders.MasterCard*, or *Tenders.AmericanExpress*, you'll get this output:

```
Display Credit Card Authorization Dialog.
```

No Fall-Through in *switch* Statements

Throughout the design phase of C#, its designers were cognizant of applying a "risk/reward" test when deciding whether a feature should be included in the language. The fall-through feature is an example of one that didn't pass the test. Normally in C++, a *case* statement runs when its *constant-expression* matches the *switch_expression*. The *switch* statement is then exited with a *break* statement. Fall-through causes the next *case* statement in the *switch* statement to execute in the absence of a *break* statement.

Though not supported in C#, fall-through is typically used in situations in which you have two case labels and the second label represents an operation that will be done in either case. For example, I once wrote a database editor in C++ that allowed end users to create their tables and fields graphically. Each of these tables was displayed in a tree view in a Windows Explorer–like user interface. If the end user right-clicked the tree view, I wanted to display a menu with options such as Print All Tables and Create New Table. If the end user right-clicked a specific table, I wanted to display a context menu for that table. However, that menu also needed to include all the tree view options as well. Conceptually my code was similar to the following:

```
// Dynamically create menu in C++.
switch(itemSelected)
{
```

```
    case TABLE:
    // Add menu options based on current table;
    // break left out intentionally.

    case TREE_VIEW:
    // Add menu options for tree view.
    break;
}
// Display menu.
```

The first case label amounts to a combination of the two labels without me having to duplicate code or insert two calls to the same method. However, the C# language designers decided that although this feature can be handy, its reward wasn't worth the risk involved because the majority of the time a *break* statement is left out unintentionally, which results in bugs that are difficult to track down. To accomplish this in C#, you'd probably be better off using an *if* statement instead:

```
// Dynamically create menu.
if (itemSelected == TABLE)
{
    // Add menu options based on current table.
}
// Add menu options for tree view.
// Display menu.
```

Iteration Statements

In C#, the *while*, *do/while*, *for*, and *foreach* statements enable you to perform controlled iteration, or looping. In each case, a specified simple or compound statement is executed until a Boolean expression resolves to *true*, except for the case of the *foreach* statement, which is used to iterate through a list of objects.

The *while* Statement

The *while* statement takes the following form:

> while (*Boolean-expression*)
> *embedded-statement*

Using the number-guessing example from earlier in the chapter, we could rewrite the example, as beginning on the next page, with a *while* statement such that you could continue the game until you either guessed the correct number or decided to quit.

```
using System;

class WhileApp
{
    const int MIN = 1;
    const int MAX = 10;
    const string QUIT_CHAR = "Q";

    public static void Main()
    {
        Random rnd = new Random();
        double correctNumber;

        string inputString;
        int userGuess;

        bool correctGuess = false;
        bool userQuit = false;

        while (!correctGuess && !userQuit)
        {
            correctNumber = rnd.NextDouble() * MAX;
            correctNumber = Math.Round(correctNumber);

            Console.Write
                ("Guess a number between {0} and {1}...({2} to quit)",
                MIN, MAX, QUIT_CHAR);
            inputString = Console.ReadLine();

            if (0 == string.Compare(inputString, QUIT_CHAR, true))
                userQuit = true;
            else
            {
                userGuess = inputString.ToInt32();
                correctGuess = (userGuess == correctNumber);

                Console.WriteLine
                    ("The correct number was {0}\n",
                    correctNumber);
            }
        }

        if (correctGuess && !userQuit)
        {
            Console.WriteLine("Congratulations!");
        }
        else
```

```
        {
            Console.WriteLine("Maybe next time!");
        }
    }
}
```

Coding and running this application will result in output similar to the following:

```
C:\>WhileApp
Guess a number between 1 and 10...(Q to quit)3
The correct number was 5

Guess a number between 1 and 10...(Q to quit)5
The correct number was 5

Congratulations!

C:\>WhileApp
Guess a number between 1 and 10...(Q to quit)q
Maybe next time!
```

The *do/while* Statement

Looking back at the syntax for the *while* statement, you can see the possibility for one problem. The *Boolean-expression* is evaluated before the *embedded-statement* is executed. For this reason, the application in the previous section initialized the *correctGuess* and *userQuit* variables to *false* to guarantee that the *while* loop would be entered. From there, those values are controlled by whether the user correctly guesses the number or quits. However, what if we want to make sure that the *embedded-statement* always executes at least once without having to set the variables artificially? This is what the *do/while* statement is used for.

The *do/while* statement takes the following form:

> do
> *embedded-statement*
> while (*Boolean-expression*)

Because the evaluation of the *while* statement's *Boolean-expression* occurs after the *embedded-statement*, you're guaranteed that the *embedded-statement* will be executed at least one time. The number-guessing application rewritten to use the *do/while* statement appears on the following page.

```csharp
using System;

class DoWhileApp
{
    const int MIN = 1;
    const int MAX = 10;
    const string QUIT_CHAR = "Q";

    public static void Main()
    {
        Random rnd = new Random();
        double correctNumber;

        string inputString;
        int userGuess = -1;

        bool userHasNotQuit = true;

        do
        {
            correctNumber = rnd.NextDouble() * MAX;
            correctNumber = Math.Round(correctNumber);

            Console.Write
                ("Guess a number between {0} and {1}...({2} to quit)",
                MIN, MAX, QUIT_CHAR);
            inputString = Console.ReadLine();

            if (0 == string.Compare(inputString, QUIT_CHAR, true))
                userHasNotQuit = false;
            else
            {
                userGuess = inputString.ToInt32();
                Console.WriteLine
                    ("The correct number was {0}\n", correctNumber);
            }
        } while (userGuess != correctNumber
            && userHasNotQuit);

        if (userHasNotQuit
            && userGuess == correctNumber)
        {
            Console.WriteLine("Congratulations!");
        }
        else // wrong answer!
        {
            Console.WriteLine("Maybe next time!");
        }
    }
}
```

The functionality of this application will be the same as the *while* sample. The only difference is how the loop is controlled. In practice, you'll find that the *while* statement is used more often than the *do/while* statement. However, because you can easily control entry into the loop with the initialization of a Boolean variable, choosing one statement over the other is a choice of personal preference.

The *for* Statement

By far, the most common iteration statement that you'll see and use is the *for* statement. The *for* statement is made up of three parts. One part is used to perform initialization at the beginning of the loop—this part is carried out only once. The second part is the conditional test that determines whether the loop is to be run again. And the last part, called "stepping," is typically (but not necessarily) used to increment the counter that controls the loop's continuation—this counter is what is usually tested in the second part. The *for* statement takes the following form:

for (*initialization; Boolean-expression; step*)
    embedded-statement

Note that any of the three parts (*initialization, Boolean-expression, step*) can be empty. When *Boolean-expression* evaluates to *false*, control is passed from the top of the loop to the next line following the *embedded-statement*. Therefore, the *for* statement works just like a *while* statement except that it gives you the additional two parts (*initialization* and *step*). Here's an example of a *for* statement that displays the printable ASCII characters:

```
using System;

class ForTestApp
{
    const int StartChar = 33;
    const int EndChar = 125;

    static public void Main()
    {
        for (int i = StartChar; i <= EndChar; i++)
        {
            Console.WriteLine("{0}={1}", i, (char)i);
        }
    }
}
```

The order of events for this *for* loop is as follows:

1. A value-type variable (*i*) is allocated on the stack and initialized to 33. Note that this variable will be out of scope once the *for* loop concludes.

229

2.   The embedded statement will execute while the variable *i* has a value less than 126. In this example, I used a compound statement. However, because this *for* loop consists of a single line statement, you could also write this code without the braces and get the same results.

3.   After each iteration through the loop, the *i* variable will be incremented by 1.

Nested Loops

In the *embedded-statement* of a *for* loop, you can also have other *for* loops, which are generally referred to as *nested loops*. Using the example from the previous section, I've added a nested loop that causes the application to print three characters per line, instead of one per line:

```
using System;

class NestedForApp
{
    const int StartChar = 33;
    const int EndChar = 125;
    const int CharactersPerLine = 3;

    static public void Main()
    {
        for (int i = StartChar; i <= EndChar; i+=CharactersPerLine)
        {
            for (int j = 0; j < CharactersPerLine;  j++)
            {
                Console.Write("{0}={1} ", i+j, (char)(i+j));
            }
            Console.WriteLine("");
        }
    }

}
```

Note that the variable *i* that was defined in the outer loop is still in scope for the internal loop. However, the variable *j* is not available to the outer loop.

Using the Comma Operator

A comma can serve not only as a separator in method argument lists, but also as an operator in a *for* statement. In both the *initialization* and *step* portions of a *for* statement, the comma operator can be used to delimit multiple statements that are processed sequentially. In the following example, I've taken the nested loop example from the previous section and converted it to a single *for* loop by using the comma operator:

```
using System;

class CommaOpApp
{
    const int StartChar = 33;
    const int EndChar = 125;

    const int CharactersPerLine = 3;

    static public void Main()
    {
        for (int i = StartChar, j = 1; i <= EndChar; i++, j++)
        {
            Console.Write("{0}={1} ", i, (char)i);
            if (0 == (j % CharactersPerLine))
            {
                // New line if j is divisible by 3.
                Console.WriteLine("");
            }
        }
    }
}
```

Using the comma operator in the *for* statement can be powerful, but it can also lead to ugly and difficult-to-maintain code. Even with the addition of constants, the following code is an example of using the comma operator in a technically correct, but inappropriate, manner:

```
using System;

class CommaOp2App
{
    const int StartChar = 33;
    const int EndChar = 125;

    const int CharsPerLine = 3;
    const int NewLine = 13;
    const int Space = 32;

    static public void Main()
    {
        for (int i = StartChar, extra = Space;
            i <= EndChar;
            i++, extra = ((0 == (i - (StartChar-1)) % CharsPerLine)
            ? NewLine : Space))
        {
            Console.Write("{0}={1} {2}", i, (char)i, (char)extra);
        }
    }
}
```

The *foreach* Statement

For years, languages such as Visual Basic have had a special statement specifically designed for the iteration of arrays and collections. C# also has such a construct, the *foreach* statement, which takes the following form:

foreach (*type* in *expression*)
embedded-statement

Take a look at the following array class:

```
class MyArray
{
    public ArrayList words;

    public MyArray()
    {
        words = new ArrayList();
        words.Add("foo");
        words.Add("bar");
        words.Add("baz");
    }
}
```

From the different iteration statements you've already seen, you know that this array can be traversed using any of several different statements. However, to most Java and C++ programmers, the most logical way to write this application would be like this:

```
using System;
using System.Collections;

class MyArray
{
    public ArrayList words;

    public MyArray()
    {
        words = new ArrayList();
        words.Add("foo");
        words.Add("bar");
        words.Add("baz");
    }
}

class Foreach1App
{
    public static void Main()
```

```
    {
        MyArray myArray = new MyArray();

        for (int i = 0; i < myArray.words.Count; i++)
        {
            Console.WriteLine("{0}", myArray.words[i]);
        }
    }
}
```

But this approach is fraught with potential problems:

■ If the *for* statement's initialization variable (*i*) isn't initialized properly, the entire list won't be iterated.

■ If the *for* statement's Boolean expression isn't correct, the entire list won't be iterated.

■ If the *for* statement's step isn't correct, the entire list won't be iterated.

■ Collections and arrays have different methods and properties for accessing their count.

■ Collections and arrays have different semantics for extracting a specific element.

■ The *for* loop's embedded statement needs to extract the element into a variable of the correct type.

The code can go wrong many ways. Using the *foreach* statement, you can avoid these problems and iterate through any collection or array in a uniform manner. With the *foreach* statement, the previous code would be rewritten as follows:

```
using System;
using System.Collections;

class MyArray
{
    public ArrayList words;

    public MyArray()
    {
        words = new ArrayList();
        words.Add("foo");
        words.Add("bar");
        words.Add("baz");
    }
}
```

(continued)

```
class Foreach2App
{
    public static void Main()
    {
        MyArray myArray = new MyArray();

        foreach (string word in myArray.words)
        {
            Console.WriteLine("{0}", word);
        }
    }
}
```

Notice how much more intuitive using the *foreach* statement is. You're guaranteed to get every element because you don't have to manually set up the loop and request the count, and the statement automatically places the element in a variable that you name. You need only refer to your variable in the embedded statement.

Branching with Jump Statements

Inside the embedded statements of any of the iteration statements covered in the previous sections, you can control the flow of execution with one of several statements collectively known as jump statements: *break, continue, goto,* and *return*.

The *break* Statement

You use the *break* statement to terminate the current enclosing loop or conditional statement in which it appears. Control is then passed to the line of code following that loop's or conditional statement's embedded statement. Having the simplest syntax of any statement, the *break* statement has no parentheses or arguments and takes the following form at the point that you want to transfer out of a loop or conditional statement:

```
break
```

In the following example, the application will print each number from 1 to 100 that is equally divisible by 6. However, when the count reaches 66, the *break* statement will cause the *for* loop to discontinue.

```
using System;

class BreakTestApp
{
    public static void Main()
```

```
    {
        for (int i = 1; i <= 100; i ++)
        {
            if (0 == i % 6)
            {
                Console.WriteLine(i);
            }

            if (i == 66)
            {
                break;
            }
        }
    }
}

}
```

Breaking Out of Infinite Loops

Another use for the *break* statement is to create an infinite loop in which control is transferred out of the loop only by a *break* statement being reached. The following example illustrates a method of writing the number-guessing game presented earlier in the chapter with a *break* statement used to quit the loop once the user enters the letter *Q*. Notice that I changed the *while* statement to *while(true)* such that it will not end until a *break* statement is encountered.

```
using System;

class InfiniteLoopApp
{
    const int MIN = 1;
    const int MAX = 10;
    const string QUIT_CHAR = "Q";

    public static void Main()
    {
        Random rnd = new Random();
        double correctNumber;

        string inputString;
        int userGuess;

        bool correctGuess = false;
        bool userQuit = false;
```

(continued)

```
        while(true)
        {
            correctNumber = rnd.NextDouble() * MAX;
            correctNumber = Math.Round(correctNumber);

            Console.Write
                ("Guess a number between {0} and {1}...({2} to quit)",
                MIN, MAX, QUIT_CHAR);
            inputString = Console.ReadLine();

            if (0 == string.Compare(inputString, QUIT_CHAR, true))
            {
                userQuit = true;
                break;
            }
            else
            {
                userGuess = inputString.ToInt32();
                correctGuess = (userGuess == correctNumber);

                if ((correctGuess = (userGuess == correctNumber)))
                {
                    break;
                }
                else
                {

                    Console.WriteLine
                        ("The correct number was {0}\n", correctNumber);
                }
            }
        }

        if (correctGuess && !userQuit)
        {
            Console.WriteLine("Congratulations!");
        }
        else
        {
            Console.WriteLine("Maybe next time!");
        }
    }
}
```

One last point: I could have used an empty *for* statement here with the form *for (;;)* instead of *while(true)*. They work the same, so it comes down to a matter of taste.

The *continue* Statement

Like the *break* statement, the *continue* statement enables you to alter the execution of a loop. However, instead of ending the current loop's embedded statement, the *continue* statement stops the current iteration and returns control back to the top of the loop for the next iteration. In the following example, I have an array of strings that I want to check for duplicates. One way to accomplish that is to iterate through the array with a nested loop, comparing one element against the other. However, I certainly don't want to compare an element to itself or I'll register an invalid number of duplicates. Therefore, if one index into the array (*i*) is the same as the other index into the array (*j*), it means that I have the same element and don't want to compare those two. In that case, I use the *continue* statement to discontinue the current iteration and pass control back to the top of the loop.

```
using System;
using System.Collections;

class MyArray
{
    public ArrayList words;

    public MyArray()
    {
        words = new ArrayList();
        words.Add("foo");
        words.Add("bar");
        words.Add("baz");
        words.Add("bar");
        words.Add("ba");
        words.Add("foo");
    }
}

class ContinueApp
{
    public static void Main()
    {
        MyArray myArray = new MyArray();
        ArrayList dupes = new ArrayList();

        Console.WriteLine("Processing array...");
        for (int i = 0; i < myArray.words.Count; i++)
        {
            for (int j = 0; j < myArray.words.Count; j++)
```

(continued)

```
    {
        if (i == j) continue;

        if (myArray.words[i] == myArray.words[j]
            && !dupes.Contains(j))
        {
            dupes.Add(i);
            Console.WriteLine("'{0}' appears on lines {1} and {2}",
                myArray.words[i],
                i + 1,
                j + 1);
        }
    }
}
Console.WriteLine("There were {0} duplicates found",
    ((dupes.Count > 0) ? dupes.Count.ToString() : "no"));
    }
}
```

Notice that I could have used a *foreach* loop to iterate through the array. However, in this particular case, I wanted to keep track of which element I was on, so using a *for* loop was the best way.

The Infamous *goto* Statement

Probably no other construct in programming history is as maligned as the *goto* statement. Therefore, before we get into the syntax for and some uses of the *goto* statement, let's look at why some people feel so strongly about not using this statement and the types of problems that can be solved by using it.

The *goto* Statement: A (Very) Brief History

The *goto* statement was cast into disfavor with the publication of a paper titled "Go To Statement Considered Harmful," by Edsger W. Dijkstra, in 1968. At that particular time in programming history, a debate was raging over the issue of structured programming. Unfortunately, less attention was focused on the overall issues raised by structured programming than on a relatively small detail: whether particular statements, such as *go to* (now usually the *goto* keyword), should be present in modern programming languages. As is too often the case, many people took Dijkstra's advice and ran to the extreme, concluding that all uses of *goto* were bad and that use of *goto* should be avoided at all costs.

The problem with using *goto* isn't the keyword itself—rather, it's the use of *goto* in inappropriate places. The *goto* statement can be a useful tool in structuring program flow and can be used to write more expressive code than that resulting from other branching and iteration mechanisms. One such example is the "loop-and-a-half" problem, as coined by Dijkstra. Here is the traditional flow of the loop-and-a-half problem in pseudocode:

```
loop
    read in a value
    if value == sentinel then exit
    process the value
end loop
```

The exit from the loop is accomplished only by the execution of the *exit* statement in the middle of the loop. This *loop/exit/end loop* cycle, however, can be quite disturbing to some people who, acting on the notion that all uses of *goto* are evil, would write this code as follows:

```
read in a value
while value != sentinel
    process the value
    read in a value
end while
```

Unfortunately, as Eric S. Roberts of Stanford University points out, this second approach has two major drawbacks. First, it requires the duplication of the statement(s) required to read in a value. Any time you duplicate code, this results in an obvious maintenance problem in that any change to one statement must be made to the other. The second problem is more subtle and probably more damning. The key to writing solid code that's easy to understand, and therefore maintain, is to write code that reads in a natural manner. In any noncode description of what this code is attempting to do, one would describe the solution as follows: First, I need to read in a value. If that value is a sentinel, I stop. If not, I process that value and continue to the next value. Therefore, it's the code omitting the *exit* statement that's actually counterintuitive because that approach reverses the natural way of thinking about the problem. Now, let's look at some situations in which a *goto* statement can result in the best way to structure control flow.

Using the *goto* Statement

The *goto* statement can take any of the following forms:

goto *identifier*
goto case *constant-expression*
goto default

In the first usage of the *goto* statement here, the target of the *identifer* is a label statement. The label statement takes the form

identifer:

If that label doesn't exist in the current method, a compile-time error will result. Another important rule to remember is that the *goto* statement can be used to jump out of a nested loop. However, if the *goto* statement is not within the scope of the label, a compile-time error will result. Therefore, you cannot jump into a nested loop.

In the following example, the application is iterating through a simple array, reading each value until it reaches a sentinel value whereupon it exits the loop. Notice that the *goto* statement really just acts like the *break* statement in that it causes the program flow to jump out of the *foreach* loop.

```
using System;
using System.Collections;

class MyArray
{
    public ArrayList words;
    public const string TerminatingWord = "stop";

    public MyArray()
    {
        words = new ArrayList();

        for (int i = 1; i <= 5; i++) words.Add(i.ToString());
        words.Add(TerminatingWord);
        for (int i = 6; i <= 10; i++) words.Add(i.ToString());
    }
}

class Goto1App
{
    public static void Main()
    {
        MyArray myArray = new MyArray();

        Console.WriteLine("Processing array...");

        foreach (string word in myArray.words)
        {
            if (word == MyArray.TerminatingWord) goto finished;
            Console.WriteLine(word);
        }

        finished:
            Console.WriteLine("Finished processing array");
    }
}
```

Regarding this use of the *goto* statement, one could argue that a *break* statement could have been used just as effectively and a label wouldn't have been necessary. We'll look at the other forms of the *goto* statement, and you'll see that the problems at hand can be resolved only with the *goto* statement.

In the section on the *switch* statement, I discussed the fact that fall-throughs are not supported in C#. Even if fall-throughs were supported, it wouldn't solve the following problem. Let's say we have a *Payment* class (reused from earlier in the chapter) that accepted several forms of payment, or tenders: Visa, American Express, MasterCard, cash, and charge off (basically a credit). Because Visa, American Express, and MasterCard are all credit cards, we could combine them into a single case label and process them all in the same manner. In the case of the charge off, we would need to call methods specific to it, and in the case of the cash purchase, we'd only want to print a receipt. Also, we would want to print a receipt in all cases. How could we have three distinct case labels but have the first two cases—the credit card and the charge back cases—both branch to the cash label when done? As you can see in the following code, this problem is a good example of when to use the *goto* statement:

```
using System;

enum Tenders : int
{
    ChargeOff,
    Cash,
    Visa,
    MasterCard,
    AmericanExpress
};

class Payment
{
    public Payment(Tenders tender)
    {
        this.Tender = tender;
    }

    protected Tenders tender;
    public Tenders Tender
    {
        get
        {
            return this.tender;
        }
    }
```

(continued)

```
        set
        {
            this.tender = value;
        }
    }

    protected void ChargeOff()
    {
        Console.WriteLine("Charge off.");
    }

    protected bool ValidateCreditCard()
    {
        Console.WriteLine("Card approved.");
        return true;
    }

    protected void ChargeCreditCard()
    {
        Console.WriteLine("Credit Card charged");
    }

    protected void PrintReceipt()
    {
        Console.WriteLine("Thank you and come again.");
    }

    public void ProcessPayment()
    {
        switch ((int)(this.tender))
        {
            case (int)Tenders.ChargeOff:
                ChargeOff();
                goto case Tenders.Cash;

            case (int)Tenders.Visa:
            case (int)Tenders.MasterCard:
            case (int)Tenders.AmericanExpress:
                if (ValidateCreditCard())
                    ChargeCreditCard();
                goto case Tenders.Cash;

            case (int)Tenders.Cash:
                PrintReceipt();
                break;
```

```
                    default:
                        Console.WriteLine("\nSorry - Invalid tender.");
                        break;
                }
        }
}

class GotoCaseApp
{
    public static void Main()
    {
        Payment payment = new Payment(Tenders.Visa);
        payment.ProcessPayment();
    }
}
```

Instead of having to solve the problem counterintuitively, we simply tell the compiler that when a credit card or charge off case is finished, we want to branch to the cash label. One last thing to note here is that if you branch out of a case label in C#, you should not use a *break* statement, which would result in a compiler error for "unreachable code."

The last form of the *goto* statement enables you to branch to the *default* label in a *switch* statement, thereby giving you another means of writing a single code block that can be executed as a result of multiple evaluations of the *switch* statement.

The *return* Statement

The *return* statement has two functions. It specifies a value to be returned to the caller of the currently executed code (when the current code is not defined as returning *void*), and it causes an immediate return to the caller. The *return* statement is defined with the following syntax:

return [*return-expression*]

When the compiler encounters a method's *return* statement that specifies a *return-expression*, it evaluates whether the *return-expression* can be implicitly converted into a form compatible with the current method's defined return value. It's the result of that conversion that is passed back to the caller.

When using the *return* statement with exception handling, you have to be sure that you understand some rules. If the *return* statement is a *try* block that contains an associated *finally* block, control is actually passed to the first line of the *finally* block, and when that block of code finishes, control is passed back to the caller. If the *try* block is nested in another *try* block, control will continue back up the chain in this fashion until the final *finally* block has executed.

Summary

The C# conditional statements enable you to control program flow. The three different categories of flow statements include the selection statements, such as *if* and *switch,* the iteration statements (*while, for,* and *foreach*) and the different jump statements (*break, continue, goto,* and *return*). Determining the best statements to use based on the material in this chapter will help you write better structured and more maintainable applications.

12

Error Handling with Exceptions

One of the main goals of the .NET Common Language Runtime (CLR) is for run-time errors to either be avoided (through features such as automatic memory and resource management when using managed code) or at least caught at compile time (by a strongly typed system). However, certain errors can be caught only at run time, and therefore a consistent means of dealing with errors must be used across all the languages that comply with the Common Language Specification (CLS). To that extent, this chapter focuses on the error-handling system implemented by the CLR—exception handling.

In this chapter, you'll first learn the general mechanics and basic syntax of exception handling. Once you have this baseline knowledge, you'll see how exception handling compares with the more prevalent methods of error handling today and you'll discover the advantages that exception handling has over these other techniques. We'll then dive into some of the more specific .NET exception-handling issues, such as using the *Exception* class and deriving your own exception classes. Finally, the last part of this chapter will deal with the issue of properly designing your system to use exception handling.

Overview of Exception Handling

Exceptions are error conditions that arise when the normal flow of a code path— that is, a series of method calls on the call stack—is impractical or imprudent. It's imperative to understand the difference here between an exception and an expected event (such as reaching the end of a file). If you have a method that is sequentially reading through a file, you know that at some point it's going to reach the end of the file. Therefore, this event is hardly *exceptional* in nature and certainly doesn't prevent the application from continuing. However, if you're attempting to read through a file and the operating system alerts you to the fact that a disk error has been detected, this is certainly an exceptional situation and definitely one that will affect the normal flow of your method's attempt to continue reading the file.

Most exceptions also involve another problem: *context*. Let's look at an example. Assuming that you're writing tightly cohesive code—code in which one method is responsible for one action—your (pseudo)code might look like this:

```
public void Foo()
{
    File file = OpenFile(String fileName);
    while (!file.IsEOF())
    {
        String record = file.ReadRecord();
    }
CloseFile();
}
public void OpenFile(String fileName)
{
    // Attempt to lock and open file.
}
```

Note that if the *OpenFile* method fails, it cannot handle the error. This is because its only responsibility is to open files. It can't determine whether the inability to open the specified file constitutes a catastrophic error or a minor annoyance. Therefore, *OpenFile* can't handle the error condition because the method is said to not be in the correct context.

This is the entire reason for the existence of exception handling: one method determines that an exception condition has been reached and happens not to be in the correct context to deal with the error. It signals to the runtime that an error has occurred. The runtime traverses back up the call stack until it finds a method that can properly deal with the error condition. Obviously, this becomes even more important if the code path is five methods deep with the fifth method reaching an error condition and the first method being the only method that can deal with the error correctly. Now let's look at the syntax used in exception handling.

Basic Exception-Handling Syntax

Exception handling consists of only four keywords: *try*, *catch*, *throw*, and *finally*. The way the keywords work is simple and straightforward. When a method fails its objective and cannot continue—that is, when it detects an exceptional situation—it throws an exception to the calling method by using the *throw* keyword. The calling method, assuming it has enough context to deal with the exception, then receives this exception via the *catch* keyword and decides what course of action to take. In the following sections, we'll look at the language semantics governing how to throw and catch exceptions as well as some code snippets that will illustrate how this works.

Throwing an Exception

When a method needs to notify the calling method that an error has occurred, it uses the *throw* keyword in the following manner:

throw *statement*:
throw *expression* opt;

We'll get into the different ways in which you can throw exceptions a bit later. For now, it's enough to realize that when you throw an exception, you're required to throw an object of type *System.Exception* (or a derived class). Following is an example of a method that has determined that an unrecoverable error has occurred and that it needs to throw an exception to the calling method. Notice how it instantiates a new *System.Exception* object and then throws that newly created object back up the call stack.

```
public void SomeMethod()
{
// Some error determined.
throw new Exception();
}
```

Catching an Exception

Obviously, because a method can throw an exception, there must be a reciprocal part of this equation where something has to catch the thrown exception. The *catch* keyword defines a block of code that is to be processed when an exception of a given type is caught. The code in this block is referred to as an *exception handler*.

One thing to keep in mind is that not every method needs to deal with every possible thrown exception, especially because a method might not have the context required to do anything with the error information. After all, the point of exception handling is that errors are to be handled by code that has enough context to correctly do so—see "Handling Errors in the Correct Context," later in this chapter. For now let's deal with situations in which a method is going to catch any thrown exceptions from the method being called. We use two keywords to catch an exception: *try* and *catch*.

To catch an exception, you need to bracket the code you're attempting to execute in a *try* block and then specify which types of exceptions the code within that *try* block is capable of handling in a *catch* block. All the statements in the *try* block will be processed in order as usual unless an exception is thrown by one of the methods being called. If that happens, control is passed to the first line of the appropriate *catch* block. By "appropriate catch block," I mean the block that's defined as catching the type of exception that is thrown. Here's an example of a method (*Foo*) calling and catching an exception being thrown by another method (*Bar*):

```
public void Foo()
{
    try
    {
        Bar();
    }
    catch(System.Exception e)
    {
        // Do something with error condition.
    }
}
```

Now your next question might be, "What happens if *Bar* throws an exception and *Foo* doesn't catch it?" (This would also be the case if the call to *Bar* were not in a *try* block.) The result depends on the design of the application. When an exception is thrown, control is passed back up the call stack until a method is found that has a *catch* block for the type of exception being thrown. If a method with an appropriate *catch* block is not located, the application aborts. Therefore, if a method calls another method that does throw an exception, the design of the system must be such that some method in the call stack must handle the exception.

Rethrowing an Exception

There will be times after a method has caught an exception and done everything it can in its context that it then *rethrows* the exception back up the call stack. This is done very simply by using the *throw* keyword. Here's an example of how that looks:

```
using System;

class RethrowApp
{
    static public void Main()
    {
        Rethrow rethrow = new Rethrow();

        try
        {
            rethrow.Foo();
        }
        catch(Exception e)
        {
            Console.WriteLine(e.Message);
        }
    }

    public void Foo()
    {
        try
        {
            Bar();
        }
        catch(Exception)
        {
            // Handle error.
            throw;
        }
    }

    public void Bar()
    {
        throw new Exception("thrown by Rethrow.Bar");
    }
}
```

In this example, *Main* calls *Foo*, which calls *Bar*. *Bar* throws an exception that *Foo* catches. *Foo* at this point does some preprocessing and then rethrows the exception back up the call stack to *Main* by using the *throw* keyword.

Cleaning Up with *finally*

One sticky issue with exception handling is ensuring that a piece of code is always run regardless of whether an exception is caught. For example, suppose you allocate a resource such as a physical device or a data file. Then suppose that you open this resource and call a method that throws an exception. Regardless of whether your method can continue working with the resource, you still need to deallocate or close that resource. This is when the *finally* keyword is used, like so:

```csharp
using System;

public class ThrowException1App
{
    public static void ThrowException()
    {
        throw new Exception();
    }

    public static void Main()
    {
        try
        {
            Console.WriteLine("try...");
        }
        catch(Exception e)
        {
            Console.WriteLine("catch...");
        }
        finally
        {
            Console.WriteLine("finally");
        }
    }
}
```

As you can see, the existence of the *finally* keyword prevents you from having to put this cleanup code both in the *catch* block and after the *try/catch* blocks. Now, despite whether an exception is thrown, the code in the *finally* block will be executed.

Comparing Error-Handling Techniques

Now that you've seen the basics of throwing and catching exceptions, let's take a few minutes to compare the different approaches to error handling taken in programming languages.

The standard approach to error handling has typically been to return an error code to the calling method. The calling method is then left with the responsibility of deciphering the returned value and acting accordingly. The return value can be as simple as a basic C or C++ type or it can be a pointer to a more robust object containing all the information necessary to fully appreciate and understand the error. More elaborately designed error-handling techniques involve an entire error subsystem in which the called method indicates the error condition to the subsystem and then returns an error code to the caller. The caller then calls a global function exported from the error subsystem in order to determine the cause of the last error registered with the subsystem. You can find an example of this approach in the Microsoft Open Database Connectivity (ODBC) SDK. However, regardless of the exact semantics, the basic concept remains the same: the calling method in some way calls a method and inspects the returned value to verify the relative success or failure of the called method. This approach, although being the standard for many years, is severely flawed in a number of important ways. The following sections describe a few of the ways exception handling provides tremendous benefits over using return codes.

The Benefits of Exception Handling Over Return Codes

When using return codes, the called method returns an error code and the error condition is handled by the calling method. Because the error handling occurs outside the scope of the called method, there is no guarantee that the caller will check the returned error code. As an example, let's say that you write a class called *CommaDelimitedFile* that wraps the functionality of reading and writing standard comma-delimited files. Part of what your class would have to expose includes methods to open and read data from the file. Using the older return code method of reporting errors, these methods would return some variable type that would have to be checked by the caller to verify the success of the method call. If the user of your class called the *CommaDelimitedFile.Open* method and then attempted to call the *CommaDelimitedFile.Read* method without checking whether the *Open* call succeeded, this could—and probably would in the case of a demo in front of your most important client—cause less than desirable results. However, if the class's *Open* method throws an exception, the caller would be forced to deal with the fact that the *Open* method failed. This is because each time a method throws an exception, control is passed back up the call stack until it's caught. Here's an example of what that code might look like:

```
using System;

class ThrowException2App
{
    class CommaDelimitedFile
    {
        protected string fileName;

        public void Open(string fileName)
        {
            this.fileName = fileName;
```

(continued)

```
            // Attempt to open file
            // and throw exception upon error condition.
            throw new Exception("open failed");
        }

        public bool Read(string record)
        {
            // Code to read file.
            return false; // EOF
        }
    }

    public static void Main()
    {
        try
        {
            Console.WriteLine("attempting to open file");

            CommaDelimitedFile file = new CommaDelimitedFile();
            file.Open("c:\\test.csv");

            string record = "";

            Console.WriteLine("reading from file");

            while (file.Read(record) == true)
            {
                Console.WriteLine(record);
            }

            Console.WriteLine("finished reading file");
        }
        catch (Exception e)
        {
            Console.WriteLine(e.Message);
        }
    }
}
```

In this example, if either the *CommaDelimitedFile.Open* method or the *CommaDelimitedFile.Read* method throws an exception, the calling method is forced to deal with it. If the calling method does not catch the exception and no other method in the current code path attempts to catch an exception of this type, the application will abort. Pay particular attention to the fact that because the *Open* method call is placed in a block, an invalid read (using our example in which the *Open* method has thrown an exception) would not be attempted. This is because programmatic control would be passed from the *Open* call in the *try* block to the first line of the *catch* block. Therefore, one of the biggest benefits of exception handling over return codes is that exceptions are programmatically more difficult to ignore.

Handling Errors in the Correct Context

One general principle of good programming is the practice of *tight cohesion,* which refers to the objective or purpose of a given method. Methods that demonstrate tight cohesion are those that perform a single task. The main benefit of using tight cohesion in your programming is that a method is more likely to be portable and used in different scenarios when it performs only a single action. A method that performs a single action is also certainly easier to debug and maintain. However, tightly cohesive code does cause one major problem with regards to error handling. Let's look at an example to illustrate the problem and how exception handling solves it.

In this example, a class (*AccessDatabase*) is used to generate and manipulate Microsoft Access databases. Let's say this class has a static method called *GenerateDatabase*. Because the *GenerateDatabase* method would be used to create new Access databases, it would have to perform several tasks to create the database. For example, it would have to create the physical database file, create the specified tables (including any rows and columns your application needs), and define any necessary indexes and relations. The *GenerateDatabase* method might even have to create some default users and permissions.

The programmatic design problem is as follows: if an error were to occur in the *CreateIndexes* method, which method would handle it and how? Obviously, at some point, the method that originally called the *GenerateDatabase* method would have to handle the error, but how could it? It would have no idea how to handle an error that occurred several method calls deep in the code path. As we've seen, the calling method is said to not be in the correct context to handle the error. In other words, the only method that could logically create any meaningful error information about the error is the method that failed. Having said that, if return codes were used in our *AccessDatabase* class, each method in the code path would have to check for every single error code that every other method *might* return. One obvious problem with this is that the calling method would potentially have to handle a ridiculously large number of error codes. In addition, maintenance would be difficult. Every time an error condition was added to any of the methods in the code path, every other instance in the application where a method calls that method would have to be updated to handle the new error code. Needless to say, this is not an inexpensive proposition in terms of software total cost of ownership (TCO).

Exception handling resolves all of these issues by enabling the calling method to trap for a given type of exception. In the example we're using, if a class called *AccessDatabaseException* were derived from *Exception*, it could be used for any types of errors that occur within any of the *AccessDatabase* methods. (I'll discuss the *Exception* class and deriving your own exception classes later in this chapter in "Using the *System.Exception* Class.") Then, if the *CreateIndexes* method failed, it would construct and throw an exception of type *AccessDatabseException*. The calling method would catch that exception and be able to inspect the *Exception* object to decipher what exactly went wrong. Therefore, instead of handling every possible type of return code that *GenerateDatbase* and any of its called methods could return, the calling method would be assured that if *any* of the methods in that code path failed, the proper error information would be returned. Exception handling provides an additional bonus: because the error information is contained within a class, new error conditions can be added and the calling method will remain unchanged. And wasn't extensibility—being able to build something and then add to it without changing or breaking existing code—one of the original promises of object-oriented programming to begin with? For these reasons, the concept of catching and dealing with errors in the correct context is the most significant advantage to using exception handling.

Improving Code Readability

When using exception-handling code, code readability improves enormously. This directly relates to reduced costs in terms of code maintenance. The way in which return codes are handled vs. the exception-handling syntax is the source of this improvement. If you used return codes with the *AccessDatabase.GenerateDatbase* method mentioned previously, code similar to the following would be required to handle error conditions:

```
public bool GenerateDatabase()
{
    if (CreatePhysicalDatabase())
    {
        if (CreateTables())
        {
            if (CreateIndexes())
            {
                return true;
            }
            else
            {
                // Handle error.
                return false;
            }
        }
```

```
        }
        else
        {
            // Handle error.
            return false;
        }
    }
    else
    {
        // Handle error.
        return false;
    }
}
```

Add a few other validations to the preceding code and you wind up with a tremendous amount of error validation code mixed in with your business logic. If you indent your code 4 spaces per block, the first character of a line of code might not appear until column 20 or greater. None of this is disastrous for the code itself, but it does make the code more difficult to read and maintain, and the bottom line is that code that's difficult to maintain is a breeding ground for bugs. Let's look at how this same example would look if exception handling were used:

```
// Calling code.
try
{
    AccessDatabase accessDb = new AccessDatabase();
    accessDb.GenerateDatabase();
}
catch(Exception e)
{
    // Inspect caught exception.
}

// Definition of AccessDatabase.GenerateDatabase method.
public void GenerateDatabase()
{
    CreatePhysicalDatabase();
    CreateTables();
    CreateIndexes();
}
```

Notice how much cleaner and more elegant the second solution is. This is because error detection and recovery code are no longer mixed with the logic of the calling code itself. Because exception handling has made this code more straightforward, maintaining the code has been made much easier.

Throwing Exceptions From Constructors

Another major advantage that exceptions have over other error-handling techniques is in the area of object construction. Because a constructor cannot return values, there's simply no easy, intuitive means of signaling to the constructor's calling method that an error occurred during object construction. Exceptions, however, can be used because the calling method need only wrap the construction of the object in a *try* block, as in the following code:

```
try
{
    // If the AccessDatabase object fails to construct
    // properly and throws an exception, it will now be caught.
    AccessDatabase accessDb = new AccessDatabase();
}
catch(Exception e)
{
    // Inspect the caught exception.
}
```

Using the *System.Exception* Class

As mentioned earlier, all exceptions that are to be thrown must be of the type (or derived from) *System.Exception*. In fact, the *System.Exception* class is the base class of several exception classes that can be used in your C# code. Most of the classes that inherit from *System.Exception* do not add any functionality to the base class. So why does C# bother with derived classes if the derived classes aren't going to significantly differ from their base class? The reason is that a single *try* block can have multiple *catch* blocks with each *catch* block specifying a specific exception type. (You'll see this shortly.) This enables the code to handle different exceptions in a manner applicable to a specific exception type.

Constructing an *Exception* Object

As of this writing, there are four different constructors for the *System.Exception* class:

```
public Exception ();
public Exception(String);
protected Exception(SerializationInfo, StreamingContext);
public Exception(String, Exception);
```

The first constructor listed above is the default constructor. It takes no arguments and simply defaults all member variables. This exception is typically thrown as follows:

```
// Error condition reached.
throw new Exception();
```

The second exception constructor takes as its only argument a *String* value that identifies an error message and is the form that you've seen in most of the examples in this chapter. This message is retrieved by the code catching the exception via the *System.Exception.Message* property. Here's a simple example of both sides of this exception propagation:

```
using System;

class ThrowException3
{
    class FileOps
    {
        public void FileOpen(String fileName)
        {
            // ...
            throw new Exception("Oh bother");
        }

        public void FileRead()
        {
        }
    }

    public static void Main()
    {
        // Code catching exception.
        try
        {
            FileOps fileOps = new FileOps();

            fileOps.FileOpen("c:\\test.txt");
            fileOps.FileRead();
        }
        catch(System.Exception e)
        {
            Console.WriteLine(e.Message);
        }
    }
}
```

The third constructor initializes an instance of the *Exception* class with serialized data.

Finally, the last constructor enables you to specify not only an error message but also what's known as an *inner exception*. The reason for this is that when handling exceptions, at times you'll want to *massage* the exception a bit at one level of the call stack before passing it further up the call stack. Let's look at an example of how you might use this feature.

Let's say that in order to ease the burden on your class's client, you decide to throw only one type of exception. That way the client only has to catch one exception and reference the exception's *InnerException* property. This has the added benefit that if you decide to modify a given method to throw a new type of exception after the client code has been written, the client doesn't have to be updated unless it wants to do something specific with this exception.

In the following example, notice that the client code catches the top-level *System.Exception* and prints a message contained in that exception's inner exception object. If at later date the *DoWork* method throws other kinds of exceptions—as long as it does so as inner exceptions of an *System.Exception* object— the client code will continue to work.

```
using System;
using System.Globalization;

class FooLib
{
    protected bool IsValidParam(string value)
    {
        bool success = false;

        if (value.Length == 3)
        {
            char c1 = value[0];
            if (Char.IsNumber(c1))
            {
                char c2 = value[2];
                if (Char.IsNumber(c2))
                {
                    if (value[1] == '.')
                        success = true;
                }
            }
        }

        return success;
    }
```

```
    public void DoWork(string value)
    {
        if (!IsValidParam(value))throw new Exception
            ("", new FormatException("Invalid parameter specified"));
        Console.WriteLine("Work done with '{0}'", value);
    }
}

class FooLibClientApp
{
    public static void Main(string[] args)
    {
        FooLib lib = new FooLib();
        try
        {
            lib.DoWork(args[0]);
        }
        catch(Exception e)
        {
            Exception inner = e.InnerException;
            Console.WriteLine(inner.Message);
        }
    }
}
```

Using the *StackTrace* Property

Another useful property of the *System.Exception* class is the *StackTrace* property. The *StackTrace* property enables you to determine—at any given point at which you have a valid *System.Exception* object—what the current call stack looks like. Take a look at the following code:

```
using System;

class StackTraceTestApp
{
    public void Open(String fileName)
    {
        Lock(fileName);
        // ...
    }
    public void Lock(String fileName)
```

(continued)

```
    {
        // Error condition raised.
        throw new Exception("failed to lock file");
    }
    public static void Main()
    {
        StackTraceTestApp test = new StackTraceTestApp();

        try
        {
            test.Open("c:\\test.txt");
            // Use file.
        }
        catch(Exception e)
        {
            Console.WriteLine(e.StackTrace);
        }
    }
}
```

In this example, what prints out is the following:

```
at StackTraceTest.Main()
```

Therefore, the *StackTrace* property returns the call stack at the point that the exception is caught, which can be useful for logging and debugging scenarios.

Catching Multiple Exception Types

In various situations, you might want a *try* block to catch different exception types. For example, a given method might be documented as throwing several different exception types, or you might have several method calls in a single *try* block where each method being called is documented as being able to throw a different exception type. This is handled by adding a *catch* block for each type of exception that your code needs to handle:

```
try
{
    Foo(); // Can throw FooException.
    Bar(); // Can throw BarException.
}
catch(FooException e)
{
    // Handle the error.
}
catch(BarException e)
{
    // Handle the error.
}
```

```
catch(Exception e)
{
}
```

Each exception type can now be handled with its distinct *catch* block (and error-handling code). However, one extremely important detail here is the fact that the base class is handled last. Obviously, because all exceptions are derived from *System.Exception*, if you were to place that *catch* block first, the other *catch* blocks would be unreachable. To that extent, the following code would be rejected by the compiler:

```
try
{
    Foo(); // Can throw FooException.
    Bar(); // Can throw BarException.
}
catch(Exception e)
{
    // ***ERROR - THIS WON'T COMPILE
}
catch(FooException e)
{
    // Handle the error.
}
catch(BarException e)
{
    // Handle the error.
}
```

Deriving Your Own *Exception* Classes

As I've said, there might be times when you want to provide extra information or formatting to an exception before you throw it to the client code. You might also want to provide a base class for that situation so that your class can publish the fact that it throws only one type of exception. That way, the client only need concern itself with catching this base class.

Yet another example of when you might want to derive your own *Exception* class is if you wanted to perform some action—such as logging the event or sending an email to someone at the help desk—every time an exception was thrown. In this case, you would derive your own *Exception* class and put the needed code in the class constructor, like this:

```
using System;

public class TestException : Exception
```

(continued)

```
    {
        // You would probably have extra methods and properties
        // here that augment the .NET Exception that you derive from.

        // Base Exception class constructors.
        public TestException()
            :base() {}
        public TestException(String message)
            :base(message) {}
        public TestException(String message, Exception innerException)
            :base(message, innerException) {}
    }
    public class DerivedExceptionTestApp
    {
        public static void ThrowException()
        {
            throw new TestException("error condition");
        }
        public static void Main()
        {
            try
            {
                ThrowException();
            }
            catch(Exception e)
            {
                Console.WriteLine(e.ToString());
            }
        }
    }
```

Deriving Your Own Exception Classes

Although not a hard-and-fast rule, it's good programming practice—and consistent with most C# code you'll see—to name your exception classes such that the name ends with the word "Exception." For example, if you wanted to derive an *Exception* class for a class called *MyFancyGraphics*, you could name the class *MyFancyGraphicsException*.

Another rule of thumb when creating or deriving your own exception classes is to implement all three *System.Exception* constructors. Once again, this isn't absolutely necessary, but it does improve consistency with other C# code that your client will be using.

This code will generate the following output. Note that the *ToString* method results in a combination of properties being displayed: the textual representation of the exception class name, the message string passed to the exception's constructor, and the *StackTrace*.

```
TestException: error condition
   at DerivedExceptionTestApp.Main()
```

Designing Your Code with Exception Handling

So far, we've covered the basic concepts of using exception handling and the semantics related to the throwing and catching of exceptions. Now let's look at an equally important facet of exception handling: understanding how to design your system with exception handling in mind. Suppose you have three methods: *Foo*, *Bar*, and *Baz*. *Foo* calls *Bar*, which calls *Baz*. If *Baz* publishes the fact that it throws an exception, does *Bar* have to catch that exception even if it can't, or won't, do anything with it? How should code be split with regards to the *try* and *catch* blocks?

Design Issues with the *try* Block

You know how to catch an exception that a called method might throw, and you know that control passes up the call stack until an appropriate *catch* block is found. So the question is, should a *try* block catch every possible exception that a method within it can throw? The answer is no, to maintain the biggest benefits of using exception handling in your applications: reduced coding and lower maintenance costs. The following example illustrates a program where a catch is rethrown, to be handled by another catch block.

```
using System;

class WhenNotToCatchApp
{
    public void Foo()
    {
        try
        {
            Bar();
        }
        catch(Exception e)
        {
            Console.WriteLine(e.Message);
        }
```

(continued)

```
        }

        public void Bar()
        {
            try
            {
                Baz();
            }
            catch(Exception e)
            {
// Bar should catch this because it
// doesn't do anything but rethrow it.

throw;
            }
        }

        public void Baz()
        {
            throw new Exception("Exception originally thrown by Baz");
        }

        public static void Main()
        {
            WhenNotToCatchApp test = new WhenNotToCatchApp();
            test.Foo(); // This method will ultimately
                        // print the error message.
        }
}
```

In this example, *Foo* catches the exception that *Baz* throws even though it then does nothing except rethrow the exception back up to *Bar*. *Bar* then catches the rethrown exception and does something with the information—in this case, displaying the *Exception* object's error message property. Following are a few reasons why methods that simply rethrow an exception should not catch that exception in the first place:

■   Because the method doesn't do anything with the exception, you'd be left with a *catch* block in the method that is superfluous at best. Obviously, it's never a good idea for code to exist when it has absolutely no function.

■   If the exception type being thrown by *Baz* were to change, you'd have to go back and change both the *Bar catch* block and the *Foo catch* block. Why put yourself in a situation in which you'd have to alter code that doesn't even do anything?

Because the CLR automatically continues up the call stack until a method catches the exception, intermediate methods can ignore the exceptions that they cannot process. Just make sure in your design that *some* method catches the exception because, as mentioned earlier, if an exception is thrown and no *catch* block is found in the current call stack, the application will abort.

Design Issues with the *catch* Block

The only code that should appear in a *catch* block is code that will at least partially process the caught exception. For example, at times a method will catch an exception, do what it can to process that exception, and then rethrow that exception so that further error handling can occur. The following example illustrates this. *Foo* has called *Bar*, which will do some database work on *Foo*'s behalf. Because commitment control, or transactions, are being used, *Bar* needs to catch any error that occurs and rollback the uncommitted changes before rethrowing the exception back to *Foo*.

```
using System;

class WhenToCatchApp
{
    public void Foo()
    {
        try
        {
            Bar();
        }
        catch(Exception e)
        {
            Console.WriteLine(e.Message);
        }
    }

    public void Bar()
    {
        try
        {
            // Call method to set a "commitment boundary."
            Console.WriteLine("setting commitment boundary");

            // Call Baz to save data.
            Console.WriteLine("calling Baz to save data");
            Baz();

            Console.WriteLine("commiting saved data");
```

(continued)

```
        }
        catch(Exception)
        {
                // In this case, Bar should catch the exception
                // because it's doing something significant
                //(rolling back uncommitted database changes).

                Console.WriteLine("rolling back uncommited changes " +
                        "and then rethrowing exception");

            throw;
        }
    }

    public void Baz()
    {
        throw new Exception("db failure in Baz");
    }

    public static void Main()
    {
        WhenToCatchApp test = new WhenToCatchApp();
        test.Foo(); // This method will ultimately print
                    // the error msg.
    }
}
```

Bar needed to catch the exception to do its own error processing. When finished, it then rethrew the exception back up the call stack, where *Foo* caught it and was able to do its error processing. This ability of each level of the call stack to do just the amount of error processing that it's capable of, given its context, is one example of what makes exception handling so important to the design of your system.

Summary

The C# exception-handling syntax is simple and straightforward, and implementing exception handling in your applications is as easy as designing your methods ahead of time. A primary goal of the .NET CLR is to help prevent run-time errors through a strong type system and to handle gracefully any run-time errors that do occur. The use of exception-handling code in your applications will make them more robust, dependable, and ultimately easier to maintain.

13

Operator Overloading and User-Defined Conversions

In Chapter 7, "Properties, Arrays, and Indexers," you learned how to use the [] operator with a class to programmatically index an object as if it were an array. In this chapter, we'll look at two closely related features of C# that provide the ability to create structure and class interfaces that are easier and more intuitive to use: operator overloading and user-defined conversions. I'll start with a general overview of operator overloading in terms of the benefits it provides you and then look at the actual syntax for redefining the default behaviors of operators as well as a realistic example application in which I overload the + operator to aggregate multiple *Invoice* objects. After that, you'll see a listing of which binary and unary operators are overloadable as well as some of the restrictions involved. The operator overloading discussion will end with some design guidelines to take into account when deciding whether to overload operators in your classes. Once we've finished with operator overloading, you'll learn about a new concept, user-defined conversions. Once again, I'll start with broad strokes, explaining the basics of this feature, and then I'll dive into a class that illustrates how you can use conversions to enable the casting of a *struct* or *class* to a different *struct*, *class*, or basic C# type.

Operator Overloading

Operator overloading allows existing C# operators to be redefined for use with user-defined types. Operator overloading has been called "syntactic sugar," owing to the fact that the overloaded operator is simply another means of calling a method. It's also been said that the feature doesn't fundamentally add anything to the language. Although this is technically true, operator overloading does aid in one of the most important aspects of object-oriented programming: abstraction.

Suppose that you want to aggregate a collection of invoices for a particular customer. Using operator overloading, you can write code similar to the following in which the += operator is overloaded:

```
Invoice summaryInvoice = new Invoice();
foreach (Invoice invoice in customer.GetInvoices())
{
    summaryInvoice += invoice;
}
```

The benefits of such code include its very natural syntax and the fact that the client is abstracted from having to understand the implementation details of how the invoices are being aggregated. Simply put, operator overloading aids in creating software that is less expensive to write and maintain.

Syntax and Example

As I've said, operator overloading is a means of calling a method. To redefine an operator for a class, you need only use the following pattern, where *op* is the operator you're overloading:

public static *retval* operator*op* (*object1* [, *object2*])

Keep in mind the following facts when using operator overloading:

■ All overloaded operator methods must be defined as *public* and *static*.

■ Technically, *retval* (the return value) can be any type. However, it's common practice to return the type for which the method is being defined with the exception of the *true* and *false* operators, which should always return a Boolean value.

■ The number of arguments passed (*object1*, *object2*) depends on the type of operator being overloaded. If a unary operator (an operator having a single operand) is being overloaded, there will be one argument. If a binary operator (an operator taking two operands) is being overloaded, two arguments are passed.

■ In the case of a unary operator, the argument to the method must be the same type as that of the enclosing class or struct. In other words, if you redefine the ! unary operator for a class called *Foo*, that method must take as its only argument a variable of type *Foo*.

■   If the operator being overloaded is a binary operator, the first argu-
    ment must be the same type as that of the enclosing class and the
    second argument can be any type.

In the previous section's pseudocode, I used the += operator with an *Invoice*
class. For reasons you'll soon understand, you can't actually overload these compound operators. You can overload only the "base" operator—in this case, the +.
Here's the syntax used to define the *Invoice* class's *operator+* method:

```
public static Invoice operator+ (Invoice invoice1, Invoice invoice2)
{
    // Create a new Invoice object.
    // Add the desired contents from
    // invoice1 to the new Invoice object.
    // Add the desired contents from
    // invoice2 to the new Invoice object.
    // Return the new Invoice object.
}
```

Let's look at a more substantial example now, one with two main classes:
Invoice and *InvoiceDetailLine*. The *Invoice* class has a member variable of type
ArrayList that represents a collection of all invoice detail lines. To allow for the
aggregation of detail lines for multiple invoices, I've overloaded the + operator.
(See the *operator+* method below for details.) The *Invoice.operator+* method
creates a new *Invoice* object and iterates through both invoice objects' arrays of
invoice detail lines, adding each detail line to the new *Invoice* object. This *Invoice*
object is then returned to the caller. Obviously, in a real-world invoicing module,
this would be much more complex, but the point here is to show somewhat
realistically how operator overloading could be used.

```
using System;
using System.Collections;

class InvoiceDetailLine
{
    double lineTotal;
    public double LineTotal
    {
        get
        {
            return this.lineTotal;
        }
    }
```

(continued)

269

```
        public InvoiceDetailLine(double LineTotal)
        {
            this.lineTotal = LineTotal;
        }
    }

class Invoice
{
    public ArrayList DetailLines;

    public Invoice()
    {
        DetailLines = new ArrayList();
    }

    public void PrintInvoice()
    {
        Console.WriteLine("\nLine Nbr\tTotal");

        int i = 1;
        double total = 0;
        foreach(InvoiceDetailLine detailLine in DetailLines)
        {
            Console.WriteLine("{0}\t\t{1}", i++, detailLine.LineTotal);
            total += detailLine.LineTotal;
        }

        Console.WriteLine("=====\t\t===");
        Console.WriteLine("Total\t\t{1}", i++, total);
    }

    public static Invoice operator+ (Invoice invoice1, Invoice invoice2)
    {
        Invoice returnInvoice = new Invoice();

        foreach (InvoiceDetailLine detailLine in invoice1.DetailLines)
        {
            returnInvoice.DetailLines.Add(detailLine);
        }

        foreach (InvoiceDetailLine detailLine in invoice2.DetailLines)
        {
            returnInvoice.DetailLines.Add(detailLine);
        }
        return returnInvoice;
    }
}
```

```
class InvoiceAddApp
{
    public static void Main()
    {
        Invoice i1 = new Invoice();
        for (int i = 0; i < 2; i++)
        {
            i1.DetailLines.Add(new InvoiceDetailLine(i + 1));
        }

        Invoice i2 = new Invoice();
        for (int i = 0; i < 2; i++)
        {
            i2.DetailLines.Add(new InvoiceDetailLine(i + 1));
        }

        Invoice summaryInvoice = i1 + i2;

        summaryInvoice.PrintInvoice();
    }
}
```

Overloadable Operators

Only the following unary and binary operators can be overloaded.

Unary operands: +, -, !, ~, ++, --, *true, false*

Binary operands: +, -, *, /, %, &, |, ^, <<, >>, ==, !=, >, <, >=, <=

Note   The comma is used here to separate the different overloadable operators. The comma operator, which is used in the *for* statement and in method calls, cannot be overloaded.

Restrictions on Operator Overloading

It is not possible to overload the = assignment operator. However, when you overload a binary operator, its compound assignment equivalent is implicitly overloaded. For example, if you overload the + operator, the += operator is implicitly overloaded in that the user-defined *operator+* method will be called.

The [] operators can't be overloaded. However, as you saw in Chapter 7, user-defined object indexing is supported through indexers.

The parentheses used to perform a cast are also not overloadable. Instead, you should use conversion operators, which are also referred to as user-defined conversions, the subject of the second half of this chapter.

Operators that are currently not defined in the C# language cannot be overloaded. You can't, for example, define ** as a means of defining exponentiation because C# does not define a ** operator. Also, an operator's syntax can't be modified. You can't change the binary * operator to take three arguments when, by definition, its syntax calls for two operands. Finally, an operator's precedence can't be altered. The rules of precedence are static—see Chapter 10, "Expressions and Operators," for more on these rules.

Design Guidelines

You've seen what operator overloading is and how to use it in C#, so let's examine an often-ignored aspect of this useful feature: design guidelines. What you want to stay away from is the natural tendency to want to use a new feature for the sake of using it. This phenomenon is sometimes referred to as "a solution in search of a problem." But it's always a good design approach to remember the adage, "Code is read more than it is written." Keep the class's client in mind when determining if and when to overload an operator or set of operators. Here's a rule of thumb: you should overload an operator only if it makes the class's interface more intuitive to use. For example, it makes perfect sense to be able to add invoices together.

In addition, don't forget that you have to think as a client of your class would. Let's say you're writing an *Invoice* class and you want the client to be able to discount the invoice. You and I might know that a credit line item will be added to the invoice, but the point of encapsulation is that your clients don't have to know the exact implementation details of the class. Therefore, overloading the * operator—as shown here—might be a good idea because it would serve to make the *Invoice* class's interface natural and intuitive:

```
invoice *= .95; // 5% discount.
```

User-Defined Conversions

Earlier I mentioned that the parentheses used for casting cannot be overloaded and that user-defined conversions must be used instead. In short, user-defined conversions enable you to declare conversions on structures or classes such that the *struct* or *class* can be converted to other structures, classes, or basic C# types. Why and when would you want to do that? Let's say you needed to use the standard Celsius and Fahrenheit temperature scales in your application such that you could easily convert between the two. By creating user-defined conversions, you could use the following syntax:

```
Fahrenheit f = 98.6F;
Celsius c = (Celsius)f; // User-defined conversion.
```

This doesn't provide any functional benefits over the following syntax, but it is more intuitive to write and easier to read.

```
Fahrenheit f = 98.6F;
Celsius c = f.ConvertToCelsius();
```

Syntax and Example

The syntax of the user-defined conversion uses the *operator* keyword to declare user-defined conversions:

> public static implicit operator *conv-type-out* (*conv-type-in operand*)

> public static explicit operator *conv-type-out* (*conv-type-in operand*)

There are only a couple of rules regarding the syntax of defining conversions:

- Any conversion method for a *struct* or *class*—you can define as many as you need—must be *static*.

- Conversions must be defined as either *implicit* or *explicit*. The *implicit* keyword means that the cast is not required by the client and will occur automatically. Conversely, using the *explicit* keyword signifies that the client must explicitly cast the value to the desired type.

- All conversions either must take (as an argument) the type that the conversion is being defined on or must return that type.

- As with operator overloading, the *operator* keyword is used in the conversion method signature but without any appended operator.

I know the first time I read these rules, I didn't have the foggiest idea what to do, so let's look at an example to crystallize this. In this example, we have two structures (*Celsius* and *Fahrenheit*) that enable the client to convert a value of type *float* to either temperature scale. I'll first present the *Celsius* structure and make some points about it, and then you'll see the complete working application.

```
struct Celsius
{
    public Celsius(float temp)
    {
        this.temp = temp;
    }

    public static implicit operator Celsius(float temp)
    {
        Celsius c;
        c = new Celsius(temp);
        return(c);
    }

    public static implicit operator float(Celsius c)
    {
        return(((((c.temp - 32) / 9) * 5)));
    }

    public float temp;
}
```

The first decision that you see was the one to use a structure instead of a class. I had no real reason for doing that other than the fact that using classes is more expensive than using structures—in terms of how the classes are allocated—and a class is not really necessary here because the *Celsius* structure doesn't need any C# class-specific features, such as inheritance.

Next notice that I've declared a constructor that takes a float as its only argument. This value is stored in a member variable named *temp*. Now look at the conversion operator defined immediately after the structure's constructor. This is the method that will be called when the client attempts to cast a float to *Celsius* or use a float in a place, such as with a method, where a *Celsius* structure is expected. This method doesn't have to do much, and in fact this is fairly formulaic code that can be used in most basic conversions. Here I simply instantiate a *Celsius* structure and then return that structure. That return call is what will cause the last method defined in the structure to be called. As you can see, the method simply provides the mathematical formula for converting from a Fahrenheit value to a Celsius value.

Here's the entire application, including a *Fahrenheit* structure:

```
using System;

struct Celsius
{
    public Celsius(float temp)
```

```
    {
        this.temp = temp;
    }

    public static implicit operator Celsius(float temp)
    {
        Celsius c;
        c = new Celsius(temp);
        return(c);
    }

    public static implicit operator float(Celsius c)
    {
        return((((c.temp - 32) / 9) * 5));
    }

    public float temp;
}

struct Fahrenheit
{
    public Fahrenheit(float temp)
    {
        this.temp = temp;
    }

    public static implicit operator Fahrenheit(float temp)
    {
        Fahrenheit f;
        f = new Fahrenheit(temp);
        return(f);
    }

    public static implicit operator float(Fahrenheit f)
    {
        return((((f.temp * 9) / 5) + 32));
    }

    public float temp;
}

class Temp1App
{
    public static void Main()
```

(continued)

```
    {
        float t;

        t=98.6F;
        Console.Write("Conversion of {0} to Celsius = ", t);
        Console.WriteLine((Celsius)t);

        t=0F;
        Console.Write("Conversion of {0} to Fahrenheit = ", t);
        Console.WriteLine((Fahrenheit)t);
    }
}
```

If you compile and execute this application, you get this output:

```
Conversion of 98.6 to Celsius = 37
Conversion of 0 to Fahrenheit = 32
```

This works pretty well, and being able to write *(Celsius)98.6F* is certainly more intuitive than calling some static class method. But note that you can pass only values of type *float* to these conversion methods. For the application above, the following won't compile:

```
Celsius c = new Celsius(55);
Console.WriteLine((Fahrenheit)c);
```

Also, because there's no Celsius conversion method that takes a *Fahrenheit* structure (or vice versa), the code has to assume that the value being passed in is a value that needs converting. In other words, if I call *(Celsius)98.6F*, I will receive the value 37. However, if that value is then passed back to the conversion method again, the conversion method has no way of knowing that the value has already been converted and logically already represents a valid Celsius temperature—to the conversion method, it's just a float. As a result, the value gets converted again. Therefore, we need to modify the application so that each structure can take as a valid argument the other structure.

When I originally thought of doing this, I cringed at the thought because I worried about how difficult this task would be. As it turns out, it's extremely easy. Here's the revised code with ensuing comments:

```
using System;

class Temperature
{
    public Temperature(float Temp)
    {
        this.temp = Temp;
    }
```

```
    protected float temp;
    public float Temp
    {
        get
        {
            return this.temp;
        }
    }
}

class Celsius : Temperature
{
    public Celsius(float Temp)
        : base(Temp) {}

    public static implicit operator Celsius(float Temp)
    {
        return new Celsius(Temp);
    }

    public static implicit operator Celsius(Fahrenheit F)
    {
        return new Celsius(F.Temp);
    }

    public static implicit operator float(Celsius C)
    {
        return((((C.temp - 32) / 9) * 5));
    }
}

class Fahrenheit : Temperature
{
    public Fahrenheit(float Temp)
        : base(Temp) {}

    public static implicit operator Fahrenheit(float Temp)
    {
        return new Fahrenheit(Temp);
    }

    public static implicit operator Fahrenheit(Celsius C)
    {
        return new Fahrenheit(C.Temp);
    }

    public static implicit operator float(Fahrenheit F)
```

(continued)

```
    {
        return(((((F.temp * 9) / 5) + 32));
    }
}

class Temp2App
{
    public static void DisplayTemp(Celsius Temp)
    {
        Console.Write("Conversion of {0} {1} to Fahrenheit = ",
            Temp.ToString(), Temp.Temp);
        Console.WriteLine((Fahrenheit)Temp);
    }

    public static void DisplayTemp(Fahrenheit Temp)
    {
        Console.Write("Conversion of {0} {1} to Celsius = ",
            Temp.ToString(), Temp.Temp);
        Console.WriteLine((Celsius)Temp);
    }

    public static void Main()
    {
        Fahrenheit f = new Fahrenheit(98.6F);
        DisplayTemp(f);

        Celsius c = new Celsius(0F);
        DisplayTemp(c);
    }
}
```

The first thing to note is that I changed the *Celsius* and *Fahrenheit* types from *struct* to *class*. I did that so that I would have two examples—one using *struct* and one using *class*. But a more practical reason for doing so is to share the *temp* member variable by having the *Celsius* and *Fahrenheit* classes derive from the same *Temperature* base class. I can also now use the inherited (from *System.Object*) *ToString* method in the application's output.

The only other difference of note is the addition of a conversion for each temperature scale that takes as an argument a value of the other temperature scale. Notice how similar the code is between the two Celsius conversion methods:

```
public static implicit operator Celsius(float temp)
{
    Celsius c;
    c = new Celsius(temp);
    return(c);
}
```

```
public static implicit operator Celsius(Fahrenheit f)
{
    Celsius c;
    c = new Celsius(f.temp);
    return(c);
}
```

The only tasks I had to do differently were change the argument being passed and retrieve the temperature from the passed object instead of a hard-coded value of type *float*. This is why I noted earlier how easy and formulaic conversion methods are once you know the basics.

Summary

Operator overloading and user-defined conversions are useful for creating intuitive interfaces for your classes. When using overloaded operators, keep in mind the associated restrictions while designing your classes. For example, while you can't overload the = assignment operator, when a binary operator is overloaded its compound assignment equivalent is implicitly overloaded. Follow the design guidelines for deciding when to use each feature. Keep the class's client in mind when determining whether or not to overload an operator or set of operators. With a little insight into how your clients would use your classes, you can use these very powerful features to define your classes such that certain operations can be performed with a more natural syntax.

14

Delegates and Event Handlers

Another useful innovation of the C# language is something called delegates, which basically serve the same purpose as function pointers in C++. However, delegates are type-safe, secure managed objects. This means that the runtime guarantees that a delegate points to a valid method, which further means that you get all the benefits of function pointers without any of the associated dangers, such as an invalid address or a delegate corrupting the memory of other objects. In this chapter, we'll be looking at delegates, how they compare to interfaces, the syntax used to define them, and the different problems that they were designed to address. We'll also see several examples of using delegates with both callback methods and asynchronous event handling.

In Chapter 9, "Interfaces," we saw how interfaces are defined and implemented in C#. As you'll recall, from a conceptual standpoint interfaces are simply contracts between two disparate pieces of code. However, interfaces are much like classes in that they're defined at compile time and can include methods, properties, indexers, and events. Delegates, on the other hand, refer only to single methods and are defined at run time. Delegates have two main usages in C# programming: callbacks and event handling. Let's start off by talking about callback methods.

Using Delegates as Callback Methods

Used extensively in programming for Microsoft Windows, callback methods are used when you need to pass a function pointer to another function that will then call you back (via the passed pointer). An example would be the Win32 API

EnumWindows function. This function enumerates all the top-level windows on the screen, calling the supplied function for each window. Callbacks serve many purposes, but the following are the most common:

- **Asynchronous processing**   Callback methods are used in asynchronous processing when the code being called will take a good deal of time to process the request. Typically, the scenario works like this: Client code makes a call to a method, passing to it the callback method. The method being called starts a thread and returns immediately. The thread then does the majority of the work, calling the callback function as needed. This has the obvious benefit of allowing the client to continue processing without being blocked on a potentially lengthy synchronous call.

- **Injecting custom code into a class's code path**   Another common use of callback methods is when a class allows the client to specify a method that will be called to do custom processing. Let's look at an example in Windows to illustrate this. Using the *Listbox* class in Windows, you can specify that the items be sorted in ascending or descending order. Besides some other basic sort options, the *Listbox* class can't really give you any latitude and remain a generic class. Therefore, the *Listbox* class also enables you to specify a callback function for sorting. That way, when *Listbox* sorts the items, it calls the callback function and your code can then do the custom sorting you need.

Now let's look at an example of defining and using a delegate. In this example, we have a database manager class that keeps track of all active connections to the database and provides a method for enumerating those connections. Assuming that the database manager is on a remote server, it might be a good design decision to make the method asynchronous and allow the client to provide a callback method. Note that for a real-world application you'd typically create this as a multithreaded application to make it truly asynchronous. However, to keep the example simple—and because we haven't covered multithreading yet— let's leave multithreading out.

First, let's define two main classes: *DBManager* and *DBConnection*.

```
class DBConnection
{
    ⋮
}
```

```
class DBManager
{
  static DBConnection[] activeConnections;

  ⋮

  public delegate void EnumConnectionsCallback(DBConnection connection);
    public static void EnumConnections(EnumConnectionsCallback callback)
    {
        foreach (DBConnection connection in activeConnections)
        {
            callback(connection);
        }
    }
}
```

The *EnumConnectionsCallback* method is the delegate and is defined by placing the keyword *delegate* in front of the method signature. You can see that this delegate is defined as returning *void* and taking a single argument: a *DBConnection* object. The *EnumConnections* method is then defined as taking an *EnumConnectionsCallback* method as its only argument. To call the *DBManager.EnumConnections* method, we need only pass to it an instantiated *DBManager.EnumConnectionCallback* delegate.

To do that, you *new* the delegate, passing to it the name of method that has the same signature as the delegate. Here's an example of that:

```
DBManager.EnumConnectionsCallback myCallback =
    new DBManager.EnumConnectionsCallback(ActiveConnectionsCallback);

DBManager.EnumConnections(myCallback);
```

Also note that you can combine this into a single call like so:

```
DBManager.EnumConnections(new
    DBManager.EnumConnectionsCallback(ActiveConnectionsCallback));
```

That's all there is to the basic syntax of delegates. Now let's look at the full example application:

```
using System;

class DBConnection
{
    public DBConnection(string name)
    {
        this.name = name;
    }
```

(continued)

```
            protected string Name;
            public string name
            {
                get
                {
                    return this.Name;
                }
                set
                {
                    this.Name = value;
                }
            }
        }


    class DBManager
    {
        static DBConnection[] activeConnections;
        public void AddConnections()
        {
            activeConnections = new DBConnection[5];
            for (int i = 0; i < 5; i++)
            {
                activeConnections[i] =
new DBConnection("DBConnection " + (i + 1));
            }
        }

         public delegate void EnumConnectionsCallback(DBConnection connection);
        public static void EnumConnections(EnumConnectionsCallback callback)
        {
            foreach (DBConnection connection in activeConnections)
            {
                callback(connection);
            }
        }
    }

    class Delegate1App
    {
        public static void ActiveConnectionsCallback(DBConnection connection)
        {
            Console.WriteLine("Callback method called for "
                            + connection.name);
        }

        public static void Main()
```

```
    {
        DBManager dbMgr = new DBManager();
        dbMgr.AddConnections();

    DBManager.EnumConnectionsCallback myCallback =
      new DBManager.EnumConnectionsCallback(ActiveConnectionsCallback);

    DBManager.EnumConnections(myCallback);
    }
}
```

Compiling and executing this application results in the following output:

```
Callback method called for DBConnection 1
Callback method called for DBConnection 2
Callback method called for DBConnection 3
Callback method called for DBConnection 4
Callback method called for DBConnection 5
```

Defining Delegates as Static Members

Because it's kind of clunky that the client has to instantiate the delegate each time the delegate is to be used, C# allows you to define as a static class member the method that will be used in the creation of the delegate. Following is the example from the previous section, changed to use that format. Note that the delegate is now defined as a static member of the class named *myCallback*, and also note that this member can be used in the *Main* method without the need for the client to instantiate the delegate.

```
using System;

class DBConnection
{
    public DBConnection(string name)
    {
        this.name = name;
    }

    protected string Name;
    public string name
    {
        get
        {
            return this.Name;
        }
```

(continued)

```
            set
            {
                this.Name = value;
            }
        }
    }

class DBManager
{
    static DBConnection[] activeConnections;
    public void AddConnections()
    {
        activeConnections = new DBConnection[5];
        for (int i = 0; i < 5; i++)
        {
            activeConnections[i] = new
DBConnection("DBConnection " + (i + 1));
        }
    }

    public delegate void EnumConnectionsCallback(DBConnection connection);
    public static void EnumConnections(EnumConnectionsCallback callback)
    {
        foreach (DBConnection connection in activeConnections)
        {
            callback(connection);
        }
    }
}

class Delegate2App
{
    public static DBManager.EnumConnectionsCallback myCallback =
        new DBManager.EnumConnectionsCallback(ActiveConnectionsCallback);

    public static void ActiveConnectionsCallback(DBConnection connection)
    {
        Console.WriteLine ("Callback method called for " +
                            connection.name);
    }

    public static void Main()
    {
        DBManager dbMgr = new DBManager();
        dbMgr.AddConnections();

        DBManager.EnumConnections(myCallback);
    }
}
```

Note   Because the standard naming convention for delegates is to append the word *Callback* to the method that takes the delegate as its argument, it's easy to mistakenly use the method name instead of the delegate name. In that case, you'll get a somewhat misleading compile-time error that states that you've denoted a method where a class was expected. If you get this error, remember that the actual problem is that you've specified a method instead of a delegate.

Creating Delegates Only When Needed

In the two examples you've seen so far, the delegate is created whether or not it's ever used. That was fine in those examples because I knew that it would always be called. However, when defining your delegates, it's important to consider when to create them. Let's say, for example, that the creation of a particular delegate is time-consuming and not something you want to do gratuitously. In these situations in which you know the client won't typically call a given callback method, you can put off the creation of the delegate until it's actually needed by wrapping its instantiation in a property. To illustrate how to do this, a modification of the *DBManager* class follows that uses a read-only property—because only a getter method is present—to instantiate the delegate. The delegate will not be created until this property is referenced.

```
using System;

class DBConnection
{
    public DBConnection(string name)
    {
        this.name = name;
    }

    protected string Name;
    public string name
    {
        get
        {
            return this.Name;
        }
        set
```

(continued)

```
            {
                this.Name = value;
            }
        }
    }

    class DBManager
    {
        static DBConnection[] activeConnections;
        public void AddConnections()
        {
            activeConnections = new DBConnection[5];
            for (int i = 0; i < 5; i++)
            {
                activeConnections[i] = new
                    DBConnection("DBConnection " + (i + 1));
            }
        }

        public delegate void EnumConnectionsCallback(DBConnection connection);
        public static void EnumConnections(EnumConnectionsCallback callback)
        {
            foreach (DBConnection connection in activeConnections)
            {
                callback(connection);
            }
        }
    }

    class Delegate3App
    {
        public DBManager.EnumConnectionsCallback myCallback
        {
            get
            {
                return new DBManager.EnumConnectionsCallback
                        (ActiveConnectionsCallback);
            }
        }

        public static void ActiveConnectionsCallback(DBConnection connection)
        {
            Console.WriteLine
                ("Callback method called for " + connection.name);
        }
```

```
public static void Main()
{
    Delegate3App app = new Delegate3App();

    DBManager dbMgr = new DBManager();
    dbMgr.AddConnections();

    DBManager.EnumConnections(app.myCallback);
}
}
```

Delegate Composition

The ability to compose delegates—by creating a single delegate out of multiple delegates—is one of those features that at first doesn't seem very handy, but if you ever need it you'll be happy that the C# design team thought of it. Let's look at some examples in which delegate composition is useful. In the first example, you have a distribution system and a class that iterates through the parts for a given location, calling a callback method for each part that has an "on-hand" value of less than 50. In a more realistic distribution example, the formula would take into account not only "on-hand" but also "on order" and "in transit" in relation to the lead times, and it would subtract the safety stock level, and so on. But let's keep this simple: if a part's on-hand value is less than 50, an exception has occurred.

The twist is that we want two distinct methods to be called if a given part is below stock: we want to log the event, and then we want to email the purchasing manager. So, let's take a look at how you programmatically create a single composite delegate from multiple delegates:

```
using System;
using System.Threading;

class Part
{
    public Part(string sku)
    {
        this.Sku = sku;

        Random r = new Random(DateTime.Now.Millisecond);
        double d = r.NextDouble() * 100;

        this.OnHand = (int)d;
    }
```

(continued)

```
        protected string Sku;
        public string sku
        {
            get
            {
                return this.Sku;
            }
            set
            {
                this.Sku = value;
            }
        }

        protected int OnHand;
        public int onhand
        {
            get
            {
                return this.OnHand;
            }
            set
            {
                this.OnHand = value;
            }
        }
    }

class InventoryManager
{
    protected const int MIN_ONHAND = 50;

    public Part[] parts;
    public InventoryManager()
    {
        parts = new Part[5];
        for (int i = 0; i < 5; i++)
        {
            Part part = new Part("Part " + (i + 1));

            Thread.Sleep(10); // Randomizer is seeded by time.

            parts[i] = part;
            Console.WriteLine("Adding part '{0}' on-hand = {1}",
                            part.sku, part.onhand);
        }
    }
```

```csharp
        public delegate void OutOfStockExceptionMethod(Part part);
        public void ProcessInventory(OutOfStockExceptionMethod exception)
        {
            Console.WriteLine("\nProcessing inventory...");
            foreach (Part part in parts)
            {
                if (part.onhand < MIN_ONHAND)
                {
                    Console.WriteLine
                        ("{0} ({1}) is below minimum on-hand {2}",
                        part.sku, part.onhand, MIN_ONHAND);

                    exception(part);
                }
            }
        }
    }

    class CompositeDelegate1App
    {
        public static void LogEvent(Part part)
        {
            Console.WriteLine("\tlogging event...");
        }

        public static void EmailPurchasingMgr(Part part)
        {
            Console.WriteLine("\temailing Purchasing manager...");
        }

        public static void Main()
        {
            InventoryManager mgr = new InventoryManager();

            InventoryManager.OutOfStockExceptionMethod LogEventCallback =
                new InventoryManager.OutOfStockExceptionMethod(LogEvent);

            InventoryManager.OutOfStockExceptionMethod
                EmailPurchasingMgrCallback = new
                InventoryManager.OutOfStockExceptionMethod(EmailPurchasingMgr);

            InventoryManager.OutOfStockExceptionMethod
                OnHandExceptionEventsCallback =
                EmailPurchasingMgrCallback + LogEventCallback;

            mgr.ProcessInventory(OnHandExceptionEventsCallback);
        }
    }
```

Running this application produces results like the following:

```
Adding part 'Part 1' on-hand = 16
Adding part 'Part 2' on-hand = 98
Adding part 'Part 3' on-hand = 65
Adding part 'Part 4' on-hand = 22
Adding part 'Part 5' on-hand = 70

Processing inventory...
Part 1 (16) is below minimum on-hand 50
    logging event...
    emailing Purchasing manager...
Part 4 (22) is below minimum on-hand 50
    logging event...
    emailing Purchasing manager...
```

Therefore, using this feature of the language, we can dynamically discern which methods comprise a callback method, aggregate those methods into a single delegate, and pass the composite delegate as though it were a single delegate. The runtime will automatically see to it that all of the methods are called in sequence. In addition, you can also remove desired delegates from the composite by using the minus operator.

However, the fact that these methods get called in sequential order does beg one important question: why can't I simply chain the methods together by having each method successively call the next method? In this section's example, where we have only two methods and both are always called as a pair, we could do that. But let's make the example more complicated. Let's say we have several store locations with each location dictating which methods are called. For example, Location1 might be the warehouse, so we'd want to log the event and email the purchasing manager, whereas a part that's below the minimum on-hand quantity for all other locations would result in the event being logged and the manager of that store being emailed.

We can easily address these requirements by dynamically creating a composite delegate based on the location being processed. Without delegates, we'd have to write a method that not only would have to determine which methods to call, but also would have to keep track of which methods had already been called and which ones were yet to be called during the call sequence. As you can see in the following code, delegates make this potentially complex operation very simple.

```
using System;

class Part
{
    public Part(string sku)
```

```
    {
        this.Sku = sku;

        Random r = new Random(DateTime.Now.Millisecond);
        double d = r.NextDouble() * 100;

        this.OnHand = (int)d;
    }

    protected string Sku;
    public string sku
    {
        get
        {
            return this.Sku;
        }
        set
        {
            this.Sku = value;
        }
    }

    protected int OnHand;
    public int onhand
    {
        get
        {
            return this.OnHand;
        }
        set
        {
            this.OnHand = value;
        }
    }
}

class InventoryManager
{
    protected const int MIN_ONHAND = 50;

    public Part[] parts;
    public InventoryManager()
    {
        parts = new Part[5];
        for (int i = 0; i < 5; i++)
```

(continued)

```
                    {
                        Part part = new Part("Part " + (i + 1));
                        parts[i] = part;
                        Console.WriteLine
                            ("Adding part '{0}' on-hand = {1}",
                             part.sku, part.onhand);
                    }
                }

                public delegate void OutOfStockExceptionMethod(Part part);
                public void ProcessInventory(OutOfStockExceptionMethod exception)
                {
                    Console.WriteLine("\nProcessing inventory...");
                    foreach (Part part in parts)
                    {
                        if (part.onhand < MIN_ONHAND)
                        {
                            Console.WriteLine
                                ("{0} ({1}) is below minimum onhand {2}",
                                 part.sku, part.onhand, MIN_ONHAND);

                            exception(part);
                        }
                    }
                }
            }

            class CompositeDelegate2App
            {
                public static void LogEvent(Part part)
                {
                    Console.WriteLine("\tlogging event...");
                }

                public static void EmailPurchasingMgr(Part part)
                {
                    Console.WriteLine("\temailing Purchasing manager...");
                }

                public static void EmailStoreMgr(Part part)
                {
                    Console.WriteLine("\temailing store manager...");
                }

                public static void Main()
                {
                    InventoryManager mgr = new InventoryManager();
```

```
InventoryManager.OutOfStockExceptionMethod[] exceptionMethods
    = new InventoryManager.OutOfStockExceptionMethod[3];

exceptionMethods[0] = new
    InventoryManager.OutOfStockExceptionMethod
        (LogEvent);
exceptionMethods[1] = new
    InventoryManager.OutOfStockExceptionMethod
        (EmailPurchasingMgr);
exceptionMethods[2] = new
    InventoryManager.OutOfStockExceptionMethod
        (EmailStoreMgr);

int location = 1;

InventoryManager.OutOfStockExceptionMethod compositeDelegate;

if (location == 2)
{
    compositeDelegate =
        exceptionMethods[0] + exceptionMethods[1];
}
else
{
    compositeDelegate =
        exceptionMethods[0] + exceptionMethods[2];
}

mgr.ProcessInventory(compositeDelegate);
    }
}
```

Now the compilation and execution of this application will yield different results based on the value you assign the *location* variable.

Defining Events with Delegates

Almost all applications for Windows have some sort of asynchronous event processing needs. Some of these events are generic, such as Windows sending messages to the application message queue when the user has interacted with the application in some fashion. Some are more problem domain–specific, such as printing the invoice for an order being updated.

Events in C# follow the publish-subscribe design pattern in which a class publishes an event that it can "raise" and any number of classes can then subscribe to that event. Once the event is raised, the runtime takes care of notifying each subscriber that the event has occurred.

The method called as a result of an event being raised is defined by a delegate. However, keep in mind some strict rules concerning a delegate that's used in this fashion. First, the delegate must be defined as taking two arguments. Second, these arguments always represent two objects: the object that raised the event (the publisher) and an event information object. Additionally, this second object must be derived from the .NET Framework's *EventArgs* class.

Let's say we wanted to monitor changes to inventory levels. We could create a class called *InventoryManager* that would always be used to update inventory. This *InventoryManager* class would publish an event that would be raised any time inventory is changed via such actions as the receipt of inventory, sales, and physical inventory updates. Then, any class needing to be kept updated would subscribe to the event. Here's how this would be coded in C# by using delegates and events:

```
using System;

class InventoryChangeEventArgs : EventArgs
{
    public InventoryChangeEventArgs(string sku, int change)
    {
        this.sku = sku;
        this.change = change;
    }

    string sku;
    public string Sku
    {
        get
        {
            return sku;
        }
    }

    int change;
    public int Change
    {
        get
        {
            return change;
        }
    }
}

class InventoryManager // Publisher.
{
    public delegate void InventoryChangeEventHandler
        (object source, InventoryChangeEventArgs e);
    public event InventoryChangeEventHandler OnInventoryChangeHandler;
```

```csharp
    public void UpdateInventory(string sku, int change)
    {
        if (0 == change)
            return; // No update on null change.

        // Code to update database would go here.

        InventoryChangeEventArgs e = new
            InventoryChangeEventArgs(sku, change);

        if (OnInventoryChangeHandler != null)
            OnInventoryChangeHandler(this, e);
    }
}

class InventoryWatcher // Subscriber.
{
    public InventoryWatcher(InventoryManager inventoryManager)
    {
        this.inventoryManager = inventoryManager;
        inventoryManager.OnInventoryChangeHandler += new
InventoryManager.InventoryChangeEventHandler(OnInventoryChange);
    }
    void OnInventoryChange(object source, InventoryChangeEventArgs e)
    {
        int change = e.Change;
        Console.WriteLine("Part '{0}' was {1} by {2} units",
            e.Sku,
            change > 0 ? "increased" : "decreased",
            Math.Abs(e.Change));
    }
    InventoryManager inventoryManager;
}

class Events1App
{
    public static void Main()
    {
        InventoryManager inventoryManager =
            new InventoryManager();

        InventoryWatcher inventoryWatch =
            new InventoryWatcher(inventoryManager);

        inventoryManager.UpdateInventory("111 006 116", -2);
        inventoryManager.UpdateInventory("111 005 383", 5);
    }
}
```

Let's look at the first two members of the *InventoryManager* class:

```
public delegate void InventoryChangeEventHandler
                        (object source, InventoryChangeEventArgs e);
public event InventoryChangeEventHandler OnInventoryChangeHandler;
```

The first line of code is a delegate, which by now you know is a definition for a method signature. As mentioned earlier, all delegates that are used in events must be defined as taking two arguments: a publisher object (in this case, *source*) and an event information object (an *EventArgs*-derived object). The second line uses the *event* keyword, a member type with which you specify the delegate and the method (or methods) that will be called when the event is raised.

The last method in the *InventoryManager* class is the *UpdateInventory* method, which is called anytime inventory is changed. As you can see, this method creates an object of type *InventoryChangeEventArgs*. This object is passed to all subscribers and is used to describe the event that took place.

Now look at the next two lines of code:

```
if (OnInventoryChangeHandler != null)
    OnInventoryChangeHandler(this, e);
```

The conditional *if* statement checks to see whether the event has any subscribers associated with the *OnInventoryChangeHandler* method. If it does—in other words, *OnInventoryChangeHandler* is not *null*—the event is raised. That's really all there is on the publisher side of things. Now let's look at the subscriber code.

The subscriber in this case is the class called *InventoryWatcher*. All it needs to do is perform two simple tasks. First, it adds itself as a subscriber by instantiating a new delegate of type *InventoryManager.InventoryChangeEventHandler* and adding that delegate to the *InventoryManager.OnInventoryChangeHandler* event. Pay special attention to the syntax used—it's using the *+=* compound assignment operator to add itself to the list of subscribers so as not to erase any previous subscribers.

```
inventoryManager.OnInventoryChangeHandler
+= new InventoryManager.InventoryChangeEventHandler(OnInventoryChange);
```

The only argument that needs to be supplied here is the name of the method that will be called if and when the event is raised.

The only other task the subscriber needs to do is implement its event handler. In this case, the event handler is *InventoryWatcher.OnInventoryChange*, which prints a message stating the part number and the change in inventory.

Finally, the code that runs this application instantiates *InventoryManager* and *InventoryWatcher* classes and, every time the *InventoryManager.UpdateInventory* method is called, an event is automatically raised that causes the *Inventory-Watcher.OnInventoryChanged* method to be called.

Summary

Delegates in C# are type-safe, secure managed objects that serve the same purpose as function pointers in C++. Delegates are different from classes and interfaces in that rather than being defined at compile time, they refer to single methods and are defined at run time. Delegates are commonly used to perform asynchronous processing and to inject custom code into a class's code path. Delegates can be used for a number of general purposes, including using them as callback methods, defining static methods, and using them to define events.

Part IV

Advanced C#

15

Multithreaded Programming

Technically speaking, threads are not specific to C#; most C# books tend to stay away from the topic for that reason. Although I've tried to stay very specific to C#, the general subject of multithreading is one most programmers should be familiar with when learning this new language. I certainly can't cover the entire range of threading-related issues in one chapter, but I will cover the basics and even some intermediate-to-advanced issues regarding the aborting, scheduling, and lifetime management of threads. I'll also discuss thread synchronization with the *System.Monitor* and *System.Mutex* classes and the C# *lock* statement.

Threading Basics

Using a single-threaded application is like shopping in a supermarket with a single cashier. Employing only one cashier is less expensive for the store owner and the cashier can handle relatively low levels of traffic, but once the store announces double-coupon day and the checkout line gets longer and longer, some customers become extremely unhappy. What we have here is your standard bottleneck scenario: too much data and too small a conduit. The answer, of course, is to hire more cashiers.

And so it is for threading and applications. Multithreading allows an application to divide tasks such that they work independently of each other to make the most efficient use of the processor and the user's time. However, if you're new to multithreaded programming, there's a caveat: *threading is not the right choice for all applications and can sometimes even slow an application down.* So, it's paramount that along with learning the syntax of multithreading you also understand when to use it. To that end, I've included a section at the end of this chapter ("Threading Guidelines") to help you determine when creating multiple threads in your applications is the way to go. For now, let's start looking at how threading is implemented in the Microsoft .NET Framework.

Threads and Multitasking

A thread is a unit of processing, and multitasking is the simultaneous execution of multiple threads. Multitasking comes in two flavors: cooperative and preemptive. Very early versions of Microsoft Windows supported cooperative multitasking, which meant that each thread was responsible for relinquishing control to the processor so that it could process other threads. For those of us with backgrounds in other operating systems—in my case, IBM System/38 (CPF) and OS/2—each of us has our own story of the day we hung the computer because we didn't place a call to *PeekMessage* in our code to allow other threads in the system to be served by the CPU. "I have to do what?!" was our typical response.

However, Microsoft Windows NT—and, later, Windows 95, Windows 98, and Windows 2000—support the same preemptive multitasking that OS/2 does. With preemptive multitasking, the processor is responsible for giving each thread a certain amount of time in which to execute—a *timeslice*. The processor then switches among the different threads, giving each its timeslice, and the programmer doesn't have to worry about how and when to relinquish control so that other threads can run. Because .NET will only work only on preemptive multitasking operating systems, this is what I'll be focusing on.

By the way, even with preemptive multitasking, if you're running on a single processor machine, you don't really have multiple threads executing at the same time. Because the processor is switching between processes at intervals that number in the milliseconds, it just "feels" that way. If you want to run true multiple threads concurrently, you'll need to develop and run your code on a machine with multiple processors.

Context Switching

Context switching is integral to threading and a difficult concept for some, so let me give a brief overview here in the "Threading Basics" section.

The processor uses a hardware timer to determine when a timeslice has ended for a given thread. When the hardware timer signals the interrupt, the processor saves all registers for the current thread onto the stack. Then the processor moves those same registers from the stack into a data structure called a *CONTEXT* structure. When the processor wants to switch back to a previously executing thread, it reverses this procedure and restores the registers from the *CONTEXT* structure associated with the thread. This entire procedure is called context switching.

A Multithreaded Application in C#

Before examining some of the different ways you can use threads in C#, let's see how easy it is to create a secondary thread in C#. After discussing the example, I'll look more closely at the *System.Threading* namespace and, specifically, the *Thread* class. In this example, I'm creating a second thread from the *Main* method. The method associated with the second thread then outputs a string showing that the thread has been called.

```
using System;
using System.Threading;

class SimpleThreadApp
{
    public static void WorkerThreadMethod()
    {
        Console.WriteLine("Worker thread started");
    }

    public static void Main()
    {
        ThreadStart worker = new ThreadStart(WorkerThreadMethod);

        Console.WriteLine("Main - Creating worker thread");

        Thread t = new Thread(worker);
        t.Start();

    Console.WriteLine
        ("Main - Have requested the start of worker thread");
    }
}
```

If you compile and execute this application, you'll see that the message from the *Main* method prints before the message from the worker thread, proving that the worker thread is indeed working asynchronously. Let's dissect what's going on here.

The first new item to note is the inclusion of the *using* statement for the *System.Threading* namespace. We'll get to know that namespace shortly. For now, it's enough to understand that this namespace contains the different classes necessary for threading in the .NET environment. Now take a look at the first line of the *Main* method:

```
ThreadStart WorkerThreadMethod = new ThreadStart(WorkerThreadMethod);
```

Any time you see the following form, you can be sure that *x* is a delegate or—as you learned in Chapter 14, "Delegates and Event Handlers"—a definition of a method signature:

x varName = new *x*(*methodName*);

So, we know that *ThreadStart* is a delegate. But it's not just any delegate. Specifically, it's the delegate that must be used when creating a new thread, and it's used to specify the method that you want called as your thread method. From there, I instantiate a *Thread* object where the constructor takes as its only argument a *ThreadStart* delegate, like so:

```
Thread t = new Thread(worker);
```

After that, I call my *Thread* object's *Start* method, which results in a call to the *WorkerThreadMethod*.

That's it! Three lines of code to set up and run the thread and the thread method itself, and you're off and running. Now let's look deeper into the *System.Threading* namespace and its classes that make all this happen.

Working with Threads

All creation and management of threads is achieved through use of the *System.Threading.Thread* class, so we'll start there.

AppDomain

In .NET, threads run in something called an *AppDomain*. You'll sometimes hear that an *AppDomain* is analogous to a Win32 process in that it offers many of the same benefits, including fault tolerance and the ability to be independently started and stopped. This is a good comparison, but the comparison breaks down in relation to threads. In Win32, a thread is confined to a single process, as you saw when I described context switching earlier. A thread in one process cannot invoke a method in a thread that belongs to another process. In .NET, however, threads can cross *AppDomain* boundaries, and a method in one thread can call a method in another *AppDomain*. Therefore, here's a better definition of an *AppDomain*: a logical process inside of a physical process.

The *Thread* Class

Most everything you do with threads you'll do using the *Thread* class. This section looks at using the *Thread* class to carry out basic threading tasks.

Creating Threads and Thread Objects

You can instantiate a *Thread* object in two ways. You've already seen one way: creating a new thread and, in that process, getting a *Thread* object with which to manipulate the new thread. The other way to obtain a *Thread* object is by calling the static *Thread.CurrentThread* method for the currently executing thread.

Managing Thread Lifetimes

There are many different tasks you might need to perform to manage the activity or life of a thread. You can manage all these tasks by using the different *Thread* methods. For example, it's quite common to need to pause a thread for a given period of time. To do this, you can call the *Thread.Sleep* method. This method takes a single argument that represents the amount of time, in milliseconds, that you want the thread to pause. Note that the *Thread.Sleep* method is a static method and cannot be called with an instance of a *Thread* object. There's a very good reason for this. You're not allowed to call *Thread.Sleep* on any other thread except the currently executing one. The static *Thread.Sleep* method calls the static *CurrentThread* method, which then pauses that thread for the specified amount of time. Here's an example:

```
using System;
using System.Threading;

class ThreadSleepApp
{
    public static void WorkerThreadMethod()
    {
        Console.WriteLine("Worker thread started");

        int sleepTime = 5000;

        Console.WriteLine("\tsleeping for {0} seconds", sleepTime / 1000);
        Thread.Sleep(sleepTime); // Sleep for five seconds.
        Console.WriteLine("\twaking up");
    }
```

(continued)

```
public static void Main()
{
    ThreadStart worker = new ThreadStart(WorkerThreadMethod);

    Console.WriteLine("Main - Creating worker thread");

    Thread t = new Thread(worker);
    t.Start();

    Console.WriteLine
        ("Main - Have requested the start of worker thread");
}
}
```

There are two more ways to call the *Thread.Sleep* method. First, by calling *Thread.Sleep* with the value *0*, you'll cause the current thread to relinquish the unused balance of its timeslice. Passing a value of *Timeout.Infinite* results in the thread being paused indefinitely until the suspension is interrupted by another thread calling the suspended thread's *Thread.Interrupt* method.

The second way to suspend the execution of a thread is by using the *Thread.Suspend* method. There are some major difference between the two techniques. First, the *Thread.Suspend* method can be called on the currently executing thread or another thread. Second, once a thread is suspended in this fashion, only another thread can cause its resumption, with the *Thread.Resume* method. Note that once a thread suspends another thread, the first thread is not blocked. The call returns immediately. Also, regardless of how many times the *Thread.Suspend* method is called for a given thread, a single call to *Thread.Resume* will cause the thread to resume execution.

Destroying Threads

If the need should arise to destroy a thread, you can accomplish this with a call to the *Thread.Abort* method. The runtime forces the abortion of a thread by throwing a *ThreadAbortException*. Even if the method attempts to catch the *ThreadAbortException*, the runtime won't let it. However, the runtime will execute the code in the aborted thread's *finally* block, if one's present. The following code illustrates what I mean. The *Main* method pauses for two seconds to make sure that the runtime has had time to start the worker thread. Upon being started, the worker thread starts counting to ten, pausing for a second in between each number. When the *Main* method resumes execution after its two-second pause, it aborts the worker thread. Notice that the *finally* block is executed after the abort.

```
using System;
using System.Threading;
```

```
class ThreadAbortApp
{
    public static void WorkerThreadMethod()
    {
        try
        {
            Console.WriteLine("Worker thread started");

            Console.WriteLine
                ("Worker thread - counting slowly to 10");
            for (int i = 0; i < 10; i++)
            {
                Thread.Sleep(500);
                Console.Write("{0}...", i);
            }

            Console.WriteLine("Worker thread finished");
        }
        catch(ThreadAbortException e)
        {
        }
        finally
        {
            Console.WriteLine
                ("Worker thread -
                    I can't catch the exception, but I can cleanup");
        }
    }

    public static void Main()
    {
        ThreadStart worker = new ThreadStart(WorkerThreadMethod);

        Console.WriteLine("Main - Creating worker thread");

        Thread t = new Thread(worker);
        t.Start();

        // Give the worker thread time to start.
        Console.WriteLine("Main - Sleeping for 2 seconds");
        Thread.Sleep(2000);

        Console.WriteLine("\nMain - Aborting worker thread");
        t.Abort();
    }
}
```

When you compile and execute this application, the following output results:

```
Main - Creating worker thread
Main - Sleeping for 2 seconds
Worker thread started
Worker thread - counting slowly to 10
0...1...2...3...
Main - Aborting worker thread
Worker thread - I can't catch the exception, but I can cleanup
```

You should also realize that when the *Thread.Abort* method is called, the thread will not cease execution immediately. The runtime waits until the thread has reached what the documentation describes as a "safe point." Therefore, if your code is dependent on something happening after the abort and you must be sure the thread has stopped, you can use the *Thread.Join* method. This is a synchronous call, meaning that it will not return until the thread has been stopped. Lastly, note that once you abort a thread, it cannot be restarted. In that case, although you have a valid *Thread* object, you can't do anything useful with it in terms of executing code.

Scheduling Threads

When the processor switches between threads once a given thread's timeslice has ended, the process of choosing which thread executes next is far from arbitrary. Each thread has an associated priority level that tells the processor how it should be scheduled in relation to the other threads in the system. This priority level is defaulted to *Normal*—more on this shortly—for threads that are created within the runtime. For threads that are created outside the runtime, they retain their original priority. You use the *Thread.Priority* property to view and set this value. The *Thread.Priority* property's setter takes a value of type *Thread.ThreadPriority* that is an *enum* that defines these values: *Highest, AboveNormal, Normal, BelowNormal,* and *Lowest*.

To illustrate how priorities can affect even the simplest code, take a look at the following example in which one worker thread counts from 1 to 10 and the other counts from 11 to 20. Note the nested loop within each *WorkerThread* method. Each loop is there to represent work the thread would be doing in a real application. Because these methods don't really do anything, not having those loops would result in each thread finishing its work in its first timeslice!

```
using System;
using System.Threading;
```

```
class ThreadSchedule1App
{
    public static void WorkerThreadMethod1()
    {
        Console.WriteLine("Worker thread started");

        Console.WriteLine
            ("Worker thread - counting slowly from 1 to 10");
        for (int i = 1; i < 11; i++)
        {
            for (int j = 0; j < 100; j++)
            {
                Console.Write(".");
                // Code to imitate work being done.
                int a;
                a = 15;
            }
            Console.Write("{0}", i);
        }

        Console.WriteLine("Worker thread finished");
    }

    public static void WorkerThreadMethod2()
    {
        Console.WriteLine("Worker thread started");

        Console.WriteLine
            ("Worker thread - counting slowly from 11 to 20");
        for (int i = 11; i < 20; i++)
        {
            for (int j = 0; j < 100; j++)
            {
                Console.Write(".");
                // Code to imitate work being done.
                int a;
                a = 15;
            }
            Console.Write("{0}", i);
        }

        Console.WriteLine("Worker thread finished");
    }

    public static void Main()
```

(continued)

```
    {
        ThreadStart worker1 = new ThreadStart(WorkerThreadMethod1);
        ThreadStart worker2 = new ThreadStart(WorkerThreadMethod2);

        Console.WriteLine("Main - Creating worker threads");

        Thread t1 = new Thread(worker1);
        Thread t2 = new Thread(worker2);

        t1.Start();
        t2.Start();
    }
}
```

Running this application results in the following output. Note that in the interest of brevity I've truncated the output—most of the dots are removed.

```
Main - Creating worker threads
Worker thread started
Worker thread started
Worker thread - counting slowly from 1 to 10
Worker thread - counting slowly from 11 to 20
......1......11......2......12......3......13
```

As you can see, both threads are getting equal playing time with the processor. Now alter the *Priority* property for each thread as in the following code—I've given the first thread the highest priority allowed and the second thread the lowest—and you'll see a much different result.

```
using System;
using System.Threading;

class ThreadSchedule2App
{
    public static void WorkerThreadMethod1()
    {
        Console.WriteLine("Worker thread started");

        Console.WriteLine
            ("Worker thread - counting slowly from 1 to 10");
        for (int i = 1; i < 11; i++)
        {
            for (int j = 0; j < 100; j++)
            {
                Console.Write(".");
                // Code to imitate work being done.
                int a;
                a = 15;
            }
```

```
            Console.Write("{0}", i);
        }

        Console.WriteLine("Worker thread finished");
    }

    public static void WorkerThreadMethod2()
    {
        Console.WriteLine("Worker thread started");

        Console.WriteLine
            ("Worker thread - counting slowly from 11 to 20");
        for (int i = 11; i < 20; i++)
        {
            for (int j = 0; j < 100; j++)
            {
                Console.Write(".");
                // Code to imitate work being done.
                int a;
                a = 15;
            }
            Console.Write("{0}", i);
        }

        Console.WriteLine("Worker thread finished");
    }

    public static void Main()
    {
        ThreadStart worker1 = new ThreadStart(WorkerThreadMethod1);
        ThreadStart worker2 = new ThreadStart(WorkerThreadMethod2);

        Console.WriteLine("Main - Creating worker threads");

        Thread t1 = new Thread(worker1);
        Thread t2 = new Thread(worker2);

        t1.Priority = ThreadPriority.Highest;
        t2.Priority = ThreadPriority.Lowest;

        t1.Start();
        t2.Start();
    }
}
```

The (abbreviated) results should be as shown on the next page. Notice that the second thread has been set to such a low priority that it doesn't receive any cycles until after the first thread has completed its work.

```
Main - Creating worker threads
Worker thread started
Worker thread started
Worker thread - counting slowly from 1 to 10
Worker thread - counting slowly from 11 to 20
......1......2......3......4......5......6......7......8......9......10......
11......12......13......14......15......16......17......18......19......20
```

Remember that when you tell the processor the priority you want a given thread to have, it's the operating system that eventually uses this value as part of its scheduling algorithm that it relays to the processor. In .NET, this algorithm is based on the priority level that you've just used (with the *Thread.Priority* property) as well as the process's *priority class* and *dynamic boost* values. All these values are used to create a numeric value (*0–31* on an Intel processor) that represents the thread's priority. The thread having the highest value is the thread with the highest priority.

One last note on the subject of thread scheduling: use it with caution. Let's say you have a GUI application and a couple of worker threads that are off doing some sort of asynchronous work. If you set the worker thread priorities too high, the UI might become sluggish because the main thread in which the GUI application is running is receiving fewer CPU cycles. Unless you have a specific reason to schedule a thread with a high priority, it's best to let the thread's priority default to *Normal*.

> **Note**   When you have a situation where several threads are running at the same priority, they'll all get an equal amount of processor time. This is called *round robin scheduling*.

Thread Safety and Synchronization

When programming for a single-threaded environment, it's common to write methods in such a way that at several points in the code the object is in a temporarily invalid state. Obviously, if only one thread is accessing the object at a time, you're guaranteed that each method will complete before another method is called—meaning that the object is always in a valid state to any of the object's clients. However, when multiple threads are thrown into the mix, you can easily have situations in which the processor switches to another thread while your object is in an invalid state. If that thread then also attempts to use this same object, the results can be quite unpredictable. Therefore, the term "thread safety" means that the members of an object always maintain a valid state when used concurrently by multiple threads.

So, how do we prevent this unpredictable state? Actually, as is common in programming, there are several ways to address this well-known issue. In this section, I'll cover the most common means: synchronization. Through synchronization, you specify *critical sections* of code that can be entered by only one thread at a time, thereby guaranteeing that any temporary invalid states of your object are not seen by the object's clients. We'll be looking at several means of defining critical sections, including the .NET *Monitor* and *Mutex* classes as well as the C# *lock* statement.

Protecting Code by Using the *Monitor* Class

The *System.Monitor* class enables you to serialize the access to blocks of code by means of locks and signals. For example, you have a method that updates a database and that cannot be executed by two or more threads at the same time. If the work being performed by this method is especially time-consuming and you have multiple threads, any of which might call this method, you could have a serious problem on your hands. This is where the *Monitor* class comes in. Take a look at the following synchronization example. Here we have two threads, both of which will call the *Database.SaveData* method.

```
using System;
using System.Threading;

class Database
{
    public void SaveData(string text)
    {
        Console.WriteLine("Database.SaveData - Started");

        Console.WriteLine("Database.SaveData - Working");
        for (int i = 0; i < 100; i++)
        {
            Console.Write(text);
        }

        Console.WriteLine("\nDatabase.SaveData - Ended");
    }
}

class ThreadMonitor1App
```

(continued)

```
{
    public static Database db = new Database();

    public static void WorkerThreadMethod1()
    {
        Console.WriteLine("Worker thread #1 - Started");

        Console.WriteLine
            ("Worker thread #1 -Calling Database.SaveData");
        db.SaveData("x");

        Console.WriteLine("Worker thread #1 - Returned from Output");
    }

    public static void WorkerThreadMethod2()
    {
        Console.WriteLine("Worker thread #2 - Started");

        Console.WriteLine
            ("Worker thread #2 - Calling Database.SaveData");
        db.SaveData("o");

        Console.WriteLine("Worker thread #2 - Returned from Output");
    }

    public static void Main()
    {
        ThreadStart worker1 = new ThreadStart(WorkerThreadMethod1);
        ThreadStart worker2 = new ThreadStart(WorkerThreadMethod2);

        Console.WriteLine("Main - Creating worker threads");

        Thread t1 = new Thread(worker1);
        Thread t2 = new Thread(worker2);

        t1.Start();
        t2.Start();
    }
}
```

When you compile and execute this application, you'll see that the resulting output will have a mixture of o's and x's, showing that the *Database.SaveData* method is being run concurrently by both threads. (Note that once again I've abbreviated the output.)

```
Main - Creating worker threads

Worker thread #1 - Started
Worker thread #2 - Started

Worker thread #1 - Calling Database.SaveData
Worker thread #2 - Calling Database.SaveData

Database.SaveData - Started
Database.SaveData - Started

Database.SaveData - Working
Database.SaveData - Working
xoxoxoxoxoxoxoxoxoxoxoxoxoxoxoxoxoxoxoxoxoxoxoxoxoxoxoxox
Database.SaveData - Ended
Database.SaveData - Ended

Worker thread #1 - Returned from Output
Worker thread #2 - Returned from Output
```

Obviously, if the *Database.SaveData* method needed to finish updating multiple tables before being called by another thread, we'd have a serious problem.

To incorporate the *Monitor* class in this example, we use two of its static methods. The first method is called *Enter*. When executed, this method attempts to obtain a monitor lock on the object. If another thread already has the lock, the method will block until that lock has been released. Note that there is no implicit box operation performed here, so you can supply only a reference type to this method. The *Monitor.Exit* method is then called to release the lock. Here's the example rewritten to force the serialization of access to the *Database.SaveData* method:

```
using System;
using System.Threading;

class Database
{
    public void SaveData(string text)
    {
        Monitor.Enter(this);

        Console.WriteLine("Database.SaveData - Started");

        Console.WriteLine("Database.SaveData - Working");
        for (int i = 0; i < 100; i++)
        {
            Console.Write(text);
        }
```

(continued)

```
                Console.WriteLine("\nDatabase.SaveData - Ended");

                Monitor.Exit(this);
        }
    }

    class ThreadMonitor2App
    {
        public static Database db = new Database();

        public static void WorkerThreadMethod1()
        {
            Console.WriteLine("Worker thread #1 - Started");

            Console.WriteLine
                ("Worker thread #1 - Calling Database.SaveData");
            db.SaveData("x");

            Console.WriteLine("Worker thread #1 - Returned from Output");
        }

        public static void WorkerThreadMethod2()
        {
            Console.WriteLine("Worker thread #2 - Started");

            Console.WriteLine
                ("Worker thread #2 - Calling Database.SaveData");
            db.SaveData("o");

            Console.WriteLine("Worker thread #2 - Returned from Output");
        }

        public static void Main()
        {
            ThreadStart worker1 = new ThreadStart(WorkerThreadMethod1);
            ThreadStart worker2 = new ThreadStart(WorkerThreadMethod2);

            Console.WriteLine("Main - Creating worker threads");

            Thread t1 = new Thread(worker1);
            Thread t2 = new Thread(worker2);

            t1.Start();
            t2.Start();
        }
    }
```

Notice in the following output that even though the second thread called the *Database.SaveData* method, the *Monitor.Enter* method caused it to block until the first thread had released its lock:

```
Main - Creating worker threads

Worker thread #1 - Started
Worker thread #2 - Started

Worker thread #1 - Calling Database.SaveData
Worker thread #2 - Calling Database.SaveData

Database.SaveData - Started
Database.SaveData - Working
xxxxxxxxxxxxxxxxxxxxxxxxxxxxxxxxxxxxxxxxx
Database.SaveData - Ended

Database.SaveData - Started

Worker thread #1 - Returned from Output

Database.SaveData - Working
ooooooooooooooooooooooooooooooooooooooo
Database.SaveData - Ended

Worker thread #2 - Returned from Output
```

Using Monitor Locks with the C# *lock* Statement

Although the C# *lock* statement doesn't support the full array of features found in the *Monitor* class, it does enable you to obtain and release a monitor lock. To use the *lock* statement, simply specify the *lock* statement with the code being serialized in braces. The braces indicate the starting and stopping point of the code being protected, so there's no need for an *unlock* statement. The following code will produce the same synchronized output as the previous examples:

```
using System;
using System.Threading;

class Database
{
    public void SaveData(string text)
    {
        lock(this)
```

(continued)

319

```
        {
            Console.WriteLine("Database.SaveData - Started");

            Console.WriteLine("Database.SaveData - Working");
            for (int i = 0; i < 100; i++)
            {
                Console.Write(text);
            }

            Console.WriteLine("\nDatabase.SaveData - Ended");
        }
    }
}

class ThreadLockApp
{
    public static Database db = new Database();

    public static void WorkerThreadMethod1()
    {
        Console.WriteLine("Worker thread #1 - Started");

        Console.WriteLine
            ("Worker thread #1 - Calling Database.SaveData");
        db.SaveData("x");

        Console.WriteLine("Worker thread #1 - Returned from Output");
    }

    public static void WorkerThreadMethod2()
    {
        Console.WriteLine("Worker thread #2 - Started");

        Console.WriteLine
            ("Worker thread #2 - Calling Database.SaveData");
        db.SaveData("o");

        Console.WriteLine("Worker thread #2 - Returned from Output");
    }

    public static void Main()
    {
        ThreadStart worker1 = new ThreadStart(WorkerThreadMethod1);
        ThreadStart worker2 = new ThreadStart(WorkerThreadMethod2);

        Console.WriteLine("Main - Creating worker threads");

        Thread t1 = new Thread(worker1);
        Thread t2 = new Thread(worker2);
```

```
        t1.Start();
        t2.Start();
    }
}
```

Synchronizing Code by Using the *Mutex* Class

The *Mutex* class—defined in the *System.Threading* namespace—is a run-time representation of the Win32 system primitive of the same name. You can use a mutex to serialize access to code as you can use a monitor lock, but mutexes are much slower because of their increased flexibility. The term *mutex* comes from *mutually exclusive,* and just as only one thread at a time can obtain a monitor lock for a given object, only one thread at a time can obtain a given mutex.

You can create a mutex in C# with the following three constructors:

Mutex( )
Mutex(bool *initiallyOwned*)
Mutex(bool *initiallyOwned*, string *mutexName*)

The first constructor creates a mutex with no name and makes the current thread the owner of that mutex. Therefore, the mutex is locked by the current thread. The second constructor takes only a Boolean flag that designates whether the thread creating the mutex wants to own it (lock it). And the third constructor allows you to specify whether the current thread owns the mutex and to specify the name of the mutex. Let's now incorporate a mutex to serialize access to the *Database.SaveData* method:

```
using System;
using System.Threading;

class Database
{
    Mutex mutex = new Mutex(false);

    public void SaveData(string text)
    {
        mutex.WaitOne();

        Console.WriteLine("Database.SaveData - Started");

        Console.WriteLine("Database.SaveData - Working");
        for (int i = 0; i < 100; i++)
        {
            Console.Write(text);
        }
```

(continued)

321

```
            Console.WriteLine("\nDatabase.SaveData - Ended");

            mutex.Close();
        }
    }

    class ThreadMutexApp
    {
        public static Database db = new Database();

        public static void WorkerThreadMethod1()
        {
            Console.WriteLine("Worker thread #1 - Started");

            Console.WriteLine
                ("Worker thread #1 - Calling Database.SaveData");
            db.SaveData("x");

            Console.WriteLine("Worker thread #1 - Returned from Output");
        }

        public static void WorkerThreadMethod2()
        {
            Console.WriteLine("Worker thread #2 - Started");

            Console.WriteLine
                ("Worker thread #2 - Calling Database.SaveData");
            db.SaveData("o");

            Console.WriteLine("Worker thread #2 - Returned from Output");
        }

        public static void Main()
        {
            ThreadStart worker1 = new ThreadStart(WorkerThreadMethod1);
            ThreadStart worker2 = new ThreadStart(WorkerThreadMethod2);

            Console.WriteLine("Main - Creating worker threads");

            Thread t1 = new Thread(worker1);
            Thread t2 = new Thread(worker2);

            t1.Start();
            t2.Start();
        }
    }
```

Now, the *Database* class defines a *Mutex* field. We don't want the thread to own the mutex just yet because we'd have no way of getting into the *SaveData* method. The first line of the *SaveData* method shows you how you need to attempt to acquire the mutex—with the *Mutex.WaitOne* method. At the end of the method is a call to the *Close* method, which releases the mutex.

The *WaitOne* method is also overloaded to provide more flexibility in terms of allowing you to define how much time the thread will wait for the mutex to become available. Here are those overloads:

```
WaitOne( )
WaitOne(TimeSpan time, bool exitContext)
WaitOne(int milliseconds, bool exitContext)
```

The basic difference between these overloads is that the first version—used in the example—will wait indefinitely, and the second and third versions will wait for the specified amount of time, expressed with either a *TimeSpan* value or an *int* value.

Thread Safety and the .NET Classes

One question I see quite often in the newsgroups and mailing lists is whether all the .NET *System.** classes are thread-safe. The answer is "No, and they should not be." You could severely cripple a system's performance if all classes serialized access to their functionality. For example, imagine attempting to use one of the collection classes if it obtained a monitor lock each time you called its *Add* method. Now let's say you instantiate a collection object and add about a thousand objects to it. Performance would be dismal—to the point of making the system unusable.

Threading Guidelines

When do you need to use threads, and when is it best, if ever, to avoid them like the plague? In this section, I'll describe both some common scenarios in which threads can be extremely valuable to your application and some situations in which it would be best to avoid using multiple threads.

When to Use Threads

You should use threads when you are striving for increased concurrency, simplified design, and better utilization of CPU time, as described in the following sections.

Increased Concurrency

Very often applications need to accomplish more than one task at a time. For example, I once wrote a document retrieval system for banks that accessed data from optical disks that were stored in optical disk jukeboxes. Imagine the massive amounts of data we're talking about here; picture a jukebox with one drive and 50 platters serving up gigabytes of data. It could sometimes take as long as 5 to 10 seconds to load a disk and find the requested document. Needless to say, it wouldn't exactly be the definition of productivity if my application blocked user input while it did all this. Therefore, to deal with the user input case, I spun off another thread to do the physical work of retrieving the data, allowing the user to continue working. This thread would notify the main thread when the document was loaded. This is a great example of having independent activities—loading a document and handling the UI—that can be handled with two separate threads.

Simplified Design

A popular way to simplify the design of complex systems is to use queues and asynchronous processing. Using such a design, you'd have queues set up to handle the different events that transpire in your system. Instead of methods being called directly, objects are created and placed in queues where they will be handled. At the other end of these queues are server programs with multiple threads that are set up to "listen" for messages coming in to these queues. The advantage of this type of simplified design is that it provides for reliable, robust, and extendable systems.

Better Utilization of CPU Time

Many times your application isn't really doing any work while it's still enjoying its timeslice. In my document retrieval example, one thread was waiting on the jukebox to load the platter. Obviously, this wait was a hardware issue and required no use of the CPU. Other examples of wait times include when you're printing a document or waiting on the hard disk or CD-ROM drive. In each case, the CPU is not being utilized. Such cases are candidates for being moved to background threads.

When Not to Use Threads

It's a common mistake for those new to threads to attempt to deploy them in every application. This can be much worse than not having them at all! As with any other tool in your programming arsenal, you should use threads only when it's appropriate to do so. You should avoid using multiple threads in your application in at least the following cases (described in the following sections): when costs outweigh benefits, when you haven't benchmarked both cases, and when you can't come up with a reason to use threads.

Costs Outweigh Benefits

As you saw in "Thread Safety and Synchronization," writing multithreaded applications takes a bit of time and effort in the design of the code. There will be times when the slight gains enjoyed by having multiple threads just isn't worth the extra time required to make your code thread-safe.

You Haven't Benchmarked Both Cases

If you're new to multithreaded programming, it might surprise you to find that often the overhead required by CPU thread creation and scheduling to achieve modest gains in CPU utilization can actually result in single-threaded applications running faster! It all depends on what you're doing and if you're truly splitting independent tasks into threads. For example, if you have to read three files from disk, spawning three threads won't do you any good because each has to use the same hard disk. Therefore, always be sure to benchmark a prototype of both a single-threaded and multithreaded version of your system before going through the extra time and cost of designing around a solution that might actually backfire in terms of performance.

No Good Reason Why You Should

Using multiple threads should *not* be the default. Because of the inherent complexities of writing multithreaded applications, you should always default to single-threaded code unless you have a good reason to do otherwise.

Summary

Multithreading allows applications to divide tasks so that they work independently of each other to make the most efficient use of the processor's time. However, adding multiple threads to an application is not the right choice in all situations and can sometimes slow the application down. Thread management and creation in C# is done through the *System.Threading.Thread* class. An important concept related to the creation and use of threads is thread safety. Thread safety means that the members of an object always maintain a valid state when used concurrently by multiple threads. It's important that along with learning the syntax of multithreading you also understand when to use it: to increase concurrency, to simplify design, and to better utilize CPU time.

16

Querying Metadata with Reflection

In Chapter 2, "Introducing Microsoft .NET," I touched on the fact that the compiler generates a Win32-portable executable (PE) comprising mainly MSIL and metadata. One very powerful feature of .NET is that it allows you to write code to access an application's metadata through a process known as *reflection*. Put simply, reflection is the ability to discover type information at run time. This chapter will describe the reflection API and how you can use it to iterate through an assembly's modules and types and to retrieve the different design-time characteristics of a type. You'll also see several advanced usages of reflection, such as dynamically invoking methods and use type information (through late binding) and even creating and executing MSIL code at run time!

The Reflection API Hierarchy

The .NET reflection API is actually a lattice of classes—part of which is shown in Figure 16-1—that is defined in the *System.Reflection* namespace. These classes enable you to logically traverse assembly and type information. You can start at any place in this hierarchy depending on your application's specific design needs.

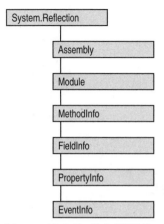

Figure 16-1 Partial .NET *System.Reflection* class hierarchy.

Note that these classes encompass a great deal of functionality. Rather than listing every method and field for each class, I will present an overview of the key classes and then show a demo that illustrates the functionality you'd most likely need to incorporate in your applications.

The Type Class

At the center of reflection is the *System.Type* class. The *System.Type* class is an abstract class that represents a type in the Common Type System (CTS) and enables you to query for type name, the type's encompassing module and namespace, and whether the type is a value type or a reference type.

Retrieving the Type of an Instance

The following example shows how to retrieve a *Type* object for an instantiated *int*:

```
using System;
using System.Reflection;

class TypeObjectFromInstanceApp
{
    public static void Main(string[] args)
    {
        int i = 6;
        Type t = i.GetType();
        Console.WriteLine(t.Name);
    }
}
```

Retrieving the Type from a Name

Besides retrieving a variable's *Type* object, you can also create a *Type* object from a type name. In other words, you don't need to have an instance of the type. Here's an example of doing this for the *System.Int32* type:

```
using System;
using System.Reflection;

class TypeObjectFromNameApp
{
    public static void Main(string[] args)
    {
        Type t = Type.GetType("System.Int32");
        Console.WriteLine(t.Name);
    }
}
```

Note that you cannot use the C# aliases when calling the *Type.GetType* method, because this method is used by all languages. Therefore, you cannot use the C# specific *int* in place of *System.Int32*.

Interrogating Types

The *System.Type* class also enables you to query a type regarding almost any of its attributes, including a types access modifier, whether the type is nested, its COM properties, and so on. The following code illustrates this by using several common types as well as some demo types:

```
using System;
using System.Reflection;

interface DemoInterface
{
}

class DemoAttr : System.Attribute
{
}

enum DemoEnum
{
}

public class DemoBaseClass
{
}
```

(continued)

329

```
public class DemoDerivedClass : DemoBaseClass
{
}

class DemoStruct
{
}

class QueryTypesApp
{
    public static void QueryType(string typeName)
    {
        try
        {
            Type type = Type.GetType(typeName);
            Console.WriteLine("Type name: {0}", type.FullName);
            Console.WriteLine("\tHasElementType = {0}",
                                type.HasElementType);
            Console.WriteLine("\tIsAbstract = {0}", type.IsAbstract);
            Console.WriteLine("\tIsAnsiClass = {0}", type.IsAnsiClass);
            Console.WriteLine("\tIsArray = {0}", type.IsArray);
            Console.WriteLine("\tIsAutoClass = {0}", type.IsAutoClass);
            Console.WriteLine("\tIsAutoLayout = {0}",
                                type.IsAutoLayout);
            Console.WriteLine("\tIsByRef = {0}", type.IsByRef);
            Console.WriteLine("\tIsClass = {0}", type.IsClass);
            Console.WriteLine("\tIsCOMObject = {0}", type.IsCOMObject);
            Console.WriteLine("\tIsContextful = {0}",
                                type.IsContextful);
            Console.WriteLine("\tIsEnum = {0}", type.IsEnum);
            Console.WriteLine("\tIsExplicitLayout = {0}",
                                type.IsExplicitLayout);
            Console.WriteLine("\tIsImport = {0}", type.IsImport);
            Console.WriteLine("\tIsInterface = {0}",
                                type.IsInterface);
            Console.WriteLine("\tIsLayoutSequential = {0}",
                                type.IsLayoutSequential);
            Console.WriteLine("\tIsMarshalByRef = {0}",
                                type.IsMarshalByRef);
            Console.WriteLine("\tIsNestedAssembly = {0}",
                                type.IsNestedAssembly);
            Console.WriteLine("\tIsNestedFamANDAssem = {0}",
                                type.IsNestedFamANDAssem);
            Console.WriteLine("\tIsNestedFamily = {0}",
                                type.IsNestedFamily);
```

```
        Console.WriteLine("\tIsNestedFamORAssem = {0}",
                            type.IsNestedFamORAssem);
        Console.WriteLine("\tIsNestedPrivate = {0}",
                            type.IsNestedPrivate);
        Console.WriteLine("\tIsNestedPublic = {0}",
                            type.IsNestedPublic);
        Console.WriteLine("\tIsNotPublic = {0}",
                            type.IsNotPublic);
        Console.WriteLine("\tIsPointer = {0}",
                            type.IsPointer);
        Console.WriteLine("\tIsPrimitive = {0}",
                            type.IsPrimitive);
        Console.WriteLine("\tIsPublic = {0}",
                            type.IsPublic);
        Console.WriteLine("\tIsSealed = {0}",
                            type.IsSealed);
        Console.WriteLine("\tIsSerializable = {0}",
                            type.IsSerializable);
        Console.WriteLine("\tIsServicedComponent = {0}",
                            type.IsServicedComponent);
        Console.WriteLine("\tIsSpecialName = {0}",
                            type.IsSpecialName);
        Console.WriteLine("\tIsUnicodeClass = {0}",
                            type.IsUnicodeClass);
        Console.WriteLine("\tIsValueType = {0}", type.IsValueType);
    }
    catch(System.NullReferenceException)
    {
        Console.WriteLine
                ("{0} is not a valid type", typeName);
    }
}


public static void Main(string[] args)
{
        QueryType("System.Int32");
        QueryType("System.Int64");
        QueryType("System.Type");

        QueryType("DemoAttr");
        QueryType("DemoEnum");
        QueryType("DemoBaseClass");
        QueryType("DemoDerivedClass");
        QueryType("DemoStruct");
    }
}
```

Working with Assemblies and Modules

Assemblies will be covered in much more detail in Chapter 18, "Working with Assemblies." For the purpose of this conversation, it's enough to know that an assembly is a physical file that consists of multiple .NET PE files. An assembly's main benefit is that it enables you to semantically group functionality for easier deployment and versioning. The .NET runtime's representation of an assembly (and the apex of the reflection object hierarchy) is the *Assembly* class.

You can do many things with the *Assembly* class. Here are some of the more common tasks that we'll be looking at:

- Iterate through an assembly's types

- List an assembly's modules

- Determine identification information, such as the assembly's physical file name and location

- Inspect versioning and security information

- Retrieve the assembly's entry point

Iterating Through the Types of an Assembly

To iterate through all of the types for a given assembly, you need only instantiate an *Assembly* object and then request the *Types* array for the that assembly. Here's an example:

```
using System;
using System.Diagnostics;
using System.Reflection;

class DemoAttr : System.Attribute
{
}

enum DemoEnum
{
}

class DemoBaseClass
{
}
```

```
class DemoDerivedClass : DemoBaseClass
{
}

class DemoStruct
{
}

class GetTypesApp
{
    protected static string GetAssemblyName(string[] args)
    {
        string assemblyName;

        if (0 == args.Length)
        {
            Process p = Process.GetCurrentProcess();
            assemblyName = p.ProcessName + ".exe";
        }
        else
            assemblyName = args[0];

        return assemblyName;
    }

    public static void Main(string[] args)
    {
        string assemblyName = GetAssemblyName(args);

        Console.WriteLine("Loading info for " + assemblyName);
        Assembly a = Assembly.LoadFrom(assemblyName);

        Type[] types = a.GetTypes();
        foreach(Type t in types)
        {
            Console.WriteLine("\nType information for: " +
                            t.FullName);
            Console.WriteLine("\tBase class = " +
                            t.BaseType.FullName);
        }
    }
}
```

> **Note** If you're attempting to run code that needs security clearance—
> such as code that uses the reflection API—over an intranet, you'll need
> to modify policy. One means of doing this is with the Code Access Se-
> curity Policy tool (caspol.exe). Here is an example of using caspol.exe:
>
> ```
> caspol -addgroup 1.2 -url "file://somecomputer/someshare/*"
>     SkipVerification
> ```
>
> This example grants additional permission—in this case, *SkipVerification*—
> based on the URL of the code being run. Note that you could also modify
> policy for all code in a given zone or only for a particular assembly, based
> on cryptographic signature or even the hash of the bits. To view the valid
> arguments for the caspol.exe utility, either type *caspol -?* at a command
> prompt or use the MSDN online documentation.

The first part of the *Main* method isn't really interesting—that code determines whether you passed an assembly name to the application. If you did not,
the *Process* class's static *GetProcessName* method is used to determine the name
of the currently executing application.

After that you start to see how easy most of the reflection tasks are. The easiest
way to instantiate an *Assembly* object is to call the *Assembly.LoadFrom* method.
This method takes a single argument: a string representing the name of the physical
file that you want to load. From there, a call to the *Assembly.GetTypes* method
returns an array of *Type* objects. At this point, we have an object describing every
single type in the entire assembly! Finally, the application prints its base class.

Here's the output from the execution of this application when you either
specify the *gettypes.exe* file or don't pass any arguments to the application:

```
Loading info for GetTypes.exe

Type information for: DemoAttr
    Base class = System.Attribute

Type information for: DemoEnum
    Base class = System.Enum

Type information for: DemoBaseClass
    Base class = System.Object
```

```
Type information for: DemoDerivedClass
    Base class = DemoBaseClass

Type information for: DemoStruct
    Base class = System.Object

Type information for: AssemblyGetTypesApp
    Base class = System.Object
```

Listing an Assembly's Modules

Although most of this book's applications consist of a single module, you can
create assemblies that are made up of multiple modules. You can retrieve modules from an *Assembly* object in two ways. The first is to request an array of all
modules. This allows you to iterate through them all and retrieve any needed
information. The second is to retrieve a specific module. Let's look at each of
these approaches.

To iterate through an assembly's modules, I need to create an assembly with
more than one module. I'll do that by moving *GetAssemblyName* into its own class
and putting that class into a file called *AssemblyUtils.netmodule*, like so:

```
using System.Diagnostics;

namespace MyUtilities
{
    public class AssemblyUtils
    {
        public static string GetAssemblyName(string[] args)
        {
            string assemblyName;

            if (0 == args.Length)
            {
                Process p = Process.GetCurrentProcess();
                assemblyName = p.ProcessName + ".exe";
            }
            else
                assemblyName = args[0];

            return assemblyName;
        }
    }
}
```

The netmodule is then built using the following command:

```
csc /target:module AssemblyUtils.cs
```

The */target:module* switch causes the compiler to generate a module for later inclusion in an assembly. The command above will create a file named AssemblyUtils.netmodule. In Chapter 18, I'll cover the different options when creating assemblies and modules in a bit more detail.

At this point, I just want to create a secondary module so that we have something to reflect upon. The application that will use the *AssemblyUtils* class follows. Note the *using* statement where the *MyUtilities* namespace is referenced.

```
using System;
using System.Reflection;
using MyUtilities;

class GetModulesApp
{
    public static void Main(string[] args)
    {
        string assemblyName = AssemblyUtils.GetAssemblyName(args);

        Console.WriteLine("Loading info for " + assemblyName);
        Assembly a = Assembly.LoadFrom(assemblyName);

        Module[] modules = a.GetModules();
        foreach(Module m in modules)
        {
            Console.WriteLine("Module: " + m.Name);
        }
    }
}
```

To compile this application and have the AssemblyUtils.netmodule added to its assembly, you'll need to use the following command-line switches:

```
csc /addmodule:AssemblyUtils.netmodule GetModules.cs
```

At this point, you have an assembly with two different modules. To see this, execute the application—the results should be as follows:

```
Loading info for GetModulesApp.exe
Module: GetModulesApp.exe
Module: AssemblyUtils.netmodule
```

As you can see from the code, I simply instantiated an *Assembly* object and called its *GetModules* method. From there I iterated through the returned array and printed the name of each one.

Late Binding with Reflection

A few years back, I worked for the IBM Multimedia division on the IBM/World Book Multimedia Encyclopedia product. One challenge we had was coming up with an application that would allow the user to configure different communications protocols for use with the World Book servers. This had to be a dynamic solution because the user could continually add and remove different protocols (for example, TCP/IP, IGN, CompuServ, and so on) from their system. However, the application had to "know" which protocols were present so that the user could select a specific protocol for configuration and use. The solution we came up with was creating DLLs with a special extension and installing them in the application folder. Then when the user wanted to see a list of installed protocols, the application would call the Win32 *LoadLibrary* function to load each DLL and then call the *GetProcAddress* function to acquire a function pointer to the desired function. This is a perfect example of late binding in standard Win32 programming in that the compiler knows nothing about these calls at build time. As you'll see in the following example, this same task could be carried out in .NET by using the *Assembly* class, type reflection, and a new class called the *Activator* class.

To get things rolling, let's create an abstract class called *CommProtocol*. I'll define this class in its own DLL so that it can be shared across multiple DLLs that want to derive from it. (Note that the command-line parameters are embedded in the code's comments.)

```
// CommProtocol.cs
// Build with the following command line switches
//          csc /t:library commprotocol.cs
public abstract class CommProtocol
{
    public static string DLLMask = "CommProtocol*.dll";
    public abstract void DisplayName();
}
```

Now, I'll create two separate DLLs, each representing a communications protocol and containing a class derived from the abstract class *CommProtocol*. Note that both need to reference the CommProtocol.dll when compiled. Here's the IGN DLL:

```
// CommProtocolIGN.cs
// Build with the following command line switches
//          csc /t:library CommProtocolIGN.cs /r:CommProtocol.dll
using System;

public class CommProtocolIGN : CommProtocol
```

(continued)

```
{
    public override void DisplayName()
    {
        Console.WriteLine("This is the IBM Global Network");
    }
}
```

And here's the TCP/IP DLL:

```
// CommProtocolTcpIp.cs
// Build with the following command line switches
//            csc /t:library CommProtocolTcpIp.cs /r:CommProtocol.dll
using System;

public class CommProtocolTcpIp : CommProtocol
{
    public override void DisplayName()
    {
        Console.WriteLine("This is the TCP/IP protocol");
    }
}
```

Let's look at how easy it is to dynamically load an assembly, search for a type, instantiate that type, and call one of its methods. (By the way, there's a command file called BuildLateBinding.cmd on this book's companion CD that will also build all these files.)

```
using System;
using System.Reflection;
using System.IO;

class LateBindingApp
{
    public static void Main()
    {

        string[] fileNames = Directory.GetFiles
                            (Environment.CurrentDirectory,
                            CommProtocol.DLLMask);
        foreach(string fileName in fileNames)
        {
            Console.WriteLine("Loading DLL '{0}'", fileName);

            Assembly a = Assembly.LoadFrom(fileName);

            Type[] types = a.GetTypes();
            foreach(Type t in types)
```

```
                {
            if (t.IsSubclassOf(typeof(CommProtocol)))
            {
                object o = Activator.CreateInstance(t);

                MethodInfo mi = t.GetMethod("DisplayName");

                Console.Write("\t");
                mi.Invoke(o, null);
            }
            else
            {
                Console.WriteLine("\tThis DLL does not have " +
                "CommProtocol-derived class defined");
            }
        }
    }
  }
}
```

First I use the *System.IO.Directory* class to find all the DLLs in the current folder with a mask of *CommProtocol*.dll*. The *Directory.GetFiles* method will return an array of objects of type *string* that represents the filenames of files that match the search criteria. I can then use a *foreach* loop to iterate through the array, calling the *Assembly.LoadFrom* method that you learned about earlier in this chapter. Once an assembly is created for a given DLL, I then iterate through all the assembly's types, calling the *Type.SubClassOf* method to determine whether the assembly has a type that is derived from *CommProtocol*. I'm assuming that if I find one of these I have a valid DLL to work with. When I do find an assembly that has a type derived from *CommProtocol*, I instantiate an *Activator* object and pass to its constructor the *type* object. As you can probably guess from its name, the *Activator* class is used to dynamically create, or activate, a type.

I then use the *Type.GetMethod* method to create a *MethodInfo* object, specifying the method name *DisplayName*. Once I've done that, I can use the *MethodInfo* object's *Invoke* method, passing to it the activated type, and—voila!— the DLL's *DisplayName* method is called.

Creating and Executing Code at Run Time

Now that you've seen how to reflect types at run time, late bind to code, and dynamically execute code, let's take the next logical step and create code on the fly. Creating types at run time involves using the *System.Reflection.Emit* namespace. Using the classes in this namespace, you can define an assembly in memory, create a module for an assembly, define new types for a module (including its members), and even emit the MSIL opcodes for the application's logic.

Although the code in this example is extremely simple, I've separated the server code—a DLL that contains a class creates a method called *HelloWorld*—from the client code, an application that instantiates the code-generating class and calls its *HelloWorld* method. (Note that the compiler switches are in the code comments.) An explanation follows for the DLL code, which is here:

```
using System;
using System.Reflection;
using System.Reflection.Emit;

namespace ILGenServer
{
    public class CodeGenerator
    {
        public CodeGenerator()
        {
            // Get current currentDomain.
            currentDomain = AppDomain.CurrentDomain;

            // Create assembly in current currentDomain.
            assemblyName = new AssemblyName();
            assemblyName.Name = "TempAssembly";

            assemblyBuilder =
                    currentDomain.DefineDynamicAssembly
                    (assemblyName, AssemblyBuilderAccess.Run);

            // create a module in the assembly
            moduleBuilder = assemblyBuilder.DefineDynamicModule
                            ("TempModule");

            // create a type in the module
            typeBuilder = moduleBuilder.DefineType
                            ("TempClass",
                             TypeAttributes.Public);
            // add a member (a method) to the type
            methodBuilder = typeBuilder.DefineMethod
                            ("HelloWorld",
                             MethodAttributes.Public,
                             null,null);
```

```
            // Generate MSIL.
            msil = methodBuilder.GetILGenerator();
            msil.EmitWriteLine("Hello World");
            msil.Emit(OpCodes.Ret);

            // Last "build" step : create type.
            t = typeBuilder.CreateType();
        }

        AppDomain currentDomain;
        AssemblyName assemblyName;
        AssemblyBuilder assemblyBuilder;
        ModuleBuilder moduleBuilder;
        TypeBuilder typeBuilder;
        MethodBuilder methodBuilder;
        ILGenerator msil;
        object o;

        Type t;
        public Type T
        {
            get
            {
                return this.t;
            }
        }
    }
}
```

First, we instantiate an *AppDomain* object from the current domain. (You'll see in Chapter 17, "Interoperating with Unmanaged Code," that app domains are functionally similar to Win32 processes.) After that we instantiate an *AssemblyName* object. The *AssemblyName* class will be covered in more detail in Chapter 18—the short version is that it's a class used by the assembly cache manager to retrieve information about an assembly. Once we have the current app domain and an initialized assembly name, we call the *AppDomain.DefineDynamicAssembly* method to create a new assembly. Note that the two arguments that we're passing are an assembly name as well as the mode in which the assembly will be accessed. *AssemblyBuilderAccess.Run* designates that the assembly can be executed from memory but cannot be saved. The *AppDomain.DefineDynamicAssembly* method returns an *AssemblyBuilder* object that we then cast to an *Assembly* object. At this point, we have a fully functional assembly in memory. Now we need to create its temporary module and that module's type.

We begin by calling the *Assembly.DefineDynamicModule* method to retrieve a *ModuleBuilder* object. Once we have the *ModuleBuilder* object, we call its *DefineType* method to create a *TypeBuilder* object, passing to it the name of the type (*"TempClass"*) and the attributes used to define it (*TypeAttributes.Public*). Now that we have a *TypeBuilder* object in hand, we can create any type of member that we want. In this case, we create a method by using the *TypeBuilder.DefineMethod* method.

Finally, we have a brand new type named *TempClass* with an embedded method called *HelloWorld*. Now all we do is decide what code to place in this method. To do this, the code instantiates an *ILGenerator* object by using the *MethodBuilder.GetILGenerator* method and calls the different *ILGenerator* methods to write MSIL code into the method.

Note that here we can use standard code such as *Console.WriteLine* by using different *ILGenerator* methods or we can emit MSIL opcodes by using the *ILGenerator.Emit* method. The *ILGenerator.Emit* method takes as its only argument an *OpCodes* class member field that directly relates to an MSIL opcode.

Finally, we call the *TypeBuilder.CreateType* method. This should always be the last step performed after you've defined the members for a new type. Then we retrieve the *Type* object for the new type by using the *Type.GetType* method. This object is stored in a member variable for later retrieval by the client application.

Now all the client has to do is retrieve the *CodeGenerator*'s *Type* member, create an Activator instance, instantiate a *MethodInfo* object from the type, and then invoke the method. Here's the code to do that, with a little error checking added to make sure things work as they should:

```
using System;
using System.Reflection;
using ILGenServer;

public class ILGenClientApp
{
    public static void Main()
    {
        Console.WriteLine("Calling DLL function to generate " +
                        "a new type and method in memory...");
        CodeGenerator gen = new CodeGenerator();

        Console.WriteLine("Retrieving dynamically generated type...");
        Type t = gen.T;
        if (null != t)
        {
            Console.WriteLine("Instantiating the new type...");
            object o = Activator.CreateInstance(t);
```

```
        Console.WriteLine("Retrieving the type's " +
                        "HelloWorld method...");
        MethodInfo helloWorld = t.GetMethod("HelloWorld");
        if (null != helloWorld)
        {
            Console.WriteLine("Invoking our dynamically " +
                            "created HelloWorld method...");
                            helloWorld.Invoke(o, null);
        }
        else
        {
            Console.WriteLine("Could not locate " +
                            "HelloWorld method");
        }
    }
    else
    {
        Console.WriteLine("Could not access Type from server");
    }
    }
}
```

Now if you build and execute this application, you will see the following output:

```
Calling DLL function to generate a new type and method in memory...
Retrieving dynamically generated type...
Instantiating the new type...
Retrieving the type's HelloWorld method...
Invoking our dynamically created HelloWorld method...
Hello World
```

Summary

Reflection is the ability to discover type information at run time. The reflection API let's you do such things as iterate an assembly's modules, iterate an assembly's types, and retrieve the different design-time characteristics of a type. Advanced reflection tasks include using reflection to dynamically invoke methods and use types (via late binding) and even to create and execute MSIL code at run time.

17

Interoperating with Unmanaged Code

A new language or development environment would be short-lived if it were to ignore legacy systems and code and provide only a means of writing new systems. Regardless of how great a new technology might be, its makers must take into account that for a time the new must exist with the old. To that end, the .NET and C# design teams have made it easy for programmers to interoperate with existing code through the use of unmanaged code. *Unmanaged code* refers to code that is not managed, or controlled, by the .NET runtime. In this chapter, I'll cover the three main examples of unmanaged code in .NET, as follows:

- **Platform Invocation Services**   These services enable .NET code to access functions, structures, and even callbacks in existing, unmanaged dynamic-link libraries (DLLs).

- **Unsafe code**   Writing unsafe code allows the C# programmer to use constructs (such as pointers) in C# applications at the expense of that code being managed by the .NET runtime.

- **COM interoperability**   This term refers to the ability of .NET code to use COM components and of COM applications to use .NET components.

Platform Invocation Services

The .NET Platform Invocation Services—sometimes referred to as *PInvoke*—allows managed code to work with functions and structures that have been exported from DLLs. In this section, we'll look at how to call DLL functions and at the attributes that are used to marshal data between a .NET application and a DLL.

Because you're not providing the source code for the DLL function to the C# compiler, you must specify to the compiler the signature of the native method as well as information about any return values and how to marshal the parameters to the DLL.

> **Note**   As you know, you can create DLLs with C# and other .NET compilers. In this section, I've avoided using the term "unmanaged Win32 DLL." You should assume that any time I refer to a DLL, I'm referring to the unmanaged variety.

Declaring the Exported DLL Function

The first issue we'll look at is how to declare a simple DLL function in C#. We'll use what's fast becoming the canonical .NET *PInvoke* example, the Win32 "MessageBox" example, to get things started. Then we'll move into the more advanced areas of parameter marshalling.

As you learned in Chapter 8, "Attributes," attributes are used to provide design-time information for a C# type. Through reflection, this information can later be queried at run time. C# makes use of an attribute to allow you to describe the DLL function that the application will call to the compiler. This attribute is called the *DllImport* attribute, and its syntax is shown here:

```
[DllImport(dllName)]
accessModifier static extern retValue dllFunction(param1, param2,...);
```

As you can see, importing a DLL function is as easy as attaching the *DllImport* attribute (passing the DLL name to its constructor) to the DLL function you want to call. Pay particular attention to the fact that the *static* and *extern* modifiers must also be used on the function that you're defining. Here's the *MessageBox* example showing how easy *PInvoke* is to use:

```
using System;
using System.Runtime.InteropServices;
```

```
class PInvoke1App
{
    [DllImport("user32.dll")]
    static extern int MessageBoxA(int hWnd,
                                  string msg,
                                  string caption,
                                  int type);

    public static void Main()
    {
        MessageBoxA(0,
                    "Hello, World!",
                    "This is called from a C# app!",
                    0);
    }
}
```

Running this application results in the expected message box popping up with the "Hello, World!" statement.

Notice the *using* statement that refers to the *System.Runtime.InteropServices* namespace. This is the namespace that defines the *DllImport* attribute. After that, note that I've defined a *MessageBoxA* method that's called in the *Main* method. But what if you want to call your internal C# method something other than the name of the DLL function? You can accomplish this by using one of the *DllImport* attribute's named parameters.

What's happening in the following code is that I'm telling the compiler that I want my method to be called *MessageBoxA*. Because I didn't specify the name of the DLL function in the *DllImport* attribute, the compiler assumes that both names are the same.

```
[DllImport("user32.dll")]
static extern int MessageBoxA(int hWnd,
                              string msg,
                              string caption,
                              int type);
```

To see how to change this default behavior, let's look at another example—this time using an internal name of *MsgBox* while still calling the DLL's *MessageBoxA* function.

```
using System;
using System.Runtime.InteropServices;

class PInvoke2App
```

(continued)

```
    {
        [DllImport("user32.dll", EntryPoint="MessageBoxA")]
        static extern int MsgBox(int hWnd,
                                 string msg,
                                 string caption,
                                 int type);

        public static void Main()
        {
            MsgBox(0,
                   "Hello, World!",
                   "This is called from a C# app!",
                   0);
        }
    }
```

As you can see, I need only specify the *DllImport* attribute's *EntryPoint* named parameter to be able to name my internal equivalent of the external DLL function anything I like.

The last thing we'll look at before moving on to parameter marshalling is the *CharSet* parameter. This parameter lets you specify the character set used by the DLL file. Typically, when writing C++ applications, you don't explicitly specify *MessageBoxA* or *MessageBoxW*—a *pragma* has already let the compiler know whether you're using the ANSI or Unicode character set. That's why in C++ you call *MessageBox* and the compiler determines which character set version to call. Likewise, in C# you can specify the target character set to the *DllImport* attribute and have the target set indicate which version of the *MessageBox* function to call. In the following example, the *MessageBoxA* function will still be called as a result of the value I've passed to the *DllImport* attribute through its *CharSet* named parameter.

```
using System;
using System.Runtime.InteropServices;

class PInvoke3App
{
    // CharSet.Ansi will result in a call to MessageBoxA.
    // CharSet.Unicode will result in a call to MessageBoxW.
    [DllImport("user32.dll", CharSet=CharSet.Ansi)]
    static extern int MessageBox(int hWnd,
                                 string msg,
                                 string caption,
                                 int type);
```

```
public static void Main()
{
    MessageBox(0,
               "Hello, World!",
               "This is called from a C# app!",
               0);
}
}
```

The advantage of using the *CharSet* parameter is that I can set a variable in my application and have it control which version (ANSI or Unicode) of the functions are called; I don't have to change all my code if I change from one version to the other.

Using Callback Functions with C#

Not only can a C# application call a DLL function, but the DLL function can also call designated C# methods in your application in callback scenarios. Callback scenarios comprise use of any of the Win32 *EnumXXX* functions where you call a function to enumerate something, passing it a function pointer that will be called by Windows with each item that's found. This is done through a combination of *PInvoke*—to call the DLL function—and delegates—to define your callback. If you need a refresher on delegates, have a look at Chapter 14, "Delegates and Event Handlers."

The following code enumerates and prints out the captions of all the windows in the system:

```
using System;
using System.Runtime.InteropServices;
using System.Text;

class CallbackApp
{
  [DllImport("user32.dll")]
  static extern int GetWindowText(int hWnd, StringBuilder text, int
  count);

  delegate bool CallbackDef(int hWnd, int lParam);

  [DllImport("user32.dll")]
  static extern int EnumWindows (CallbackDef callback, int lParam);

  static bool PrintWindow(int hWnd, int lParam)
```

(continued)

```
    {
        StringBuilder text = new StringBuilder(255);
        GetWindowText(hWnd, text, 255);

        Console.WriteLine("Window caption: {0}", text);
        return true;
    }

    static void Main()
    {
        CallbackDef callback = new CallbackDef(PrintWindow);
        EnumWindows(callback, 0);
    }
}
```

First I define the Win32 functions *EnumWindows* and *GetWindowText* by using the *DllImport* attribute. I then define a delegate called *CallbackDef* and a method named *PrintWindows*. After that all I need to do in *Main* is instantiate the *CallbackDef* delegate (passing to it the *PrintWindows* method) and call the *EnumWindows* method. For each window found in the system, Windows will call the *PrintWindows* method.

The *PrintWindows* method is interesting because it uses the *StringBuilder* class to create a fixed-length string that is passed to the *GetWindowText* function. This is why the *GetWindowText* function is defined as follows:

```
static extern int GetWindowText(int hWnd, StringBuilder text, int count);
```

Anyway, the reason for all this is that the DLL function is not permitted to alter a string, so you can't use that type. And even if you attempt to pass by reference, there's no way for the calling code to initialize a string to the correct size. That's where the *StringBuilder* class comes in. A *StringBuilder* object can be dereferenced and modified by the called function, as long as the length of the text does not exceed the maximum length passed to the *StringBuilder* constructor.

Marshalling and *PInvoke*

Even though you don't typically see the marshalling or define how it works, any time you call a DLL function, .NET has to marshal the parameters to that function and the return value back to the calling .NET application. I didn't have to do anything in the previous examples in this chapter to make this happen because .NET has a defined a default native type for each .NET type. For example, the second and third parameters to the *MessageBoxA* and *MessageBoxW* functions were defined as type string. However, the C# compiler knows that the equivalent of a C# string is the Win32 LPSTR. But what happens if you want to override the default .NET marshalling behavior? To do that, you use the *MarshallAs* attribute, which is also defined in the *System.Runtime.InteropServices* namespace.

In the following sample, once again I'm using *MessageBox* to keep things simple. Here I've chosen to use the Unicode version of the Win32 *MessageBox* function. As you know from the previous section, I need only specify the *CharSet.Unicode* enumeration for the *DllImport* attribute's *CharSet* named parameter. However, in this case I want the compiler to marshal the data as wide character (LPWSTR), so I use the *MarshalAs* attribute and specify with an *UnmanagedType* enumeration the type I want my type converted to. Here's the code:

```
using System;
using System.Runtime.InteropServices;

class PInvoke4App
{
    [DllImport("user32.dll", CharSet=CharSet.Unicode)]
    static extern int MessageBox(int hWnd,
                        [MarshalAs(UnmanagedType.LPWStr)]
                        string msg,
                        [MarshalAs(UnmanagedType.LPWStr)]
                        string caption,
                        int type);

    public static void Main()
    {
        MessageBox(0,
                "Hello, World!",
                "This is called from a C# app!",
                0);
    }
}
```

Note that the *MarshalAs* attribute can be attached to method parameters (as in this example), method return values, and fields of structures and classes. Note also that to change the default marshaling for a method return value, you need to attach the *MarshalAs* attribute to the method itself.

Writing Unsafe Code

One concern some people have when moving from C++ to C# relates to whether they'll have "complete control" over memory manipulation in cases where they need it, an issue related to unsafe code. Despite its ominous sounding name, *unsafe code* is not code that is inherently unsafe and untrustworthy—it's code for which the .NET runtime will not be controlling the allocation and deallocation of memory. The ability to write unsafe code is most advantageous when you're using pointers to communicate with legacy code (such as C APIs) or when your application demands the direct manipulation of memory (typically for performance reasons).

You write unsafe code by using two keywords: *unsafe* and *fixed*. The *unsafe* keyword specifies that the marked block will run in an unmanaged context. This keyword can be applied to all methods, including constructors and properties, and even to blocks of code within methods. The *fixed* keyword is responsible for the pinning of managed objects. *Pinning* is the act of specifying to the garbage collector (GC) that the object in question cannot be moved. As it happens, during the execution of an application, objects are allocated and deallocated and "spaces" in memory open up. Instead of memory becoming fragmented, the .NET runtime moves the objects around to make the most efficient use of memory. Obviously, this is not a good thing when you have a pointer to a specific memory address and then—unbeknownst to you—the .NET runtime moves the object from that address, leaving you with an invalid pointer. Because the reason the GC moves an object in memory is to increase application efficiency, you should use this keyword judiciously.

Using Pointers in C#

Let's look at some rules regarding the use of pointers and unsafe code in C#, and then we'll dive into some examples. Pointers can be acquired only for value types, arrays, and strings. Also note that in the case of arrays the first element must be a value type because C# is actually returning a pointer to the first element of the array and not the array itself. Therefore, from the compiler's perspective, it is still returning a pointer to a value type and not a reference type.

Table 17-1 illustrates how the standard C/C++ pointer semantics are upheld in C#.

Table 17-1 C/C++ Pointer Operators

Operator	Description
&	The *address-of* operator returns a pointer that represents the memory address of the variable.
*	The *dereference* operator is used to denote the value pointed at by the pointer.
->	The *dereferencing and member access* operator is used for member access and pointer dereferencing.

The following example will look familiar to any C or C++ developers. Here I'm calling a method that takes two pointers to variables for type *int* and modifies their values before returning to the caller. Not very exciting, but it does illustrate how to use pointers in C#.

```
// Compile this application with the /unsafe option.

using System;

class Unsafe1App
{
    public static unsafe void GetValues(int* x, int* y)
    {
        *x = 6;
        *y = 42;
    }

    public static unsafe void Main()
    {
        int a = 1;
        int b = 2;
        Console.WriteLine("Before GetValues() : a = {0}, b = {1}",
                          a, b);
        GetValues(&a, &b);
        Console.WriteLine("After GetValues() : a = {0}, b = {1}",
                          a, b);
    }
}
```

This sample needs to be compiled with the /unsafe compiler option. The output from this application should be the following:

```
Before GetValues() : a = 1, b = 2
After GetValues() : a = 6, b = 42
```

The *fixed* Statement

The *fixed* statement has the following syntax:

> fixed (*type* *ptr* = *expression*) *statement*

As I mentioned, the statement tells the GC not to bother with the specified variable. Note that *type* is an unmanaged type or *void*, *expression* is any expression that results in a *type* pointer, and *statement* refers to the block of code for which the pinning of the variable is applicable. A simple example follows on the next page.

```
using System;

class Foo
{
    public int x;
}

class Fixed1App
{
    unsafe static void SetFooValue(int* x)
    {
        Console.WriteLine("Dereferenced pointer to modify foo.x");
        *x = 42;
    }

    unsafe static void Main()
    {
        // Create an instance of the structure.
        Console.WriteLine("Creating the Foo class");
        Foo foo = new Foo();

        Console.WriteLine("foo.x intialized to {0}", foo.x);

        // The fixed statement pins the foo object until
        // the enclosing compound statement ends.
        Console.WriteLine("Setting pointer to foo.x");
        // Assign the address of the foo object to a Foo*.
        fixed(int* f = &foo.x)
        {
            Console.WriteLine("Calling SetFooValue passing " +
                            "pointer to foo.x");
            SetFooValue(f);
        }

        // Show that we did alter the member via its pointer.
        Console.WriteLine("After return from " +
                            "SetFooValue, foo.x = {0}", foo.x);
    }
}
```

This code instantiates a class called *Foo* and, within a *fixed* statement, pins that object while assigning the address of its first member to a variable of type *int** (the type required by the method *SetFooValue*). Note that the *fixed* statement is used only to enclose the code that will be affected if the GC were to move the *Foo* object. This is a subtle, yet important, issue for larger and longer running code blocks where you want to minimize the amount of time you have an object pinned. Compiling and executing the code above results in the following output:

```
Creating the Foo class
foo.x intialized to 0
Setting pointer to foo.x
Calling SetFooValue passing pointer to foo.x
Dereferenced pointer to modify foo.x
After return from SetFooValue, foo.x = 42
```

> **Note**   One important point about pinned variables is the fact that the C#
> compiler does not restrict access to a pinned variable to the unsafe scope.
> For example, you can use a pinned variable as an *r*-value to an *l*-value
> that is defined in a broader scope than the unsafe block. Obviously, this
> can result in an unsafe value being used outside of the unsafe block.
> In lieu of the compiler emitting a warning or error in this case, it is the
> developer's responsibility to take care when using pinned variables as
> *r*-values.

COM Interoperability

If you've been wondering how all those COM components that you've written
through the years play along with the .NET runtime, this section is for you. I'll
show you how Classic COM components—yikes, it does hurt to see COM being
called *Classic COM*—are positioned in the .NET world.

A Brave New World

As you've seen throughout this book, there's no doubt that the .NET environment
and C# language combine to form a powerful means of building componentized
systems. However, what about the tons of existing reusable COM components
that you've built through the last few years—not to mention all those cups of
coffee and sleepless nights? Does .NET spell the end for those components? Will
they work hand-in-hand with the .NET managed runtime? For those of us who
program with COM for a living, and for those who live by the "COM is good"
mantra, there is great news. COM is here to stay, and .NET framework–managed
applications can leverage existing COM components. As you're about to see, classic
COM components interoperate with the .NET runtime through an interoperability
layer (COM Interop) that handles all the plumbing for messages passed between
the managed runtime and the COM components operating in the unmanaged realm.

Getting Started

Because the whole COM Interop layer can be a bit overwhelming at first, let's forego all the technical definitions for just a minute and jump into a realistic example of when you'd want to use a COM component from a .NET application. As we proceed, I'll explain what's going on and how you can take what you learn here and use it in your own applications.

In this example, we're going to assume that I have an AirlineInfo COM component written with Microsoft Visual C++ and ATL. I won't go through all the steps needed to build this component right here because I want to concentrate on the .NET and C# angles. However, I'll explain the salient code and mention that the entire Visual C++ project is on the companion CD.

Our COM component is designed to produce the arrival details for a specific airline. For simplicity, let's say that the component returns details for the Air Scooby IC 5678 airline and will return an error for any other airline. I purposely inserted this error mechanism so that you can take a look at how the error raised by the COM component can be propagated back and be caught by the calling .NET client application.

Here's the IDL for the COM component:

```
interface IAirlineInfo : IDispatch
{
    [id(1), helpstring("method GetAirlineTiming")]
        HRESULT GetAirlineTiming([in] BSTR bstrAirline, [out,retval]
BSTR* pBstrDetails);

    [propget, id(2), helpstring("property
        LocalTimeAtOrlando")] HRESULT
        LocalTimeAtOrlando([out, retval] BSTR
        *pVal);
};
```

Nothing too exciting here, even to the most junior of COM developers. We have an interface named *IAirlineInfo* with two methods: *GetAirlineTiming* and *LocalTimeAtOrlando*. Now let's look at the actual implementation of the *GetAirlineTiming* method:

```
STDMETHODIMP CAirlineInfo::GetAirlineTiming(BSTR
    bstrAirline, BSTR *pBstrDetails)
{
    _bstr_t bstrQueryAirline(bstrAirline);
    if(NULL == pBstrDetails) return E_POINTER;

    if(_bstr_t("Air Scooby IC 5678") ==
        bstrQueryAirline)
```

```
{
    // Return the timing for this Airline.
    *pBstrDetails =
        _bstr_t(_T("16:45:00 - Will
        arrive at Terminal 3")).copy();
}
    else
    {
        // Return an error message.
        return Error(LPCTSTR(_T("Not available" )),
                    __uuidof(AirlineInfo),
                    AIRLINE_NOT_FOUND);
    }
    return S_OK;
}
```

The *GetAirlineTiming* method takes two arguments. The first (*bstrAirline*) is a *BSTR* that represents the airline, and the second (*pBstrDetails*) is an *output* parameter that returns the arrival information (local time and gate). Within the method, we check that the value of the incoming *bstrAirline* parameter is equal to *"Air Scooby IC 5678"*. If it is, we return some hard-coded arrival information. If the value is not what we're expecting, we call an error method to return the fact that we support only one airline.

With this basic overview of the component out of the way, let's take a look at generating metadata from the component's type library (typelib) so that the .NET client can use this metadata to talk to our component and invoke its methods.

Generating Metadata from a COM *typelib*

A .NET application that needs to talk to our COM component cannot directly consume the functionality that's exposed by that component. Why not? As we saw in Chapter 16, "Querying Metadata with Reflection," the .NET runtime is designed to work with components that have metadata, whereas COM is designed to work through the Registry and a series of interrogatory methods that are implemented by the component. Therefore, the first thing we need to do to enable this COM component to be used in the .NET world is generate some metadata for it. In the case of a COM component, this metadata layer is used by the runtime to determine type information. This type information is then used at run time to manufacture what's called a *runtime callable wrapper (RCW)*. (See Figure 17-1.) The RCW handles the actual activation of the COM object and handles the marshalling requirements when the .NET application interacts with it. The RCW also does tons of other chores, such as managing object identity, object lifetimes, and interface caching.

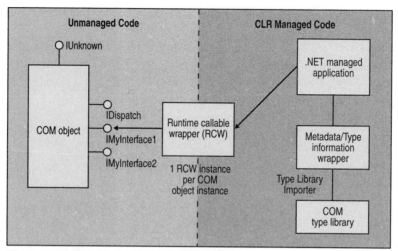

Figure 17-1 The basic components of .NET COM interoperability.

Object lifetime management is a critical issue because the .NET GC moves objects around and automatically disposes of them when they're no longer in use. The RCW serves the purpose of giving the .NET application the notion that it's interacting with a managed .NET component, and it gives the COM component in the unmanaged space the impression that it's being called by a traditional COM client. The RCW's creation and behavior varies depending on whether you're early binding or late binding to the COM object. Under the hood, the RCW is doing all the hard work and thunking down all the method invocations into corresponding vtable calls into the COM component that lives in the unmanaged world. It basically acts as an ambassador of goodwill between the managed world and the unmanaged *IUnknown* world.

Enough talk! Let's generate the metadata wrapper for our AirlineInfo COM component. To do that, we need to use a tool called the Type Library Importer (*tlbimp.exe*). This utility ships with the .NET SDK and is used to read a COM typelib and to generate the corresponding metadata wrapper containing type information that the .NET runtime can comprehend. To do this, you'll need to install the demo applications from the companion CD and locate the AirlineInfo component.

Once you've done that, type the following at a command prompt:

```
TLBIMP AirlineInformation.tlb /out:AirlineMetadata.dll
```

This command tells the *TLBIMP* to read the AirlineInfo COM typelib and to generate a corresponding metadata wrapper called AirlineMetadata.dll. If everything works as it should, you'll see the following message:

```
TypeLib imported successfully to AirlineMetadata.dll
```

So, what kind of type information does this generated metadata contain, and what does it look like? As COM folks, we have always treasured our beloved *OleView.exe* utility because of—among other things—its ability to allow us to take a peek at the contents of a *typelib*. Fortunately, the .NET SDK ships with something similar: the IL disassembler named *ILDASM*—introduced in Chapter 2, "Introducing Microsoft .NET"—which allows us to view the metadata and the MSIL code that has been generated for managed assemblies. As you learned in Chapter 16, every managed assembly contains self-describing metadata, and ILDASM is a very useful tool when you need to spelunk that metadata. Go ahead and open AirlineMetadata.dll using ILDASM. You should see results similar to those shown in Figure 17-2.

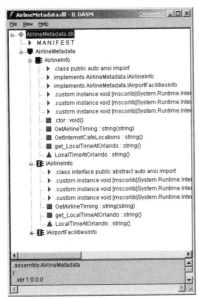

Figure 17-2 ILDASM is a great tool for viewing metadata and MSIL for managed assemblies.

From the metadata generated, you can see that the *GetAirlineTiming* method is listed as a public member for the *AirlineInfo* class. There is also a constructor that is generated for the *AirlineInfo* class. Notice that the method parameters have automatically been substituted to take their equivalent .NET counterparts. In this example, the *BSTR* has been replaced by the *System.String* parameter. Also notice that the parameter that was marked *[out,retval]* in the *GetAirlineTiming* method was converted to the actual return value of the method (returned as *System.String*). In addition, any failure *HRESULT* values that are returned back from the COM object—in case of an error or failed business logic—are raised as exceptions.

Early Binding to COM Components

Now that we've generated the metadata that's required by a .NET client, let's try invoking the *GetAirlineTiming* method in our COM object from the .NET client. Here's a C# client application that creates the COM object by using the metadata we generated earlier and invokes the *GetAirlineTiming* method. Note that in this example we're using early binding. Shortly, I'll show you two more examples that will illustrate dynamic type discovery and late binding.

```csharp
using System;
using  System.Runtime.InteropServices;
using  System.Reflection;
using  AIRLINEINFORMATIONLib;

public class AirlineClient1App
{
    public static void Main()
    {
        ///////////////////////////////////////////////
        /// EARLY BINDING EXAMPLE
        ///////////////////////////////////////////////
        String strAirline = "Air Scooby IC 5678";
        String strFoodJunkieAirline = "Air Jughead TX 1234";
        try
        {
            AirlineInfo objAirlineInfo;

            // Create a new AirlineInfo Object.
            objAirlineInfo = new AirlineInfo();

            // Display the output after calling
            // the GetAirileTiming method.
            Console.WriteLine("Details for Airline {0} --> {1}",
             strAirline,objAirlineInfo.GetAirlineTiming(strAirline));

            // ERROR: The following will result in a thrown
            // exception!
            // Console.WriteLine("Details for Airline {0} --> {1}",
            // strFoodJunkieAirline,objAirlineInfo.GetAirlineTiming
            // (strFoodJunkieAirline));
        }
        catch(COMException e)
```

```
        {
            Console.WriteLine("Oops- We encountered an error " +
                              "for Airline {0}. The Error message " +
                              "is : {1}. The  Error code is {2}",
                              strFoodJunkieAirline ,
                              e.Message,e.ErrorCode);
        }
    }
}
```

What's happening here is that the runtime is fabricating an *RCW* that maps the metadata class methods and fields to methods and properties exposed by the interface that the COM object implements. One RCW instance is created for each instance of the COM object. The .NET runtime is concerned only with managing the lifetime of the RCW and garbage collects the RCW. It's the RCW that takes care of maintaining reference counts on the COM object that it's mapped to, thereby shielding the .NET runtime from managing the reference counts on the actual COM object. As shown in Figure 17-2, the AirlineInfo metadata is defined under a namespace called *AIRLINEINFORMATIONLib*. The .NET client sees all the interface methods as if they were class members of the *AirlineInfo* class. All we need to do is create an instance of the *AirlineInfo* class by using the *new* operator and call the *public* class methods of the created object. When the method is invoked, the RCW thunks down the call to the corresponding COM method call. The RCW also handles all the marshalling and object lifetime issues. To the .NET client, it looks like nothing more than creating a typical managed object and calling one of its *public* class members!

Notice that any time the COM method raises an error, the COM error is trapped by the RCW. This error is then converted into an equivalent *COMException* class (found in the *System.Runtime.InteropServices* namespace). Of course, the COM object still needs to implement the *ISupportErrorInfo* interface for this error propagation to work and so that the RCW knows that your object provides extended error information. The error can be caught by the .NET client with the usual *try-catch* exception handling mechanism, and the client has access to the error number, description, the source of the exception, and other details that would have been available to any COM-aware client. Now let's take this example a bit further and look at some other means of binding to COM components.

Using Dynamic Type Discovery to Select COM Interfaces

So, how does the classic *QueryInterface* scenario work from the perspective of the .NET client when it wants to access another interface implemented by the COM object? To *QI* for another interface, all you need to do is cast the current object to the other interface that you need and, voila, your *QI* is done! You are now ready to invoke all the methods and properties of the desired interface. It's that simple.

Again, the RCW does the all the hard work under the covers. In a way, it's analogous to the way that the Visual Basic runtime shields COM client programmers from having to write any explicit *QueryInterface*-related code—it simply does the *QI* for you when you set one object type to an object of another associated type.

Let's see this in action to find out how easy it is. In our example, suppose you wanted to call the methods on the *IAirportFacilities* interface, which is another interface implemented by our COM object. To do this, you'd cast the *AirlineInfo* object to the *IAirportFacilities* interface. You can now call all the methods that are a part of the *IAirportFacilities* interface. But before performing the cast, you might want to check whether the object instance that you're currently holding supports or implements the interface type that you're querying for. You can do this by using the *IsInstanceOf* method in the *System.Type* class. If it returns *true*, you know that the *QI* has succeeded and you can safely perform the cast. In case you cast the object to some arbitrary interface that the object does not support, a *System.InvalidCastException* exception is thrown. This way the RCW ensures that you're casting only to interfaces that are implemented by the COM object. Here's how all that looks in code:

```
using System;
using System.Runtime.InteropServices;
using System.Reflection;
using AIRLINEINFORMATIONLib;

public class AirlineClient2App
{
    public static void Main()
    {
        ///////////////////////////////////////////////
        /// QUERY INTERFACE/ RT type Checking
        ///////////////////////////////////////////////
        try
        {
            AirlineInfo objAirlineInfo;
            IAirportFacilitiesInfo objFacilitiesInfo;
```

```
                    // Create a new AirlineInfo object.
                    objAirlineInfo = new AirlineInfo();

                    // Invoke the GetAirlineTiming method.
                    String strDetails = objAirlineInfo.GetAirlineTiming
                                            (strAirline);

                    // QI for the IAirportFacilitiesInfo interface.
                    objFacilitiesInfo =
                            (IAirportFacilitiesInfo)objAirlineInfo;

                    //Invoke a method on the IAirportFacilitiesInfo
                    //interface.
                    Console.WriteLine("{0}",
                     objFacilitiesInfo.GetInternetCafeLocations());
                }
                catch(InvalidCastException eCast)
                {
                    Console.WriteLine("We got an InvalidCast Exception " +
                                    "- Message is {0}",eCast.Message);
                }
            }
        }
    }
```

Late Binding to COM Components

The two demos that you've seen so far—*AirlineClient1App* and *AirlineClient2App*—both use the RCW metadata to early bind the .NET client to the COM object. Although early binding provides a whole smorgasbord of benefits—such as strong type checking at compile time, autocompletion capabilities from type information for development tools (such as Visual Studio.NET), and, of course, better performance—there might be instances when you don't have the compile-time metadata for the COM object that you're binding to and, therefore, you need to *late bind* to the component. For example, if the component you're attempting to use contains only a *dispinterface*, you are very much limited to late binding to use the component.

You can achieve late binding to a COM object through the reflection mechanism that you learned about in Chapter 16. To bind in this fashion to a COM component, you'll need to know the component's *ProgID*. This is because the static *CreateInstance* method of the *System.Activator* class requires a *Type* object. However, using the component's *ProgID*, you can call the *System.Type* class's *GetTypeFromProgID* method. This will return a valid .NET *Type* object that you can then use in the call to the *System.Activator.CreateInstance* method. Once you've done that, you can invoke any of the methods or properties supported by the component's default interface by using the *System.Type.InvokeMember* instance method of the *Type* object that you got back from *GetTypeFromProgID*.

All you need to know is the name of the method or property and the parameter information that the method call accepts. When you call a method of a late bound component, the way you pass parameters is by bundling them into a generic *System.Object* array and passing it to the method. You also need to set the appropriate *binding flags* depending on whether you're invoking a method or getting/setting the value of a property.

As you can see in the following code, there's a bit more work to do than with early binding. However, in cases where late binding is the only option, you're very glad to have it.

```csharp
using System;
using  System.Runtime.InteropServices;
using  System.Reflection;
using  AIRLINEINFORMATIONLib;

public class AirlineClient3App
{
    public static void Main()
    {
        ///////////////////////////////////////////////
        /// LATE BINDING
        ///////////////////////////////////////////////
        try
        {
            object objAirlineLateBound;
            Type objTypeAirline;

            object[] arrayInputParams= { "Air Scooby IC 5678" };

            objTypeAirline = Type.GetTypeFromProgID
                    ("AirlineInformation.AirlineInfo");

            objAirlineLateBound = Activator.CreateInstance
                                    (objTypeAirline);

            String str = (String)objTypeAirline.InvokeMember
                                    ("GetAirlineTiming",
                                    BindingFlags.Default |
                                    BindingFlags.InvokeMethod,
                                    null, objAirlineLateBound,
                                    arrayInputParams);
```

```
Console.WriteLine("{0}",str);

String strTime = (String)objTypeAirline.InvokeMember
                        ("LocalTimeAtOrlando",
                        BindingFlags.Default |
                        BindingFlags.GetProperty,
                        null, objAirlineLateBound,
                        new object [] {});

Console.WriteLine ("Hi there !. The Local Time in " +
                        "Orlando,Florida is: {0}", strTime);
}
catch(COMException e)
{
    Console.WriteLine("Oops- We encountered an error " +
                        "for Airline {0}. The Error message " +
                        "is : {1}. The Error code is {2}",
                        strFoodJunkieAirline,
                        e.Message,e.ErrorCode);
}
}
}
```

COM Threading Models

When most people start programming in COM, they have little or no knowledge of the COM threading models and apartments. It isn't until they become much more experienced that they realize that the free-threaded model they've been using comes at a severe performance cost when an *single-threaded apartment* (*STA*) client thread is used to create an *multithreaded apartment* (*MTA*) object. In addition, programmers new to COM frequently aren't aware of thread safety and the impending danger that awaits them when concurrent threads access their COM components.

Before a thread can call into a COM object, it has to declare its affiliation to an apartment by declaring whether it will enter an *STA* or *MTA*. *STA* client threads call *CoInitialize(NULL)* or *CoInitializeEx(0, COINIT_APARTMENTTHREADED)* to enter an *STA,* and *MTA* threads call *CoInitializeEx(0, COINIT_MULTITHREADED)* to enter an *MTA*. Similarly, in the .NET-managed world, you have the option of allowing the calling thread in the managed space to declare its apartment affinity. By default, the calling thread in a managed application chooses to live in an *MTA*. It's as if the calling thread initialized itself with *CoInitializeEx(0, COINIT_MULTITHREADED)*. But think about the overhead and the performance penalties that would be incurred if it were calling a classic *STA* COM component that was designed to be *apartment-threaded*. The incompatible apartments will incur the overhead of an additional proxy/stub pair, and this is certainly a performance penalty.

To that end, you can override the default choice of apartment for a managed thread in a .NET application by using the *ApartmentState* property of the *System.Threading.Thread* class. The *ApartmentState* property takes one of the following enumeration values:

- **MTA**   Multithreaded apartment

- **STA**   Single-threaded apartment

- **Unknown**   Equivalent to the default MTA behavior

You'll also need to specify the *ApartmentState* property for the calling thread before you make any calls to the COM object. Please note that it's not possible to change the *ApartmentState* once the COM object has been created. Therefore, it makes sense to set the thread's *ApartmentState* as early as possible in your code. The following code shows how that's done:

```
// Set the client thread ApartmentState to enter an STA.
Thread.CurrentThread.ApartmentState =
    ApartmentState.STA;

// Create our COM object through the Interop.
MySTA objSTA = new MySTA();
objSTA.MyMethod()
```

Summary

The last bit of information I'll leave you with is where these different mechanisms for working with legacy code—*PInvoke*, unsafe code, and COM Interop—fit into the overall scheme of things regarding .NET. In this chapter, you learned the following:

- With regards to using standard C-like function calls, you learned how to use *PInvoke* along with several attributes that make the issues of marshalling different types of data, including custom data, easier.

- With regards to unsafe code, you learned how to forego the benefits of managed code within a C# application for situations in which you need to have more control. These scenarios might include times when you need to manually manipulate memory for efficiency's sake or when you're moving blocks of code into a C# application and simply aren't ready yet to convert that code to managed code.

■   With regards to COM, you saw how to expose Classic COM components to .NET applications and how COM Interop seamlessly allows you to reuse existing COM components from managed code. Then, you skimmed through ways to invoke your COM component by using both early binding and late binding along with ways to do run-time type checking. Finally, you saw how managed threads declare their apartment affiliations when invoking COM components.

At this point, as a developer using one of these mechanisms for dealing with unmanaged code, you might be wondering whether it makes sense to continue using these methodologies or whether you should bite the bullet and transition directly into the .NET world by writing all your components and business logic code as managed components using a .NET language such as C#. I'll tell you that the answer depends on your current situation.

If you have tons of legacy code—whether it be C-like functions in DLLs, code that directly manipulates memory, COM components, or a combination of the three—the fact is that you're probably not going to be able to convert all your code overnight. In this case, it makes sense to leverage the different .NET mechanisms for working with legacy code. However, if you're writing new business logic code from scratch, I would most heartily advise you to write your code as managed components by using a language such as C#. That way, you can do away with the performance penalties that inevitably incur while transitioning between managed and unmanaged boundaries.

18

Working with Assemblies

This chapter describes the major advantages of using assemblies, including the packaging and versioning of your .NET components. You'll also see how to create single-file and multifile assemblies by using the Assembly Generation tool (al.exe), how to create shared assemblies by using the Strong Name tool (sn.exe), how to browse the global assembly cache by using the Assembly Cache Viewer shell extension (shfusion.dll), and how to manipulate the assembly cache with the Global Assembly Cache tool (gacutil.exe). Finally, we'll go through several demos and see what the fuss is about versioning and how assemblies and .NET versioning policies help you to avoid "DLL hell."

Assembly Overview

Chapter 16, "Querying Metadata with Reflection," described assemblies as physical files that consist of one or more portable executable (PE) files generated by a .NET compiler. In the context of that chapter, that definition was acceptable. However, assemblies are more complicated than that. Here's a more complete definition: an assembly is the packaging of a manifest, one or more modules, and, optionally, one or more resources. Using assemblies allows you to semantically group functional units into a single file for purposes of deployment, versioning, and maintenance.

All PE files that use the .NET runtime consist of an assembly or a group of assemblies. When you compile an application by using the C# compiler, you're actually creating an assembly. You might not realize that fact unless you're specifically attempting to place multiple modules in a single assembly or taking advantage of some assembly-specific feature such as versioning. However, it's important to realize that any time you build an EXE or a DLL (using the */t:library* switch), you're creating an assembly with a manifest that describes the assembly

to the .NET runtime. In addition, you can create a module (using the */t:module*
switch) that is really a DLL (with an extension of .netmodule) without a manifest. In other words, although logically it's still a DLL, it does not belong to an
assembly and must be added to an assembly either by using the */addmodule*
switch when compiling an application or by using the Assembly Generation tool.
You'll see how to do this later in the section "Building Assemblies."

Manifest Data

An assembly's manifest can be stored in different ways. If you were to compile
a stand-alone application or DLL, the manifest would be incorporated into the
resulting PE. This is known as a *single-file assembly*. A *multifile assembly* can also
be generated, with the manifest existing as either a stand-alone entity within the
assembly or as an attachment to one of the modules within the assembly.

The definition of an assembly also largely depends on how you're using
it. From a client's perspective, an assembly is a named and versioned collection
of modules, exported types, and, optionally, resources. From the assembly creator's
viewpoint, an assembly is a means of packaging related modules, types, and
resources and exporting only what should be used by a client. Having said that,
it's the manifest that provides the level of indirection between the implementation details of the assembly and what the client is meant to use. Here's a break-
down of the information that gets stored in an assembly's manifest:

■ **Assembly name**   The textual name of the assembly.

■ **Versioning information**   This string contains four distinct parts that
   make up a version number. They include a major and minor version
   number as well as a revision and build number.

■ **An (optional) shared name and signed assembly hash**   This information pertains to the deployment of assemblies and is covered
   in "Assembly Deployment" later in this chapter.

■ **Files**   This list includes all files that exist in the assembly.

■ **Referenced assemblies**   This is a list of all external assemblies that
   are directly referenced from the manifest's assembly.

■ **Types**   This is the list of all types in the assembly with a mapping to
   the module containing the type. This data is what helps the reflection
   example in Chapter 16 (that iterates through all the types in an assembly) execute so quickly.

- **Security permissions**   This is a list of security permissions that are explicitly refused by the assembly.

- **Custom attributes**   Chapter 8, "Attributes," described creating your own custom attributes. As with types, custom attributes are stored in the assembly's manifest for quicker access during reflection.

- **Product information**   This information includes Company, Trademark, Product, and Copyright values.

Benefits of Assemblies

Assemblies afford the developer numerous benefits, including packaging, deployment, and versioning.

Assembly Packaging

One advantage of the ability to package multiple modules in a single physical file is performance improvement. When you create an application and deploy it using a multifile assembly, the .NET runtime needs to load only the required modules. This has the effect of reducing the working set of the application.

Assembly Deployment

The smallest unit of deployment in .NET is the assembly. As I mentioned previously, you can create a .netmodule with the *t:module* switch, but you must include that module in an assembly if you wish to deploy it. In addition, although it's tempting to say that assemblies are a means of application deployment, this is not technically true. It's more accurate to view assemblies in .NET as a form of *class deployment* (much like a DLL in Win32), in which a single application can be made up of many assemblies.

Because assemblies are self-describing, the easiest method of deploying them is copying the assembly to the desired destination folder. Then when you attempt to run an application contained in the assembly, the manifest will instruct the .NET runtime as to the modules that are contained in the assembly. In addition, the assembly also contains references to any external assemblies that are needed by the application.

The most common means of deployment is though *private assemblies*—that is, assemblies that are copied to a folder and that are not shared. How do you specify a private assembly? This is the default and occurs automatically unless you explicitly make the assembly a *shared assembly*. Sharing assemblies takes a bit more work and is covered later in the section "Creating Shared Assemblies."

Assembly Versioning

Another great advantage to using assemblies is built-in versioning—specifically, the end of "DLL hell." "DLL hell" refers to the situation in which one application overwrites a DLL needed by another application, usually with an earlier version of the same DLL, breaking the first application. Although the Win32 resource file format does allow for a versioning resource type, the operating system doesn't enforce any versioning rules so that dependant applications will continue to function. This is solely the responsibility of application programmers.

As a means of addressing this issue, the manifest includes versioning information for the assembly as well as a list of all referenced assemblies and the versioning information for those assemblies. Because of this architecture, the .NET runtime can ensure that versioning policies are upheld and applications will continue to function even when newer, incompatible versions of shared DLLs are installed on the system. Because versioning is one of the biggest benefits of assemblies, it's covered in depth, including several examples, in "Versioning Assemblies."

Building Assemblies

If you create a DLL with the */t:library* switch, you won't be able to add it to another assembly. This is because the compiler automatically generated a manifest for the DLL, and therefore the DLL itself is an assembly. To see this in action, look at the following example. We have a DLL (Module1Server.cs) that has a dummy type called *Module1Server*.

```
// Module1Server.cs
// build with the following command line switches
//    csc /t:library Module1Server.cs
public class Module1Server
{
}
```

This DLL is then referenced by the client code (Module1Client.cs):

```
// Module1ClientApp.cs
// build with the following command line switches
//    csc Module1ClientApp.cs /r:Module1Server.dll
using System;
using System.Diagnostics;
using System.Reflection;
```

```
class Module1ClientApp
{
    public static void Main()
    {
        Assembly DLLAssembly = Assembly.GetAssembly(typeof(Module1Server));
        Console.WriteLine("Module1Server.dll Assembly Information");
        Console.WriteLine("\t" + DLLAssembly);

        Process p = Process.GetCurrentProcess();
        string AssemblyName = p.ProcessName + ".exe";
        Assembly ThisAssembly = Assembly.LoadFrom(AssemblyName);
        Console.WriteLine("Module1Client.exe Assembly Information");
        Console.WriteLine("\t" + ThisAssembly);
    }
}
```

Now let's say you built these two modules by using these switches:

```
csc /t:library Module1Server.cs
csc Module1ClientApp.cs /r:Module1Server.dll
```

Running the code at this point results in the following output and proves that both the EXE and the DLL exist in their own distinct assemblies:

```
Module1Server.dll Assembly Information
    Module1Server, Version=0.0.0.0, Culture=neutral, PublicKeyToken=null
Module1Client.dll Assembly Information
    Module1Client, Version=0.0.0.0, Culture=neutral, PublicKeyToken=null
```

In fact, if you were to change the access modifier of the *Module1Server* class from *public* to *internal*, the client code wouldn't compile because by definition the *internal* access modifier specifies that the type being modified is accessible only to other code in the same assembly.

Creating Assemblies that Have Multiple Modules

You can place both of the modules in our example into the same assembly in two ways. The first way is to change the switches used with the compiler. Here's an example:

```
// Module2Server.cs
// build with the following command line switches
//     csc /t:module Module2Server.cs
internal class Module2Server
{
}
```

Notice that we can now use the internal access modifier so that the class is only accessible to code within the assembly.

```
// Module2ClientApp.cs
// build with the following command line switches
//    csc /addmodule:Module2Server.netmodule Module2ClientApp.cs
using System;
using System.Diagnostics;
using System.Reflection;

class Module2ClientApp
{
    public static void Main()
    {
        Assembly DLLAssembly =
            Assembly.GetAssembly(typeof(Module2Server));
        Console.WriteLine("Module1Server.dll Assembly Information");
        Console.WriteLine("\t" + DLLAssembly);

        Process p = Process.GetCurrentProcess();
        string AssemblyName = p.ProcessName + ".exe";
        Assembly ThisAssembly = Assembly.LoadFrom(AssemblyName);
        Console.WriteLine("Module1Client.dll Assembly Information");
        Console.WriteLine("\t" + ThisAssembly);
    }
}
```

Notice how Module2Server.cs and Module2Client.exe are built:

> csc /t:module Module2Server.cs
> csc /addmodule:Module2Server.netmodule Module2Client.cs

First you must remove the /r switch because that switch is used only to reference assemblies and now both modules will reside in the same assembly. Then you must insert the /addmodule switch, which is used to tell the compiler which modules to add to the assembly that's being created.

Building and running the application now yields these results:

```
Module1Server.dll Assembly Information
    Module2Client, Version=0.0.0.0, Culture=neutral, PublicKeyToken=null
Module1Client.dll Assembly Information
    Module2Client, Version=0.0.0.0, Culture=neutral, PublicKeyToken=null
```

Another way to create an assembly is with the Assembly Generation tool. This tool will take as its input one or more files that are either .NET modules (containing MSIL) or resource files and image files. The output is a file with an assembly manifest. For example, you would use the Assembly Generation tool if you had several DLLs and you wanted to distribute and version them as a single unit. Assuming that your DLLs were named A.DLL, B.DLL and C.DLL, you would use the al.exe application to create the composite assembly as follows:

```
al /out:COMPOSITE.DLL A.DLL B.DLL C.DLL
```

Creating Shared Assemblies

Sharing assemblies is done when an assembly is to be used with multiple applications and versioning is important. (We'll get to versioning in the next section.) To share an assembly, you must create a *shared name* (also known as a *strong name*) for the assembly by using the Strong Name tool that accompanies the .NET SDK. The four main four benefits derived from using strong names are the following:

- It's the mechanism in .NET for generating a globally unique name.

- Because the generated key pair (explained shortly) includes a signature, you can tell whether it's been tampered with after its original creation.

- Strong names guarantee that a third party can't release a subsequent version of an assembly you built. Once again, this is because of signatures—the third party won't have your private key.

- When .NET loads an assembly, the runtime can verify that the assembly came from the publisher that the caller is expecting.

The first step to creating a strong name is to use the Strong Name tool to create a key file for the assembly. This is done by specifying the *–k* switch with the name of the output file that will contain the key. Here we'll just make something up—InsideCSharp.key—and create the file as follows:

```
sn -k InsideCSharp.key
```

Upon running this, you should get a confirmation message like the following:

```
Key pair written to InsideCSharp.key
```

Now add the *assembly:AssemblyKeyFile* attribute to the source file. Here, I've created another simple set of files to illustrate how this is done:

```
// Module3Server.cs
// build with the following command line switches
//    csc /t:module Module3Server.cs
internal class Module3Server
{
}
```

(continued)

375

```
// Module3ClientApp.cs
// build with the following command line switches
//     csc /addmodule:Module3Server.netmodule Module3ClientApp.cs
using System;
using System.Diagnostics;
using System.Reflection;

[assembly:AssemblyKeyFile("InsideCSharp.key")]

class Module3ClientApp
{
    public static void Main()
    {
        Assembly DLLAssembly =
            Assembly.GetAssembly(typeof(Module3Server));
        Console.WriteLine("Module1Server.dll Assembly Information");
        Console.WriteLine("\t" + DLLAssembly);

        Process p = Process.GetCurrentProcess();
        string AssemblyName = p.ProcessName + ".exe";
        Assembly ThisAssembly = Assembly.LoadFrom(AssemblyName);
        Console.WriteLine("Module1Client.dll Assembly Information");
        Console.WriteLine("\t" + ThisAssembly);
    }
}
```

As you can see, the *assembly:AssemblyKeyFile* attribute's constructor takes the name of the key file that was generated with the Strong Name utility and is the means by which you specify a key pair to be used to give your assembly a strong name. One more important point to understand is that this attribute is an assembly-level attribute. Therefore, technically, it can be placed in any file in the assembly and isn't attached to a specific class. However, it's customary to place this attribute just below the *using* statements and before any class definitions.

Now when you run the application, take note of the *PublicKeyToken* value of the assembly. This value was *null* in the previous two examples because those assemblies were considered to be private assemblies. However, now the assembly has been defined as a shared assembly, and so the assembly has an associated public key token.

```
Module3Server.dll Assembly Information
    Module3Client, Version=0.0.0.0, Culture=neutral,
    PublicKeyToken=6ed7cef0c0065911
Module3Client.dll Assembly Information
    Module3Client, Version=0.0.0.0, Culture=neutral,
    PublicKeyToken=6ed7cef0c0065911
```

According to the *Assembly* object that we instantiated for this demo assembly, it is shared. However, how do we know which assemblies in our .NET system are shared? The answer is the global assembly cache. In the next section, I'll cover this part of .NET and explain the role it plays in shared assemblies.

Working with the Global Assembly Cache

Every .NET installation has a code cache called the *global assembly cache*. This area serves three primary purposes:

■ It is used to store code downloaded from the Internet or other servers (both http and file servers). Note that code downloaded for a particular application is stored in the private portion of the cache—this prevents it from being accessed by others.

■ It is a data store for components shared by multiple .NET applications. Assemblies that are installed into the cache by using the Global Assembly Cache tool are stored in the global portion of the cache and are accessible by all applications on the machine.

■ One question I hear frequently is, "Where does the jitted code get stored such that my C# code is only jitted the first time it is executed?" Now you know the answer: native code versions of assemblies that have been prejitted are stored in the cache.

Viewing the Cache

Let's take a look at the cache to see the currently installed and shared assemblies. Using Microsoft Explorer, open the c:\winnt\assembly folder. To aid in viewing pertinent information about assemblies, .NET features a shell extension called the Assembly Cache Viewer (shfusion.dll). This tool enables you to view assembly information, such as the version number, culture, public key token, and even whether the assembly has been prejitted.

Another means of viewing the cache is by using the Global Assembly Cache tool. This tool enables you to perform several basic tasks by specifying any of the following (mutually exclusive) command-line switches.

■ *-i* This flag installs an assembly to the global assembly cache. An example would be the following:

```
gacutil -i HelloWorld.DLL
```

Shortly, you'll see how to add the *Module3Client* assembly to the cache by using this switch.

- ■ *-u* This flag uninstalls an assembly, including any version information, from the global assembly cache. If you don't specify the version information, *all* assemblies with the specified name are removed. Therefore, the first example here uninstalls all *HelloWorld* assemblies regardless of version number, and the second example uninstalls the specified version:

```
gacutil -u HelloWorld
gacutil -u HelloWorld, ver=1,0,0,0
```

- ■ *-l* This flag lists the contents of the global assembly cache, including the assembly name, its version number, its location, and its shared name.

> **Note** In some of the earlier .NET betas, one problem I noticed was that when exploring the c:\winnt\assembly folder, the shell extension did not execute. This was caused by the fact that the shfusion.dll extension did not register properly. If this happens on your system, open a command prompt and enter the following from the c:\winnt\Microsoft.net\framework\v*XXX* folder, where *XXX* represents the version number of the .NET Framework that you're running. Obviously, because I'm working with a beta, the folder name will change before .NET ships. Search for the shfusion.dll file, and use that folder. Here I've used the folder representing my current .NET build:
>
> c:\winnt\microsoft.net\framework\v1.0.2615>regsvr32 shfusion.dll

Now that you've created a public key file and assigned it to an assembly, let's add that assembly to the cache. To do that, type the following at the command prompt:

```
gacutil -i Module3ClientApp.exe
```

If all goes well, you should receive the following confirmation:

```
Assembly successfully added to the cache
```

At this point, you can use the *gacutil–l* command to view the assemblies listed in the cache and find the *Module3Client*, or you can use the Assembly Cache Viewer. Let's use the latter. If you open the cache in Windows Explorer (*C:\Winnt\Assembly* or *C:\Windows\Assembly*), you should now see the *Module3Client* assembly listed along with the other assemblies. Right-click that and select Properties, and you'll see things such as the public key value, version number, and physical location of the assembly on your hard disk. One point of reference is that your public key will be different than mine, but the main point is that it will be the same as that displayed by executing the Module3ClientApp application.

Versioning Assemblies

An assembly's manifest contains a version number as well as a list of all referenced assemblies with their associated version information. As you'll soon see, version numbers are divided into four segments and take the following form:

```
<major><minor><build><revision>
```

The way this works is that at run time .NET uses this version number information to decide which version of a particular assembly to use with an application. As you'll soon see, the default behavior—called the versioning policy—is that once an application is installed, .NET will automatically use the most recent version of that application's referenced assemblies if the versions match at the major and minor levels. You can change this default behavior through the use of configuration files.

Versioning pertains only to shared assemblies—private assemblies need not apply—and is probably the single most important factor in deciding to create and share assemblies. Therefore, let's look at some example code to illustrate how all this works and how to work with assembly versioning.

The example that I'm going to use here is a simpler version of the versioning example that ships with the .NET SDK, and it does not include the Windows Forms material because I want to focus on versioning and what the runtime does to enforce it.

I have two executables representing two accounting packages called Personal and Business. Both of these applications use a common shared assembly named *Account*. The only functionality that the *Account* class has is the ability to announce its version such that we can be sure our applications are using the intended version of the *Account* class. To that end, the demo will include multiple versions of the *Account* class so that you can see for yourself how the versioning works with a default version policy and how XML is used to create an association between an application and a specific version of an assembly.

To get started, create a folder called Accounting. In this folder, create a key pair that is to be used by all versions of the *Account* class. To do this, type the following at the command line in the Accounting folder:

```
sn /k account.key
```

Once that key pair has been created, create a folder within the Accounting folder called Personal. In that Personal folder, create a file called Personal.cs that looks like the following:

```
// Accounting\Personal\Personal.cs
using System;

class PersonalAccounting
{
    public static void Main()
    {
        Console.WriteLine
            ("PersonalAccounting calling Account.PrintVersion");
        Account.PrintVersion();
    }
}
```

Within that same Personal folder, create a new folder called Account1000. This folder will house the first version of the demo's *Account* class. Once you've done that, create the following file (Account.cs) in the Account1000 folder:

```
// Accounting\Personal\Account1000\Account.cs
using System;
using System.Reflection;

[assembly:AssemblyKeyFile("..\\..\\Account.key")]
[assembly:AssemblyVersion("1.0.0.0")]
public class Account
{
    public static void PrintVersion()
    {
        Console.WriteLine
            ("This is version 1.0.0.0 of the Account class");
    }
}
```

As you can see, I'm using the *AssemblyeKeyFile* and *AssemblyVersion* attributes to point the C# compiler to the key pair created earlier and to explicitly state the version of the *Account* class. Now build the Account DLL as follows:

```
csc /t:library account.cs
```

Once the *Account* class has been created, it needs to be added to the global assembly cache:

```
gacutil -i Account.dll
```

If you want, you can verify that the *Account* assembly is indeed in the assembly cache. Now go to the Personal folder and build the application like this:

```
csc Personal.cs /r:Account1000\Account.dll
```

Finally, running the application will result in the following output:

```
PersonalAccounting calling Account.PrintVersion
This is version 1.0.0.0 of the Account class
```

So far, we've done nothing new here. However, let's see what happens when another application that uses a newer version of the *Account* class is installed.

Create a new folder called Business within the Accounting folder. In the Business folder, create a folder called Account1001 to represent a new version of the *Account* class. That class will be housed in a file called Account.cs, and it will look almost identical to the previous version.

```
// Accounting\Business\Account1001\Account.cs
using System;
using System.Reflection;

[assembly:AssemblyKeyFile("..\\..\\Account.key")]
[assembly:AssemblyVersion("1.0.0.1")]
public class Account
{
    public static void PrintVersion()
    {
        Console.WriteLine
            ("This is version 1.0.0.1 of the Account class");
    }
}
```

As before, build this version of the *Account* class by using the following commands:

```
csc /t:library Account.cs
gacutil -i Account.dll
```

At this point, you should see two versions of the *Account* class in the global assembly cache. Now create the Business.cs file (in the Accounting\Business folder) as follows:

```
// Accounting\Business\Business.cs
using System;

class PersonalAccounting
{
    public static void Main()
    {
        Console.WriteLine
            ("BusinessAccounting calling Account.PrintVersion");
        Account.PrintVersion();
    }
}
```

Build the Business application by using the following command:

```
csc business.cs /r:Account1001\Account.dll
```

Running the application will produce the following, which confirms the fact that the Business application is using version 1.0.0.1 of the *Account* assembly:

```
BusinessAccounting calling Account.PrintVersion
This is version 1.0.0.1 of the Account class
```

However, now run the Personal application again and see what happens!

```
PersonalAccounting calling Account.PrintVersion
This is version 1.0.0.1 of the Account class
```

Both the Personal and Business applications are using the last version of the *Account* assembly! Why? It has to do with what is called a Quick Fix Engineering (QFE) update and the .NET default versioning policy.

QFEs and the Default Version Policy

Quick Fix Engineering updates, or hot fixes, are unscheduled fixes that are sent out to address a major problem. Because a hot fix typically doesn't modify the code's interface, the chances that client code will be adversely affected are minimal. Therefore, the default versioning policy is to automatically associate all client code to the new "fixed" version of the code unless a configuration file exists for the application that explicitly associates the application with a specific version of an assembly. A new version of an assembly is considered to be a QFE if the only part of the version number that changed is the *revision* part.

Creating a Safe Mode Configuration File

This default version policy might be fine most of the time, but what if you need to specify that the Personal application run only with the version that it shipped with? This is where XML configuration files come in. These files have the same name as the application and reside in the same folder. When the application is executed, the configuration file is read and .NET then uses the XML tags therein to dictate which version of a referenced assembly to use.

To specify that an application should always use the version of an assembly that it shipped with, you specify that you want the application's binding mode to be *"safe"*. This is sometimes colloquially referred to as putting the application in safe mode. To test this, create a file called PersonalAccounting.cfg in the Accounting/Personal folder and modify it such that it appears as follows. Take note of the *<AppBindingMode>* tag.

```
<?xml version ="1.0"?>
<Configuration>
<BindingMode>
<AppBindingMode Mode="safe"/>
</BindingMode>
</Configuration>
```

Now, if you run the Personal application again, you'll see the following output:

```
PersonalAccounting calling Account.PrintVersion
This is version 1.0.0.0 of the Account class
```

Using Specific Versions of Assemblies

Now let's look at another common issue with versioning. In the last part of this demo, we'll introduce an error into the equation. Create a folder called Account1002 in the Account\Business folder. In that folder, create the following *Account* class. Notice that this time the *AccountPrint* version is purposely programmed to throw an exception to simulate a nonworking update to the *Account* class.

```
// Accounting\Business\Account1002\Account.cs
using System;
using System.Reflection;

[assembly:AssemblyKeyFile("..\\..\\Account.key")]
[assembly:AssemblyVersion("1.0.0.2")]
public class Account
{
    public static void PrintVersion()
    {
        // This is purposely thrown to simulate code failure.
        throw new Exception();

        Console.WriteLine
            ("This is version 1.0.0.2 of the Account class");
    }
}
```

Now build this version of the *Account* assembly as follows:

```
csc /t:library Account.cs
gacutil -i Account.dll
```

Running either the Personal or Business applications will result in the uncaught exception causing the application to abort. Here I'm simulating an all-too-common phenomenon in software deployment—the installation of something that doesn't work and that winds up breaking several other applications. In the case of the Personal application, we don't want to revert to safe mode because we want to run the latest working version of *Account* (version 1.0.0.1) and safe mode would have us working with the first version (1.0.0.0).

Once again, the answer lies in the application configuration file. Now modify the Accounting\PersonalAccounting.cfg such that its XML tags look like this:

```
<?xml version ="1.0"?>
<Configuration>
<BindingPolicy>
<BindingRedir Name="Account"
              Originator="32ab35a4550339b1"
              Version="*"
              VersionNew="1.0.0.1"
              UseLatestBuildRevision="no"/>
</BindingPolicy>
</Configuration>
```

Note that the key specified for the *Originator* attribute is the one used on my system. You need to substitute the one generated when you created the Account.key file. You can locate the value needed by opening the assembly cache and locating the *Account* class.

Finally, run the Personal application again, and you'll see that it runs without any problems and that the *Account* class being used is indeed the version (1.0.0.1) that we requested.

Summary

In this chapter, I discussed the major advantages of using assemblies, including packaging, deployment, versioning, and security. I also discussed single-file and multifile assemblies and the Assembly Generation tool (al.exe), how to create and share assemblies by using the Strong Name tool (sn.exe), and the Global Assembly Cache tool (gacutil.exe). I also demonstrated how to control the default versioning policies used by .NET with the creation of XML-based configurations files.

Index

Note: Italicized page references indicate figures, tables, or code listings.

Index

Index

Index

Index

Index

Index

Tom Archer

Aside from his hobby of helping fellow developers through developer Web sites (CodeGuru and the newly formed TheCodeChannel), Tom Archer also does consulting for Microsoft Visual C++ and C# development. His clients include IBM, AT&T, Equifax, and Peachtree Software. Among his proudest accomplishments is being the lead programmer on two award-winning applications (at IBM and Peachtree). While he generally shies away from large audiences, he does currently teach C# and .NET programming to small groups (either individual or corporate) so that he can focus on more personal training.

Currently Tom lives in Atlanta, Georgia. He is an avid pool player (mainly nine-ball and bottle pool). If you're ever in the Atlanta area and want to get a good match or simply want to knock some balls around, drop him an e-mail. Tom can be reached at his Web site: *http://www.TheCodeChannel.com.*

The manuscript for this book was prepared and galleyed using Microsoft Word 98. Pages were composed by Microsoft Press using Adobe PageMaker 6.52 for Windows, with text in Garamond and display type in Helvetica Condensed. Composed pages were delivered to the printer as electronic prepress files.

Cover Designer:	Methodologie, Inc.
Interior Graphic Designer:	James D. Kramer
Principal Compositors:	Elizabeth Hansford, Barb Levy
Interior Artist:	Joel Panchot
Principal Copy Editor:	Cheryl Penner
Indexer:	Shane-Armstrong Information Systems

Get a **Free**
*e-mail newsletter, updates,
special offers, links to related books,
and more when you*

register on line!

Register your Microsoft Press® title on our Web site and you'll get
a FREE subscription to our e-mail newsletter, *Microsoft Press
Book Connections*. You'll find out about newly released and upcoming
books and learning tools, online events, software downloads, special
offers and coupons for Microsoft Press customers, and information
about major Microsoft® product releases. You can also read useful
additional information about all the titles we publish, such as detailed book descriptions, tables of contents and indexes, sample
chapters, links to related books and book series, author biographies,
and reviews by other customers.

Registration is easy. Just visit this Web page and fill in your information:

http://mspress.microsoft.com/register

Microsoft

Proof of Purchase

Use this page as proof of purchase if participating in a promotion or rebate offer on
this title. Proof of purchase must be used in conjunction with other proof(s) of
payment such as your dated sales receipt—see offer details.

Inside C#
ISBN 0-7356-1288-9

CUSTOMER NAME

Microsoft Press, PO Box 97017, Redmond, WA 98073-9830

MICROSOFT LICENSE AGREEMENT

Book Companion CD

IMPORTANT—READ CAREFULLY: This Microsoft End-User License Agreement ("EULA") is a legal agreement between you (either an individual or an entity) and Microsoft Corporation for the Microsoft product identified above, which includes computer software and may include associated media, printed materials, and "online" or electronic documentation ("SOFTWARE PRODUCT"). Any component included within the SOFTWARE PRODUCT that is accompanied by a separate End-User License Agreement shall be governed by such agreement and not the terms set forth below. By installing, copying, or otherwise using the SOFTWARE PRODUCT, you agree to be bound by the terms of this EULA. If you do not agree to the terms of this EULA, you are not authorized to install, copy, or otherwise use the SOFTWARE PRODUCT; you may, however, return the SOFTWARE PRODUCT, along with all printed materials and other items that form a part of the Microsoft product that includes the SOFTWARE PRODUCT, to the place you obtained them for a full refund.

SOFTWARE PRODUCT LICENSE

The SOFTWARE PRODUCT is protected by United States copyright laws and international copyright treaties, as well as other intellectual property laws and treaties. The SOFTWARE PRODUCT is licensed, not sold.

1. **GRANT OF LICENSE.** This EULA grants you the following rights:

   a. **Software Product.** You may install and use one copy of the SOFTWARE PRODUCT on a single computer. The primary user of the computer on which the SOFTWARE PRODUCT is installed may make a second copy for his or her exclusive use on a portable computer.

   b. **Storage/Network Use.** You may also store or install a copy of the SOFTWARE PRODUCT on a storage device, such as a network server, used only to install or run the SOFTWARE PRODUCT on your other computers over an internal network; however, you must acquire and dedicate a license for each separate computer on which the SOFTWARE PRODUCT is installed or run from the storage device. A license for the SOFTWARE PRODUCT may not be shared or used concurrently on different computers.

   c. **License Pak.** If you have acquired this EULA in a Microsoft License Pak, you may make the number of additional copies of the computer software portion of the SOFTWARE PRODUCT authorized on the printed copy of this EULA, and you may use each copy in the manner specified above. You are also entitled to make a corresponding number of secondary copies for portable computer use as specified above.

   d. **Sample Code.** Solely with respect to portions, if any, of the SOFTWARE PRODUCT that are identified within the SOFTWARE PRODUCT as sample code (the "SAMPLE CODE"):

      i. **Use and Modification.** Microsoft grants you the right to use and modify the source code version of the SAMPLE CODE, *provided* you comply with subsection (d)(iii) below. You may not distribute the SAMPLE CODE, or any modified version of the SAMPLE CODE, in source code form.

      ii. **Redistributable Files.** Provided you comply with subsection (d)(iii) below, Microsoft grants you a nonexclusive, royalty-free right to reproduce and distribute the object code version of the SAMPLE CODE and of any modified SAMPLE CODE, other than SAMPLE CODE, or any modified version thereof, designated as not redistributable in the Readme file that forms a part of the SOFTWARE PRODUCT (the "Non-Redistributable Sample Code"). All SAMPLE CODE other than the Non-Redistributable Sample Code is collectively referred to as the "REDISTRIBUTABLES."

      iii. **Redistribution Requirements.** If you redistribute the REDISTRIBUTABLES, you agree to: (i) distribute the REDISTRIBUTABLES in object code form only in conjunction with and as a part of your software application product; (ii) not use Microsoft's name, logo, or trademarks to market your software application product; (iii) include a valid copyright notice on your software application product; (iv) indemnify, hold harmless, and defend Microsoft from and against any claims or lawsuits, including attorney's fees, that arise or result from the use or distribution of your software application product; and (v) not permit further distribution of the REDISTRIBUTABLES by your end user. Contact Microsoft for the applicable royalties due and other licensing terms for all other uses and/or distribution of the REDISTRIBUTABLES.

2. **DESCRIPTION OF OTHER RIGHTS AND LIMITATIONS.**

   - **Limitations on Reverse Engineering, Decompilation, and Disassembly.** You may not reverse engineer, decompile, or disassemble the SOFTWARE PRODUCT, except and only to the extent that such activity is expressly permitted by applicable law notwithstanding this limitation.

   - **Separation of Components.** The SOFTWARE PRODUCT is licensed as a single product. Its component parts may not be separated for use on more than one computer.

   - **Rental.** You may not rent, lease, or lend the SOFTWARE PRODUCT.

   - **Support Services.** Microsoft may, but is not obligated to, provide you with support services related to the SOFTWARE PRODUCT ("Support Services"). Use of Support Services is governed by the Microsoft policies and programs described in the user manual, in "online" documentation, and/or in other Microsoft-provided materials. Any supplemental software code provided to you as part of the Support Services shall be considered part of the SOFTWARE PRODUCT and subject to the terms and conditions of this EULA. With respect to technical information you provide to Microsoft as part of the Support Services, Microsoft may use such information for its business purposes, including for product support and development. Microsoft will not utilize such technical information in a form that personally identifies you.

- **Software Transfer.** You may permanently transfer all of your rights under this EULA, provided you retain no copies, you transfer all of the SOFTWARE PRODUCT (including all component parts, the media and printed materials, any upgrades, this EULA, and, if applicable, the Certificate of Authenticity), **and** the recipient agrees to the terms of this EULA.

- **Termination.** Without prejudice to any other rights, Microsoft may terminate this EULA if you fail to comply with the terms and conditions of this EULA. In such event, you must destroy all copies of the SOFTWARE PRODUCT and all of its component parts.

3. **COPYRIGHT.** All title and copyrights in and to the SOFTWARE PRODUCT (including but not limited to any images, photographs, animations, video, audio, music, text, SAMPLE CODE, REDISTRIBUTABLES, and "applets" incorporated into the SOFTWARE PRODUCT) and any copies of the SOFTWARE PRODUCT are owned by Microsoft or its suppliers. The SOFTWARE PRODUCT is protected by copyright laws and international treaty provisions. Therefore, you must treat the SOFTWARE PRODUCT like any other copyrighted material **except** that you may install the SOFTWARE PRODUCT on a single computer provided you keep the original solely for backup or archival purposes. You may not copy the printed materials accompanying the SOFTWARE PRODUCT.

4. **U.S. GOVERNMENT RESTRICTED RIGHTS.** The SOFTWARE PRODUCT and documentation are provided with RESTRICTED RIGHTS. Use, duplication, or disclosure by the Government is subject to restrictions as set forth in subparagraph (c)(1)(ii) of the Rights in Technical Data and Computer Software clause at DFARS 252.227-7013 or subparagraphs (c)(1) and (2) of the Commercial Computer Software—Restricted Rights at 48 CFR 52.227-19, as applicable. Manufacturer is Microsoft Corporation/One Microsoft Way/Redmond, WA 98052-6399.

5. **EXPORT RESTRICTIONS.** You agree that you will not export or re-export the SOFTWARE PRODUCT, any part thereof, or any process or service that is the direct product of the SOFTWARE PRODUCT (the foregoing collectively referred to as the "Restricted Components"), to any country, person, entity, or end user subject to U.S. export restrictions. You specifically agree not to export or re-export any of the Restricted Components (i) to any country to which the U.S. has embargoed or restricted the export of goods or services, which currently include, but are not necessarily limited to, Cuba, Iran, Iraq, Libya, North Korea, Sudan, and Syria, or to any national of any such country, wherever located, who intends to transmit or transport the Restricted Components back to such country; (ii) to any end user who you know or have reason to know will utilize the Restricted Components in the design, development, or production of nuclear, chemical, or biological weapons; or (iii) to any end user who has been prohibited from participating in U.S. export transactions by any federal agency of the U.S. government. You warrant and represent that neither the BXA nor any other U.S. federal agency has suspended, revoked, or denied your export privileges.

DISCLAIMER OF WARRANTY

NO WARRANTIES OR CONDITIONS. MICROSOFT EXPRESSLY DISCLAIMS ANY WARRANTY OR CONDITION FOR THE SOFTWARE PRODUCT. THE SOFTWARE PRODUCT AND ANY RELATED DOCUMENTATION ARE PROVIDED "AS IS" WITHOUT WARRANTY OR CONDITION OF ANY KIND, EITHER EXPRESS OR IMPLIED, INCLUDING, WITHOUT LIMITATION, THE IMPLIED WARRANTIES OF MERCHANTABILITY, FITNESS FOR A PARTICULAR PURPOSE, OR NONINFRINGEMENT. THE ENTIRE RISK ARISING OUT OF USE OR PERFORMANCE OF THE SOFTWARE PRODUCT REMAINS WITH YOU.

LIMITATION OF LIABILITY. TO THE MAXIMUM EXTENT PERMITTED BY APPLICABLE LAW, IN NO EVENT SHALL MICROSOFT OR ITS SUPPLIERS BE LIABLE FOR ANY SPECIAL, INCIDENTAL, INDIRECT, OR CONSEQUENTIAL DAMAGES WHATSOEVER (INCLUDING, WITHOUT LIMITATION, DAMAGES FOR LOSS OF BUSINESS PROFITS, BUSINESS INTERRUPTION, LOSS OF BUSINESS INFORMATION, OR ANY OTHER PECUNIARY LOSS) ARISING OUT OF THE USE OF OR INABILITY TO USE THE SOFTWARE PRODUCT OR THE PROVISION OF OR FAILURE TO PROVIDE SUPPORT SERVICES, EVEN IF MICROSOFT HAS BEEN ADVISED OF THE POSSIBILITY OF SUCH DAMAGES. IN ANY CASE, MICROSOFT'S ENTIRE LIABILITY UNDER ANY PROVISION OF THIS EULA SHALL BE LIMITED TO THE GREATER OF THE AMOUNT ACTUALLY PAID BY YOU FOR THE SOFTWARE PRODUCT OR US$5.00; PROVIDED, HOWEVER, IF YOU HAVE ENTERED INTO A MICROSOFT SUPPORT SERVICES AGREEMENT, MICROSOFT'S ENTIRE LIABILITY REGARDING SUPPORT SERVICES SHALL BE GOVERNED BY THE TERMS OF THAT AGREEMENT. BECAUSE SOME STATES AND JURISDICTIONS DO NOT ALLOW THE EXCLUSION OR LIMITATION OF LIABILITY, THE ABOVE LIMITATION MAY NOT APPLY TO YOU.

MISCELLANEOUS

This EULA is governed by the laws of the State of Washington USA, except and only to the extent that applicable law mandates governing law of a different jurisdiction.

Should you have any questions concerning this EULA, or if you desire to contact Microsoft for any reason, please contact the Microsoft subsidiary serving your country, or write: Microsoft Sales Information Center/One Microsoft Way/Redmond, WA 98052-6399.